The Trainable Mentally Retarded

Thomas A. Burton

University of Georgia

Charles E. Merrill Publishing Company
A Bell & Howell Company
Columbus, Ohio 43216

For
Susanne, Rebecca, and Jon
and
AP and G

Published by
Charles E. Merrill Publishing Co.
A Bell & Howell Co.
Columbus, Ohio 43216

This book was set in Helvetica.
The production editor was Sandy Smith.
The cover was designed by Will Chenoweth.

International Standard Book Number: 0-675-08591-8

Library of Congress Catalog Card Number: 76-4440

2 3 4 5 6 7 8 9 10—81 80 79 78 77

Printed in the United States of America

Preface

After many years of effort on the part of parents, professionals, and other concerned people, the importance of program for the trainable mentally retarded is finally being recognized. This text is, in part, an expression of several years of frustration over this lack of interest and the lack of a definitive source book or text for training students to work with the trainable. Although literature has been available, it is fragmented or defines the training programs in a discreetly circumscribed manner and does not extend itself to the frontiers of new knowledge that is developing in potential areas of training and program.

Therefore, this text is intended to provide an overview of what has gone on before and to bring this and the currently emerging body of knowledge into contemporary perspective. Chapters One and Two on definitions and program are designed to give the student a background into the issues and conflicts that exist in the definition of programming for the trainable population and to elaborate on their current interpretation and significance. Chapter Three reviews the dimensions of assessment and is intended to further illustrate the complexities of defining and structuring an appropriate program. Chapters Four and Five are, perhaps, the decisive chapters in the text in their description of the "what" and "how" that appear to be appropriate in current training programs. Chapter Six is a simple statement of the mechanics of organizing a class or program. Chapter Seven describes the contemporary issues in program for the trainable adult, and Chapter Eight emphasizes the need for an extension of the training program into the home and the responsibility of professionals in assisting in stabilizing the family and in developing appropriate coping strategies to deal with the crisis of the trainable child or adult.

The issue of appropriate program for the trainable is fraught with emotion, tradition, and indecision. Therefore, it would be impossible to satisfy everyone in a text such as this. Although it recognizes the current limitations and gaps in our knowledge about this population, this text's basic orientation to program may not be universally popular. There are going to be those who want more, and those who expect less. In instances, I may be accused of pessimism or defeatism in the content of this text. This is not the intent; rather, it is my expressed intent to present a realistic and pragmatic approach to program in a constructive manner that will operate in the best interest of the trainable, their families, and society. Any departure from this level of approach may be misleading and, in fact, potentially cataclysmic if an optimism or aspiration for the trainable population that is unobtainable is expressed. We dare not, in these days of accountability, promise more than we can deliver. Much can and will be done through programs for the trainable, and, hopefully, the principle of normalization will be applied to the fullest extent in these programs. However, the principle must be kept in proper perspective so that we do not attempt to "make normal." It is my earnest desire that this text will contribute to normalization in the sense of defining a program that will insure that the trainable will be afforded the best quality of life and training available within the limitations of their handicap.

The final chapter on the trainable has certainly not been written. As time passes, the limits of our knowledge about this population becomes increasingly apparent. Rather than an end to frustration, then, this text is only the beginning of an understanding of programs for the trainable mentally retarded. Perhaps the text is also provocative enough to stimulate students to weigh the evidence and, in so doing, develop insights and purpose to seek the means of providing appropriate programs for the trainable mentally retarded.

Thomas A. Burton
Athens, Georgia

Acknowledgments

The preparation of a textbook is not a private thing and is rarely done without the patience, assistance, endurance, and commentary of those personally and professionally associated with the author. For this reason, I wish to express my general gratitude to my colleagues who have endured my intrusions and who have continually contributed time and encouragement throughout the writing of the manuscript.

Although many made contributions to the preparation of the manuscript, none contributed as much as my colleague Alfred Hirshoren. His continuing encouragement, endless hours of commentary, and sources of information and general knowledge were all indispensable and made a significant contribution to the completion of the manuscript. To Al Hirshoren, the author is eternally grateful.

Contents

The Trainable
Mentally Retarded

Chapter 1

The Trainable
Mentally Retarded

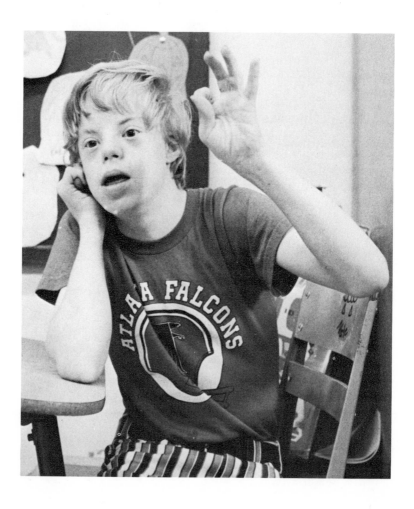

Definitions

Terms used to define persons currently referred to as "trainable mentally retarded" (TMR) have been as diverse as the circumstances extant in the trainable population. Early definitions of retardation were generic in nature. Terms such as "fools" and "monsters," along with commentaries on persons who were "lunatics" or manifested other forms of mental illness, were used to describe a population encompassing the more observable forms of retardation and mental illness.

Use of the term "fool" had its origin in the application of the Latin word *fatua*. *Fatuus* was used to define dullness, while *stultus* was used to define those who had no sense at all. The term "monster" is derived from the Middle English word *monstre* and the Latin *monstrum*, which originally meant a divine omen indicating misfortune. In this context, the term "monster" reflected an early superstition relative to the divine nature of persons so designated, and their presence was assumed to foretell the future (Kanner, 1967a).

The Growth of Knowledge

In later, Greek writings, the term *idios* ("idiocy"), meaning a private or peculiar person, came to be used to classify individuals who were mentally defective. The Romans used the term *imbecillis* ("imbecile") to identify persons who were less severely retarded than the idiot. Idiocy was ultimately separated from insanity, and idiocy became the generally accepted term used to classify all levels of retardation. In the absence of objective measures of intelligence, this term was, in all probability, applied to that level of retardate that demanded what Jordan (1972) described as the lowest level of analysis: one simply looked at a person and made a determination of intellectual level. Since the trainable population frequently represents the most observable forms of retardation, we can safely assume that the term "idiot" or "imbecile" represents the first attempt at classifying a population consisting of mentally retarded persons possessing some form of observable physical stigmata and functioning intellectually within the trainable range and below.

The label "idiot" persisted and survived other nomenclatures, such as "dunce," "fool," "buffoon," and "amentia." Until the beginning of the seventeenth century, the condition of idiocy was considered to be a homogeneous factor that was applied to all observable forms of retardation. Conditions such as endemic cretinism were originally identified and classified as being synonymous with idiocy. By 1850, however, cre-

3

tinism had been redefined as a special kind of idiocy, and delusions of homogeneity began to deteriorate. This view of the idiot witnessed a further demise in 1866, when Langdon Down differentiated mongolism from other types of idiocy. Gradually, it came to be recognized that idiocy involved a variety of heterogeneous conditions, and the rush for classification was on. Major etiological groups were subsequently identified and used to subdivide various degrees of mental retardation. These degrees of retardation were represented by an arrangement of disorders reflected by specific etiologies possessing the common end result of mental retardation. Little was known of corresponding performance levels, and a determination of specific degrees of retardation was still lacking.

The Intelligence Factor

By the end of the nineteenth century, levels of performance within the retarded population were beginning to be identified. The Binet-Simon Scale, first published in 1905, moved toward a more precise definition of mental retardation by levels of performance. The Binet-Simon Scale was revised several times before Terman (1916) defined the Intelligence Quotient (IQ) and arranged the levels of retardation according to the specific categories of Moron, Imbecile and Idiot, in descending order of intelligence. The middle group represented an IQ range from 25 to 49. An "imbecile" was defined as a person who "will probably develop some language, be trained to care for his bodily needs, and have trainability as far as his daily habits and routines are concerned" (Kirk & Johnson, 1951, p. 4). Furthermore, the imbecile-level retardate was recognized as requiring some form of supervision and care in the home or institution throughout life.

For educational purposes, "trainable" or "severely retarded" became the generally accepted terms for the imbecile level of intelligence from the 1920s through the 1950s (Robinson & Robinson, 1965). Ingram (1960) defined the trainable or severely retarded as ranging in IQ from 25 to 49, and as being "uneducable in terms of academic skills and occupational adequacy" (p. 17). However, she did indicate that they could learn to be independent in self care, in social habits, and in routine tasks by the age of fifteen or sixteen.

Since 1960, professionals have sought other nomenclatures that are more representative, descriptive, and perhaps more palatable than "trainable." Heber (1959) developed a manual of terminology and classification that was adopted in 1960 by the American Association on Mental Deficiency as their official manual of terminology and classification. In this manual, Heber (1959) defined the TMR as being incapable of achievement in academic subjects, but able to profit from training in self care, social skills, and simple job skills. However, the IQ score range for the TMR was changed to reflect an IQ from 25 or 30 to 50, and "trainable" was redefined as "moderate" (-3.01 to 4.00 σ with a Binet IQ of 36 to 51) to "severe" (-4.01 to 5.00 σ with a Binet IQ of 20 to 35) retardation. It is important to note the ambiguity of Heber's new criteria for the trainable category. The associated ranges in IQ score (that is, 25 or 30 to 50) classified the trainable, for psychometric purposes, as "moderate" *and* "severe," with a range in standard deviation units of -3.01 to 5.00. The lack of precision in this classification resulted in the terms "trainable," "moderate," and "severe" being used synonymously for this population.

In 1973, the American Association on Mental Deficiency revised the manual of terminology and classification. In this revision (Grossman, 1973), the overlapping of the categories "moderate" and "severe" was eliminated. Moderate retardation was defined as a category of retardation between three and four standard deviation units (σ) below the norm, with a Binet score of 36 to 51, encompassing "those individuals who are likely to fall into the educational category 'trainable' " (p. 18). However, a degree of ambiguity persisted, and Grossman (1973) cautioned that the categories were not absolute, and that "a child classified as mildly retarded may be better served in a 'trainable' class than an 'educable' one; some children at the severe retardation level may function successfuly in a 'trainable' group. . . . The level does not necessarily dictate the particular service need" (p. 18). This discrepancy between measured intelligence and performance levels may be further compounded by the new normative data developed for the Binet (Thorndike, 1973). It has been speculated that continued use of the Binet (1972 norms) in a psychoeducational assessment may result in a number of children obtaining lower IQ scores and an increasing number of children being classified as trainable rather than educable (Woo-Sam, Note 1).*

Whatever the terms or conditions, the value of any intellectual definition is directly related to how well it describes the level or need for program or services. To date, we have not arrived at any general consensus of opinion concerning who or what the trainable are. The term "trainable" has been much maligned by various authors (D'Amelio, 1971; Dunn, 1973) as being offensive, inaccurate, pessimistic. However, it is obvious that the terms "moderate" and "severe" are deceptive and lack clarity. By definition, moderate means "not excessive," and severe is defined as "grave" or "extreme." It must be said that a measured IQ ranging from "25 or 30 to 50," or "36 to 51" does represent

---

*Chapter 3 will elaborate on this problem.

an excessive departure from the mean intelligence, but it does not present "grave" circumstances.

Although the intellectual factor represents only one criterion in the complex problem of defining the TMR population, it is the one most frequently used in the determination of classification and assignment to a program. The most expedient practice is the continued use of the term "trainable" as a reflection of the current educational category for that population who, in terms of ultimate performance, cannot profit from an educable class and will be partially dependent upon someone for a portion of their support throughout their entire lives.

Up to this point, we have discussed definitions which were usually limited to a generic term based upon performance, behavior, or a quantitative evaluation of intelligence. Professionals have long recognized that there are clear limitations to defining the trainable—or any other level of retardation—in exclusively intellectual terms. The category "trainable" extends beyond the administration of a psychometric device. The TMR intellectual deficit is usually of a pathological origin with circumstances which distinctly indicate a consideration of the extant medical problem.

The Medical Component

Langdon Down and William Ireland were instrumental in developing the first classification and subdivision of idiocy according to pathology or etiology. Their initial classifications precipitated an era of discovery and a subsequent proliferation of identification of clinical types (Kanner, 1967b). Currently, the medical profession has identified over two hundred different etiologies resulting in some degree of retardation.

Although the majority of the retarded are mildly retarded as a result of subcultural or familial circumstances, the trainables' circumstances are usually of a pathological origin or as a result of developmental failure characterized by sensory, motor, and speech deficiencies (Davitz, Davitz, & Lorge, 1969). Because of the diverse etiologies attending individual circumstances, there is no one single criterion for a medical definition of the trainable population.

Heber (1959) developed a system of classification that was consistent with medical thought and useful to persons in other professional areas concerned with mental retardation. This sytem classified the total retarded population according to etiology where the retardation is associated with a disease entity due to conditions such as (1) infections, (2) intoxication, (3) trauma or physical agent, (4) metabolism, growth, or nutrition, (5) new growths, (6) unknown prenatal influence, (7) unknown structural reactions, and (8) uncertain causes which present a functional rather than a physical manifestation. In general, the categories (1) through (7) designate circumstances that affect physical and intellectual growth that would result in a classification of trainable or below. Category (8) defines the etiological circumstances of the cultural-familial (EMR) population and those circumstances attended by severe emotional disorders.

In the revision of Heber's manual, Grossman (1973) changed or added to some of the medical classifications in an attempt to reflect current knowledge. These revisions classified mental retardation according to circumstances such as (1) infections and intoxication, (2) trauma or physical agent, (3) disorders of metabolism or nutrition, (4) gross postnatal brain disease, (5) unknown prenatal influence, (6) chromosomal abnormality, (7) gestational disorders, (8) psychiatric disorder, (9) environmental influence, and (10) other conditions. Again, it may be noted that categories (1) through (7) would generally be expected to represent circumstances attended by a level of retardation of trainable or below. The remaining criteria would represent the educable level of retardation or severe behaviorial disorders.

The medical determinates used to define the trainable population are quite diverse in symptomatology. The criteria are usually more descriptive than functional. However, a medical definition is often useful in describing or understanding the underlying processes that affect the individual's ability to function physically, intellectually, and socially.

A determination of a TMR person's intellectual and medical circumstances is often the antecedent to a functional definition or decision relative to ultimate prognosis. What we must eventually determine is what the individual can and cannot do—the person's dependent or semidependent status. In order to arrive at this decision, we must consider a number of factors that affect the individual's ability to cope with the environment. In so doing, we may also determine her or his ultimate position in society. Heber (1960) has called the construct that represents these varied elements "adaptive behavior."

The Criterion of Adaptive Behavior

The precursor to the concept of adaptive behavior was a general concern for the status of mentally retarded people in society. Historically, these people were considered a social menace, and various measures ranging from euthanasia to sterilization and segregation were employed to bring the "menace" under control (Davies & Ecob, 1962).

Early workers subscribed to a social definition as the principal criteria for the identification of mentally retarded persons. Tredgold (1952) advocated a social criterion, based upon the individual's capacity for self-maintenance in society, as the only logical criterion for mental deficiency. Doll (1941) concurred with this attitude when he indicated that a mentally retarded person was one who was unable to adjust to the environment or was socially inadequate to the extent of being unable to manage his personal affairs. More recently, Benton (1964) has characterized social competence as the ultimate determinant in any diagnosis of mental retardation.

Heber (1959) expanded on the relationship between social competence and mental retardation. He defined this relationship as adaptive behavior, which included "a composite of many aspects of behavior" and was considered "a function of a wide range of specific abilities and disabilities" (p. 61). A person's adaptive behavior refers to the individual's ability to cope "with the natural and social demands of his environment" (p. 3). Heber further specified that impaired intellectual functioning will be reflected by impairment in adaptive behavior in different age groups by:

1. Rate of maturation in early developmental skills in infancy and early childhood.
2. Delayed learning or learning difficulties during the school years.
3. Social adjustment at the adult level in terms of employment, and the individual's ability to deal with persistent life situations.

In terms of the total life cycle, the two major facets of adaptive behavior involve:

1. The degree to which the individual is able to function and maintain himself independently, and
2. The degree to which he meets satisfactorily the culturally imposed demands of personal and social responsibility. [p. 61]

Table One

Anticipated level of adaptive behavior

Pre-school age, 0–5 Maturation & development	School-age, 6–21 Training & education	Adult, 21 and older Social & vocational adequacy
Poor motor development; speech minimal; generally unable to profit from training in self-help; little or no communication skills.	Can talk or learn to communicate; can be trained in elemental health habits; cannot learn functional academic skills; profits from systematic habit training. ("Trainable")	Can contribute partially to self-support under complete supervision; can develop self-protection skills to a minimal, useful level in controlled environment.

NOTE: Portion of a table in W. Sloan & J. A. Birch, A rationale for degrees of retardation, *American Journal of Mental Deficiency*, 1955, *60*, 262.

Table One reflects the anticipated level of adaptive behavior for the trainable from preschool to adult years. According to Heber's criteria, the TMR person's adaptive behavior is defined as Level II, or Moderate, with a definite negative deviation from the norm.

In the revision of Heber's manual, Grossman (1973) redefined mental retardation as a phenomenon that requires concurrent deficits in intellectual functioning and adaptive behavior. The implication is that deficits in adaptive behavior *and* intelligence must exist before a person can be classified as mentally retarded. Grossman also recognized the variability of adaptive behavior according to age levels which are reflected in the following progression.

Infancy and Early Childhood
1. Sensory-motor skills development and
2. Communication skills (including speech and language) and
3. Self help skills and
4. Socialization (development of ability to interact with others) and

During childhood and early adolescence in
5. Application of basic academic skills in daily life activities and
6. Application of appropriate reasoning and judgment in mastery of the environment and
7. Social skills (participation in group activities and interpersonal relationships) and

During late adolescence and adult life in
8. Vocational and social responsibilities and performance. [p. 12]

Within this continuum, Grossman anticipated that the highest level of adaptive behavior for the trainable person compared favorably with a twelve-year-old educable child.

It may well be remembered that Table Two illustrates the highest anticipated level of functioning. Subsequently, even at optimum, it is apparent that the trainable person will be seriously limited in adaptive behavior and will probably be dependent, to some degree, upon someone for a portion of their maintenance and support throughout life.

The position of the TMR in society is restricted by a composite of deficits in adaptive behavior, intelligence, and attendant organic problems. These limitations usually preclude the possibility of the person's functioning as a responsible individual, regardless of the social situation. However, the degree of this limitation is often dependent upon the upper limits of the TMR person's ability.

In general, the limited effectiveness of the TMR population necessitates establishing multiple services to support these people throughout their lives. Consequently, Farber (1968) has emphasized the TMR's position in society as a "surplus population." He contends that the presence of mental retardation limits life chances for this segment of the population, and that they subsequently become organizational surplus,

---

Table Two

Illustrations of highest level of adaptive behavior

Age & level indicated	
12 years: mild 15 years & over: moderate	*Independent functioning:* Feeds, bathes, dresses self; may select daily clothing; may prepare easy foods for self or others; combs/brushes hair; may shampoo and roll up hair; may wash and/or iron and store own clothes. *Physical:* Good body control; good gross and fine motor coordination. *Communication:* May carry on simple conversation; uses complex sentences. Recognizes words, may read sentences, ads, signs, and simple prose material with some comprehension. *Social:* May interact cooperatively and/or competitively with others. *Economic activity:* May be sent on shopping errand for several items without notes; make minor purchases; add coins to dollar with fair accuracy. *Occupation:* May do simple routine household chores (dusting, garbage disposal, dishwashing, preparing simple foods which require mixing). *Self-direction:* May initiate most of own activities; attends to task 15 to 20 minutes (or more); may be conscientious in assuming much responsibility.

NOTE: Adapted from material in H. J. Grossman, *Manual on terminology and classification in mental retardation,* American Association on Mental Deficiency, Special publication no. 2 (2nd printing), 1973, p. 31.

---

or that excess of people who are of no use to society's productiveness. In referring to the severely retarded, Farber states that they "can rarely, if ever be successful in occupation or family life regardless of the social situation" (p. 18).

If severe deficits in adaptive behavior limit the ability of the TMR to function or "behave" as responsible individuals in society, then how *do* they behave? Any description of the TMR population usually involves a statement of behaviorial characteristics, or cliches related to stereo-typed behaviors such as happy, outgoing, uninhibited, and responsive or hyperactive, querulous, and difficult to manage.

Behaviorial Implications

There appears to be some empirical basis for a behaviorial description of the TMR according to syndrome. Various authors (Domino, Goldschmid, & Kaplan, 1964; Johnson & Abelson, 1969; Moore,

Thuline, & Capes, 1968; Silverstein, 1964) have investigated the social behavior of people with Down's syndrome and found sufficient evidence to support the "mongoloid stereotype" of well-adjusted and extroverted behavior along with a generally higher competence than that shown by other TMR people in that they usually function in the upper range of the trainable population and typically pose fewer management problems. Charney (1968) also concluded from a study of teacher ratings, that teachers of the TMR considered the Down's syndrome population easier to manage and instruct. However, select studies did caution against an oversimplification of Down's syndrome behavior. It was noted that the "mongoloid stereotype" may be self-fulfilling (that is, if the expectation is that they will be "well-adjusted," these people will fulfill that expectation), and that the lack of central nervous system involvement in the Down's syndrome population may preclude the bizarre types of behavior or management problems often ascribed to the brain-damaged population. In summary, there is sufficient evidence to indicate that the behavior of the Down's syndrome population is no different than that of other retardates functioning at the trainable level (Clarke & Clarke, 1961).

Additional stereotyped behaviors have been attributed to that portion of the TMR population which is classified as brain-injured. The brain-injured person often poses some problems which have been described by Strauss and Kephart (1955) as hyperactivity, impulsivity, and overt reaction to frustration and anxiety. Stevens and Birch (1957), in a review of Strauss' early writings described the brain-injured population as "children with perceptual disturbances, disturbances in thinking and disturbances in personality" (p. 347). They further stated that these children tended to perseverate,* be hyperactive, and function in a rigidly stereotyped behavior pattern.

The behavior of brain-injured people is often considered a manifestation of the injury. However, Strauss and Kephart (1955) did indicate that the same kinds of behavior may be observed in children who were not brain-injured. Furthermore, Kennedy and Ramirez (1964) stated that they felt that there was no clear relationship between the damage and the behavioral disturbances. They offered the possibility that the symptoms were more the result of interference by the damage on the intact portion of the brain. Also on a comparative basis, Charney (1968) reported that teacher ratings indicated no difference in behaviorial characteristics between children who were brain-injured and those with Down's syndrome, and that these findings offered a caution in the generalization of the relationship between brain injury and specific behavior patterns.

---

*Involuntary persistence of one reply or one idea in response to various questions.

Such conflicting opinions should make it apparent that one must exercise restraint in stereotyping behavior based upon the diagnosis of brain injury. Much will depend upon the degree of the damage, its location in the brain, and the extent of the individual's reaction to the environment. Certainly, many of the behaviors attributed to this population exist, but the continuum of the behavior in the brain-injured TMR could range from hyperactivity to a passive, withdrawn hypoactivity level.

In addition to the etiological impact on behavior, circumstances such as psychosocial development and the parents' abilities to cope with the retardation could also have implications for the TMR. Psychosocial development is usually consistent with mental age. Therefore, it may be anticipated that TMR people will manifest behaviors, such as tantrums or reticence, that would be more consistent with the behavior of young children of similar mental ages (Begab, 1966). Furthermore, excessive demands on the part of the parents for appropriate performance or conversely, excusing the inappropriate behavior—no matter how inappropriate—because of level of retardation would have an additional impact on the behavior of the TMR child.

An additional theoretical basis for TMR behavior encompasses multiple factors. Bijou (1966) has related both constitutional and environmental factors to behavior in mental retardation. He suggests that we compound the problems of organic deficiency by restricting retardates' opportunities for development of appropriate behavioral repertoires through our withholding of stimuli or appropriate reinforcers. He proposes that the behaviorial problems ascribed to the retarded are more a result of a restriction of various forms of environmental stimulation and limited or inappropriate reinforcers.

Whatever the circumstances, the behaviorial component of a definition of the TMR population involves a consideration of multiple circumstances which precipitate varied reactions to life situations within the environment. Too often the cultural sterotype prevails. The validity of these attitudes is questionable, and the diverse nature of these reactions would preclude any simple, discrete definition of the behavior of the TMR.

Toward a Comprehensive Definition

In the preceding pages, we have discussed the various factors which have an impact on the ultimate decision concerning who and what compose the TMR population. It is obvious from this discussion that the trainable population represents a complex set of biological, psychological, and social problems which, when considered in their entirety, defy any attempt at a simple operational definition. Not only are the circumstances diverse, but there is also a difference in emphasis among professional disciplines. Therefore, a definition of the trainable must be an expression of relevant facts based on (1) measurement of intelligence, (2) cognitive development, (3) etiology, and (4) adaptive behavior. An expression of these relevant facts will only provide guidelines or criteria for decision making, rather than a specific definition of the population.

Measured Intelligence

It may be anticipated that the TMR population will have a measured IQ somewhere between 25 and 50. This is not a precise expression of current guidelines (Grossman, 1973), but it is used to provide a greater range of measurement to allow for variability as a result of other criteria (such as adaptive behavior) which may affect the decision-making process. Also, this IQ range is considered more consistent with the term "trainable" and indicates a need for training rather than education.

Cognitive Development

On the basis of measured intelligence, the TMR population could not be expected to profit from an academic program or demonstrate measurable gains in academic areas. They would be expected to develop at a rate one fourth to one half that of a normal child and learn about as efficiently as children of the same mental age. However, TMR people do not usually attain the minimum mental age necessary for the learning of academic tasks, nor are they able to reason, generalize, or form new concepts. Therefore, a program for the TMR should reflect a nonacademic curriculum devoted to habit formation and simple rote learnings in areas such as self-help and social adjustment. On the basis of anticipated cognitive development, the TMR will be expected to be semidependent/dependent on someone or on an agency for a portion of their support during their entire lifetimes.

Etiology

The TMR are usually represented by circumstances of a pathological origin. A population comprised of approximately one third Down's syndrome and two thirds brain-damaged is usually anticipated. Within this population, there are usually related disorders in areas such as communication skills, sensory defects, and physical and/or motor impairments. Speech and language disorders are often considered to be the greatest related disorder among the TMR. Further, the trainable population is usually expected to have about four times as many problems in vision and hearing than the rate usually estimated for the public school population. The severity of physical or motor problems is usually dependent upon the organicity of the extant syndrome.

Adaptive Behavior

Limited adaptive behavior is usually the sum total of all other deficits which contribute to a general inability to adapt to the social demands of the environment. The ability of the TMR to cope with persistent life situations is usually limited to such a degree as to preclude the possibility of a self-directed role in society or completely independent self-maintenance.

These guidelines or criteria are not unalterable, nor do they have universal applicability. Circumstances which contribute to the determination of a "trainable" level of functioning may vary according to the area or cultural milieu where they are applied. Intelligence is a relative construct, and what is adaptive behavior in one place, may be maladaptive in another. Therefore, the prevalence of the trainable mentally retarded, in a general population, will vary depending upon criteria and geographic area.

Prevalence

Prevalence figures are dependent upon the definition(s) or criteria used to describe a given population. The prevalence of the trainable mentally retarded has usually been determined by general estimates based on observable physical stigmata, where attendant retardation is assumed, or by an evaluation of intelligence.

Early criteria for determining idiocy were vague and inaccurate. Later criteria for determining conditions, such as cretinism and Down's syndrome, were equally capricious in that they were based on an observable condition on which there was no professional agreement or for which there was little precision in definition.

It was not until the advent of objective measures of intelligence that workers were able to impose some sort of precise criteria for the determination of an individual's level of intelligent behavior. The IQ range provided a statistical, and subsequently more precise, definition of functioning levels for various segments of the population. A test score became the principal criterion, and an IQ below 50 was used to identify that segment of the population that was considered to be trainable or below.

Early prevalence studies usually gave general estimates of the total mentally retarded population. Some of the reported findings of these studies still reflected a state of ambiguity in classification as shown in estimates of the prevalence of mental retardation ranging from 3.40 to 12.2 per 1,000 population. The obvious variance in these general estimates was usually attributed to circumstances within the geographic area surveyed, conditions of the survey, or the less than objective criteria used in the studies (Farber, 1968).

Around 1950, education began to take an increased role in providing programs for the TMR population, and prevalence figures by level of retardation consequently began to emerge for purposes of program planning. Kirk (1962) cited several studies from the decade of the 1950s which indicated that there were about two to four TMR children per 1,000 children in the school-age population. He further noted from these data that there would have to be a population of about 7,000 school-age children before it would be feasible to organize a class for the TMR.

Other general estimates have been reported by various authors. Williams (1961) summarized existing data and reported that approximately three in 1,000 of the general population were trainable. Best (1965) indicated that the Children's Bureau estimates showed that within the 3% of the population considered to be mentally retarded, 0.4% are trainable. The President's Panel on Mental Retardation (1962) estimates also reflect a figure of 0.4%. Table 3 is an analysis of the panel's figures and their relationship to the general population.

Table three includes the categories Moderate and Severe, since this analysis of the population was completed at a point in time when the current definition of "trainable" according to IQ level (20 or 30 to 50) incorporated both levels (Heber, 1960).

Table Three

Incidence of mental retardation

Degree		Total incidence	% of MR	Estimated pop. in the U.S. (Total population, 180 million)
Moderate	(IQ 35—50)	0.3	10.0	540,000
Severe	(IQ 20—35)	0.1	3.3	180,000

NOTE: Portion of a table in J. H. Rothstein, *Mental retardation: Readings and resources,* 2nd ed. (New York: Holt, Rinehart, Winston, 1971), p. 20. Based upon estimates cited in the report of The President's Panel, 1962.

Dunn (1973) summarized several prevalence studies of the 1950s and 1960s dealing with children having IQs below 50. He concluded from these surveys that school-age retarded children with IQs below 50 represented 0.25%, or approximately 50 per 20,000 of the population. In a further analysis of these data, he indicated that the segment of the population he determined as trainable (IQ 35 to 50) comprised 0.20%, or 40 per 20,000 of the population surveyed.

More recent figures (Rossmiller, Hale, & Frohreich, 1970) indicate that, depending upon geographic area, the prevalence of trainable mentally retarded varies from 0.24% to 0.18%. They further projected, on the basis of the U.S. Census Bureau information, that by 1980 the trainable will represent 0.24% of the population. For planning purposes, this would mean that by 1980, we would have approximately 48 TMR per 20,000 population in need of some sort of program or service.

The use of IQ scores has been quite convenient in the determination of the prevalence of the trainable. Although there have been some changes in terminology, the range of intelligence used to define the trainable population has not changed remarkably. Even with the recent differences between the Heber (1959) and Grossman (1973) definitions, the IQ score or range still indicates that the trainable are approximately 3 to 4 σ (standard deviation units) below the norm, and represent 0.13%, or approximately 26 per 20,000 of the general population on a normal curve or distribution of intelligence. The discrepancy between the theoretical (that is, the number derived from a normal distribution curve) and the estimated number of retardates between IQ 20 to 50 was investigated by Dingman and Tarjan (1960). Their conclusion was that various factors other than measured intelligence contributed to an actual number of TMR in excess of that which would be anticipated on the basis of a normal distribution curve.

Reported data on prevalence figures for the trainable have been

reasonably consistent. The semantic differences or changes in definition of the trainable population have not had as great an impact on
prevalence figures as have those changes involving general estimates
of the total mentally retarded population. Subsequent surveys of prevalence will become increasingly difficult to conduct, however. The introduction of adaptive behavior, by Heber (1960) and Grossman (1973), as
an additional dimension of the criteria may serve to confound future
prevalence studies. Appropriate epidemiological studies of the trainable
must now take into consideration the criteria of intelligence *and* adaptive
behavior. The IQ measure has provided a convenient, measurable
criterion for defining the trainable population. However, adaptive behavior is a nonstatistical nomenclature, without a suitable means of
measurement (Silverstein, 1973).

Additional problems in prevalence studies may also be related to
incidence. Incidence is actually the antecedent to prevalence. By definition, incidence is a measure of how often a condition or circumstance is
apt to occur, while prevalence is a measure of how extensively the
circumstances actually exist.

It has been contended that socioeconomic level has an impact on
the incidence rate of the trainable population. It has been noted that the
TMR appear to be more widely distributed than the higher level of
retardate among the various socioeconomic groups (Williams, 1961).
However, it has frequently been contended that the trainable population
tends to be more indigenous to the middle and upper-middle-class
groups, and that the educable mentally retarded are more prevalent
among the lower socioeconomic groups. This generalization of socioeconomic factors, and their relationship to the incidence of trainable
mentally retarded is the result of empirical evidence that indicates
that there is a causal relationship between the risk of impaired intellectual functioning and the unhealthy circumstances surrounding the physical and cultural environment. It is further suggested that while these
circumstances may contribute to the mild or familial levels of retardation
(that is, where one or both of the parents are retarded), the clinical
groups (such as Down's syndrome) are from different kinds of environments and parents. Consequently, the more severe the retardation, the
less probability that the parents will be retarded (Gruenberg, 1964).

One may draw several inferences from this evidence. Prevalence
more than incidence may be the factor. The prevalence of the TMR may
be predominant in middle to upper-middle-class families. However, the
incidence may be the same for all socioeconomic levels, with a lower
prevalence in the low socioeconomic groups as a result of factors such
as a higher infant mortality rate due to lack of funds for adequate medical
care. Moreover, the cultural milieu of the lower socioeconomic group

places fewer demands upon its members, and the "trainable" may not be identified as such because he or she has been able to cope adequately with the immediate environment. Wolfensberger (1967) has suggested that the assumption relative to the reported higher incidence of trainables among white middle-class families may simply be related to the fact that the various studies that have been conducted included only white middle-class parents in their sample.

Whatever the circumstances, the incidence of mental retardation at the trainable level will probably be the same at all socioeconomic levels. Socioeconomic factors may have some influence on the incidence of TMR in a population, but the conclusive data is simply not available.

Medical science provides an additional dimension that may have an impact on the incidence and prevalence of the TMR. One might anticipate a decrease in incidence as a result of improved obstetric techniques and other medical services. Genetic counseling and the availability of legal abortions may also contribute to a decrease in incidence among certain clinical types of retardation. However, these same improved medical techniques may increase the prevalence of certain clinical types by assisting them in surviving the birth trauma or by providing an extended life span with antibiotics and improved medical and surgical techniques. The impact of these various medical factors and their relationship are, as yet, undetermined.

The broadening of the knowledge base and the inclusion of additional dimensions or criteria in the definition of the trainable population will have an impact on what we can expect to report as incidence and prevalence figures. The future trend will probably be toward higher prevalence figures as a result of the inclusion of adaptive behavior in the criteria; that is, an EMR child possessing severe deficits in adaptive behavior may be reclassified as trainable.

It would be difficult to project a change in incidence because of its relationship to etiology. For practical purposes, the etiological circumstances will continue to have a major role in incidence and prevalence. Although medical science may provide some major changes in incidence through treatment and prevention, the etiology will still present a series of pervasive circumstances which will have a distinct impact on both intelligence and adaptive behavior.

Whatever changes may occur, educators will be principally concerned with prevalence figures in the planning of programs. We may also find incidence figures useful, particularly in their relationship to etiology, in grouping according to characteristics, and in determining the educational implications of the underlying causes of individual deficits.

The incidence rate of the trainable mentally retarded is reflected by a myriad of etiologies of known and unknown origin which precipitate impairment of normal development which may occur during the pre-natal, perinatal, and postnatal periods.

Etiology

The majority of the known etiologies resulting in mental retardation occur within that segment of the retarded population whose measured IQ is below 50. It is a common assumption that approximately one third of the trainable population is represented by Down's syndrome, and the remaining two thirds reflects various kinds and degrees of brain damage.

Etiological factors in mental retardation are often emphasized at the expense of other more relevant circumstances in education. Due to the number and variation of these etiologies, it would be presumptuous, and beyond the scope of this text, to discuss them all. Nevertheless, it would seem appropriate to review briefly the more representative etiologies within the trainable population.

Down's Syndrome

Down's syndrome was first described as a clinical entity by Langdon Down in 1866. It was originally designated "Mongolian Idiocy" because of the attendant physical features of a Mongolian. However, the term "Down's syndrome" is currently preferred in any description of this population.

There have been numerous explanations for the causes of Down's syndrome (Warkany, 1960). Research evidence has been relatively inconclusive, but the most promising evidence to date appears to lie in the area of chromosome research. The efforts of Dr. Joe Hin Tijo realized their fruition in the discovery of forty-six chromosomes as the exact number of chromosomes in man, and Dr. Jerome Lejune is responsible for the discovery of anomalies in this count that are as-sociated with Down's syndrome.

Chromosome errors can now be determined by sorting and pairing, and the most common of the birth defects attributed to autosome anomalies is Down's syndrome. The major emphasis in research on Down's syndrome has been directed toward these anomalies. Down's syndrome as a clinical entity may be attributed to a chromosomal anomaly manifested by a total of forty-seven instead of the normal forty-six chromosomes, where there are three instead of two Chromo-somes No. 21. This extra chromosome or "trio" in Chromosome No. 21 is often designated a "trisomic disorder" and accounts for the majority of the Down's syndrome patients studied (Polani, 1963).

Other chromosome errors resulting in Down's syndrome may be attributed to a translocation of chromosome material which will account for an array of forty-five or forty-six chromosomes. The translocation may be partial or complete. A translocation of material from Chromosome No. 21 to chromosome group 13–15, may still leave forty-six chromosomes, but the translocation from Chromosome No. 21 may be sufficient to result in forty-five chromosomes, leaving only one Chromosome No. 21 (Carter, 1966).

There may also be a nondysjunction of Chromosome No. 21. This results in a rare condition known as mosaicism. This is a rare chromosomal anomaly where the nondysjunction of Chromosome No. 21 produces a new line of cells along with normal developing cells. The result is a concurrent development of cells with forty-six *and* forty-seven chromosomes. The symptoms of mosaicism range from typical Down's syndrome to intellectually normal individuals with only peripheral symptoms (Robinson & Robinson, 1965).

A second interesting feature in the etiology of Down's syndrome is its apparent relationship to maternal age. In most conditions attributed to maternal age, it is believed that the aging of the mother, or her ova, results in the production of germ cells with two instead of one Chromosome No. 21. Women of twenty-five have approximately one chance in 2,000 of having a Down's syndrome child, but by the age of forty-five, the expectation increases to one in fifty (Polani, 1963). Further evidence indicates that the incidence of Down's syndrome is 75% greater in the forty to fifty year maternal age group than in expectant mothers of the twenty to twenty-five age group, and that mothers giving birth to a Down's syndrome child will have a mean age of thirty-six (Carter, 1966; Penrose, 1963).

Although there are known factors which contribute to Down's syndrome, the total etiology remains an enigma. The greater incidence is often attributed to factors of unknown origin which results in the development of the condition sometime early in the gestation period (Dunn, 1964). Whatever the etiology, Down's syndrome has been described as the most common of the known pathologies that cause retardation. It has a reported birth frequency of about one in 700 babies, and represents approximately 6% of all the retarded and 10% to 20% of admissions to institutions (Masland, 1963).

The clinical manifestations of Down's syndrome are numerous and do not all exist in any one case. The degree or number of physical characteristics and the level of intellectual functioning may be quite variable. The most frequent physical characteristics are (1) a short stature, (2) a flat broad head, (3) almond-shaped eyes, (4) a tongue too large for the oral cavity—often protruding and deeply fissured, (5) a transverse palmar crease, and (6) a distinct separation of the first and second toes. Concomitantly, the child with Down's syndrome frequently has congenital heart defects as well as a greater propensity for upper respiratory infections. The level of intellectual functioning is usually dependent upon a number of factors. The optimum anticipated level of intelligence would usually be within the trainable range, but Jordan (1972) reported instances of children with Down's syndrome having Binet IQs as high as 68 to 70. However, these instances are rare, and the IQ of a child with Down's syndrome would usually be somewhere between 25 to 50, with corresponding deficits in adaptive behavior.

Down's syndrome, by comparison, is perhaps the most visible clinical entity within the trainable population. The remaining population of the TMR usually represents a number of undifferentiated types of brain injury, with the single common denominator of severe intellectual impairment. There are, however, some recognizable syndromes within this population that represent visible clinical entities.

Other Clinical Syndromes

There are many cranial anomalies, but two of the more prominent syndromes are represented by conditions such as hydrocephaly and microcephaly.

Hydrocephaly

The brain is bathed in a cerebrospinal fluid which circulates freely throughout the central nervous system. An increased volume of this fluid will result in a condition known as hydrocephaly. The increased volume is usually caused by an obstruction in the circulation of the fluid (intraventricular-noncommunicating) or in the mechanisms that absorb the fluid back into the bloodstream (extraventricular-communicating). Whatever the locus of the obstruction, there is a dilation of the ventricles (hollow portions of the brain) with the resultant clinical manifestation of an enlarged head (Ransohoff & Shulman, 1963). Treatment of the hydrocephalic usually involves surgical intervention to remove the obstruction or the insertion of a ventricular shunt. In some instances, intervention is not necessary, and there is a spontaneous remission of the condition. In either case, the cranial expansion or dilation is arrested. Prognosis is dependent upon the amount of brain damage that has occurred before the condition is arrested. Weaver (1965) reported a variation of prognosis ranging from death to normal mental and physical development. However, he cautioned that "little or no improvement in mental and intellectual capacities can be expected if the hydrocephalus progresses to the point that increased intracranial pressure produces irrepairable brain damage" (p. 304).

Microcephaly

Microcephaly is also a cranial anomaly whose clinical manifestation is concerned with head size. Characteristically, the microcephalic has an unusually small head and a subsequent decrease in brain mass. Clarke and Clarke (1961) have stated that an adult head circumference of less than seventeen inches constitutes microcephaly. Penrose (1963) indicated that traditionally, regardless of age, microcephaly is extant when the head measures less than thirteen inches in circumference and that at this level retardation is inevitable. However, Rubenstein (1965) states that there is considerable discussion as to clinical criteria for diagnosis of microcephaly, and he contends that the severity of retardation has a poor correlation with head size, except in the extreme.

The causes of microcephaly are often obscure. It has frequently been attributed to a genetic base, or irradiation of the mother during the first trimester of pregnancy. In addition, viral insults during gestation, such as maternal rubella, have been thought to contribute to the incidence of microcephaly. The intellectual capacity of the microcephalic is often as unpredictable as the cause. Microcephalics are typically considered to function within the trainable range of intelligence. However, there are reported instances of the microcephalic functioning well within the educable range (Clarke & Clarke, 1961).

Other than cranial anomalies, there are factors manifested by brain injury that represent a recognizable syndrome or condition where the retardation is ancillary to the disability. Williams (1963) has reported on a small but consistent percentage of trainables being cerebral palsied. Although cerebral palsy, by definition, is principally a motor problem (Perlstein, 1963), various authors (Jordan, 1972; Levinson & Bigler, 1960) have offered evidence of retardation within this population.

Cerebral Palsy

The etiology of cerebral palsy, like many other forms of brain injury, begins with prenatal, perinatel, and postnatal determiners encompassing factors such as genetic disorders, uterine insults, or mechanical damage. If the locus of the damage is limited to the pyramidal tracts or motor areas of the brain, then cerebral palsy exists without severe impairment to intellectual functioning. The principal manifestations of the motor disability may involve (1) spasticity, (2) rigidity, (3) athetosis, and (4) ataxia, all of which usually overlap into a clinical picture presenting problems in limited movement and ambulation. However, the damage is not often discretely localized and will subsequently affect other areas of the brain that control various intellectual functions. While cerebral palsy is not considered tantamount to retardation, the IQ of a cerebral-palsied population tends to cluster around a mean of -2σ

(standard deviation units) below the normal mean of intelligence. Therefore, we could at least anticipate a moderate level of intellectual deficit among the cerebral-palsied population (Jordan, 1972).

There are a number of other etiologies that contribute to the trainable population. These are often represented by obscure circumstances which range from identifiable syndromes to undifferentiated conditions. It would be beyond the scope of this text to provide a detailed discussion of such conditions as the Lawrence-Moon-Biedl syndrome or Von Recklinghausen's disease. It would also be difficult, if not impossible, to describe that population where no recognizable syndrome exists. However, a cursory understanding of the causative factors is often necessary for the educator to function within a multidisciplinary environment. The rationale of this classification is to enhance communication.

A Classification of Causative Factors

The nomenclature of the American Association on Mental Deficiency (Grossman, 1973) provides an organized classification system that reflects contemporary medical knowledge in mental retardation. Within this nomenclature, the causative factors are listed according to etiological agent or primary disorder. For the purposes of discussion, the Grossman (1973) classification will be used to delineate the causative factors. Although the nomenclature is not inclusive, it is reasonably comprehensive and serves to bring order to a complex set of contingencies which may contribute to mental retardation.

Conditions Following Infection and Intoxication

This classification is concerned with infectious diseases and intoxicants that can affect the development of the child prenatally and postnatally. Maternal infections such as rubella, syphilis, or toxoplasmosis may precipitate brain damage or severe malformations of the child while *in utero*. Brain damage may also occur from prenatal intoxication as a result of conditions such as toxemia and Rh incompatibility, or other maternal intoxication from drugs, chemicals, or poisons. Postnatal factors principally involve brain damage as a result of cerebral infections following the onset of conditions such as mumps, measles, or rubella, or as a result of inoculation with certain types of serum or vaccine. Other postnatal brain damage may occur from the ingestion of intoxicants such as lead or various drugs, or the inhalation of toxic agents like carbon monoxide.

Conditions Following Trauma or Physical Agent

The principal manifestation of this category is brain damage as a result of influences occurring prenatally, perinatally, or postnatally. Prenatal injury may be precipitated by factors such as irradiation, prenatal oxygen deficiency, or other trauma during the gestation period. Perinatal factors are concerned with injury occurring during the birth process as a result of difficulties in labor, presentation, oxygen deprivation, hemorrhage, or twisted cord. Postnatal injury can be attributed to oxygen deficiency as a result of conditions such as shock, poisoning, and convulsions or to severe trauma as a result of a blow to the head.

Disorders of Metabolism or Nutrition

Problems related to metabolic disorders, nutrition, and endocrinology are all included in this category. Disorders of metabolism and endocrinology involve rare syndromes like Tay-Sachs disease, Niemann-Pick disease, Hurler's disease, Glactosemia, Phenylketonuria (PKU), and cretinism. These are all represented by a variety of physical disorders or stigmata which are attended by retardation. Nutritional disorders are generally attributed to retardation as a result of poor diet or problem feeding.

Conditions Associated with Gross Postnatal Brain Damage

This category encompasses conditions with a genetic or hereditary base with etiologies of known and unknown orgin. The resultant circumstances have a wide variety of manifestations such as tumors, "port wine stain," and seizures, all with some degree of mental impairment. Clinically, the underlying causes may result in cerebellar signs like ataxia, or spasticity, hemiplegia, choreiform movements, and parkinsonian facies. In some instances conditions within this category terminate in early death.

Conditions of Unknown Prenatal Influence

Etiology of unknown orgin, occurring before birth, are included in this category. The resultant factors involve cranial anomalies and other congenital defects. The cranial malformations range from anancephaly (partial or complete absence of the cerebrum), to conditions such as microcephaly, hydrocephaly, and macrocephaly. Other features within this category involve craniostenosis, encephaloceles, multiple malformations, and other disorders with no recognizable syndrome.

Conditions Related to Chromosomal Abnormality

The manifestations of chromosomal aberrations in this category are usually confined to recognizable syndromes such as Down's syndrome, Klienfelter's syndrome, Turner's syndrome, or the Cri-Du-Chat syndrome. Other abnormalities which are related to numerical or structural aberrations may also produce a wide range of undifferentiated conditions associated with retardation. Other common abnormalities within this classification include cleft lip and palate, congenital defects, and visual or auditory anomalies.

Conditions Resulting from Gestational Disorders

The incidence of defects in this category are principally related to problems of prematurity or low birth weight, or a gestation period that exceeds normal gestation by seven days or more.

The remaining causative factors listed by Grossman (1973) are related to retardation following a psychiatric disorder, or environmental influences and conditions of unknown etiology. Retardation following a psychiatric disorder or as a result of environmental influences usually lacks any cerebral pathology, and is principally concerned with intellectual functioning at the educable level of retardation. Unknown etiology, of course, encompasses any condition attended by retardation where there is no known evidence of the cause.

The previous discussion of specific etiologies represents only a brief synthesis of the current knowledge. For the student interested in a detailed discussion of the etiology of mental retardation, there are several excellent texts (Jordan, 1972; Robinson & Robinson, 1965) designed for this purpose. In addition, Grossman (1973) elaborates on this information and provides a glossary to assist in understanding terminology.

Summary

Early definitions of the trainable mentally retarded were of a common genus, expressed in terms like "fools" or "monsters," and later "idiocy." The advent of the intelligence test defined specific divisions of mental retardation as Moron, Imbecile and Idiot, in descending order of intelligence. The Imbecile level was interpreted in educational terms as "trainable," to include that population of mentally retarded who could not profit from an academic program but could learn the rudiments of self-care. Recent definitions have incorporated the criteria of medical diagnosis and adaptive behavior, and use the psychoeducational terms of moderate and/or severe. However, "trainable" still appears to be the term that best reflects the educational prognosis of this population.

Although there has been considerable discussion and modification in defining the trainable mentally retarded, the prevalence estimates have remained rather consistent. Future changes in criteria or definition could alter the prevalence figures, but current estimates indicate that the trainable represent approximately 0.24% of the population.

The majority of the known etiologies leading to mental retardation are found within the trainable range. The etiological circumstances are usually represented by clinical conditions such as Down's syndrome or factors which contribute to some form of brain injury. However, there are also a number of conditions that represent no known etiology or syndrome that may also contribute to the trainable population.

References

Begab, M. J. Emotional impact of mental retardation. In I. Phillips (Ed.), *Prevention and treatment of mental retardation*. New York: Basic Books, 1966.

Benton, A. L. Psychological evaluation and differential diagnosis. In H. Stevens & R. Heber (Eds.), *Mental retardation, a review of research*. Chicago: University of Chicago Press, 1964.

Best, H. *Public provisions for the mentally retarded in the United States*. Worcester, Mass.: Heffernon Press, 1965.

Bijou, S. W. A functional analysis of retarded development. In N. R. Ellis (Ed.), *Research in mental retardation*. New York: Academic Press, 1966.

Carter, C. H. *Handbook of mental retardation syndromes*. Springfield, Ill.: Charles C. Thomas, 1966.

Charney, L. The trainable mentally retarded. In O. Johnson & H. Blank (Eds.), *Exceptional children research review*. Washington, D.C.: Council for Exceptional Children, 1968.

Clarke, A. M., & Clarke, A. D. B. *Mental deficiency, the changing outlook*. Glencoe, Ill.: The Free Press, 1961.

D'Amelio, D. *Severely retarded children: Wider horizons*. Columbus, Oh.: Charles E. Merrill, 1971.

Davies, S. P., & Ecob, K. G. *The mentally retarded in society*. New York: Columbia University Press, 1962.

Davitz, J. R., Davitz, L. J., & Lorge, I. *Terminology and concepts in mental retardation*. New York: Columbia University Press, 1969.

Dingman, H. F., and Tarjan, G. Mental retardation and the normal distribution curve. *American Journal of Mental Deficiency*, 1960, *64*, 991–994.

Doll, E. A. The essentials of an inclusive concept in mental deficiency. *American Journal on Mental Deficiency*, 1941, *46*, 214–219.

Domino, G., Goldschmid, M., & Kaplan, M. Personality traits of institutionalized mongoloid girls. *American Journal of Mental Deficiency*, 1964, *68*, 498–502.

Dunn, L. M. Trainable mentally retarded children. In L. M. Dunn (Ed.), *Exceptional children in the schools*. Boston: Houghton Mifflin, 1964.

Dunn, L. M. Children with moderate and severe general learning disabilities. In L. M. Dunn (Ed.), *Exceptional children in the schools: Special education in transition*. New York: Holt, Rinehart, & Winston, 1973.

Farber, B. *Mental retardation: Its social context and social consequences*. Boston: Houghton-Mifflin, 1968.

Grossman, H. J. Manual on terminology and classification in mental retardation. *American Association on Mental Deficiency Special Publication*, 1973 (Series No. 2).

Gruenberg, E. M. Epidemiology. In H. A. Stevens & R. Heber (Eds.), *Mental retardation, a review of research*. Chicago: University of Chicago Press, 1964.

Heber, R. A manual on terminology and classification in mental retardation. *American Association on Mental Deficiency Monograph Supplement*, 1959.

Ingram, C. P. *Education of the slow learning child* (3rd ed.). New York: Ronald Press, 1960.

Johnson, R. C., & Abelson, R. B. The behaviorial competence of mongoloid and non-mongoloid retardates. *American Journal of Mental Deficiency*, 1969, 73, 856-857.

Jordan, T. E. *The mentally retarded* (3rd ed.). Columbus, Oh.: Charles E. Merrill, 1972.

Kanner, L. *A history of the study and care of the mentally retarded*. Springfield, Ill.: Charles C. Thomas, 1967. (a)

Kanner, L. Medicine in the history of mental retardation: 1800-1965. *American Journal of Mental Deficiency*, 1967, 72, 165-170. (b)

Kennedy, C., & Ramirez, L. S. Brain damage as a cause of behavior disturbance in children. In H. G. Birch (Ed.), *Brain damage in children: The biological and social aspects*. Baltimore: Williams & Wilkins, 1964.

Kirk, S. A. *Educating exceptional children*. Boston: Houghton Mifflin, 1962.

Kirk, S. A., & Johnson, G. O. *Educating the retarded child*. Cambridge, Mass.: Houghton Mifflin, 1951.

Levinson, A., & Bigler, J. A. *Mental retardation in infants and children*. Chicago: Year Book Publishers, 1960.

Masland, R. L. Mental retardation. In M. Fishbein (Ed.), *Birth defects*. Philadelphia: J. B. Lippincott, 1963.

Moore, B. C., Thuline, H. C., & Capes, L. Mongoloid and non-mongoloid retardates: A behaviorial comparison. *American Journal of Mental Deficiency*, 1968, 73, 433-436.

Penrose, L. S. *The biology of mental defect*. New York: Grune & Stratton, 1963.

Perlstein, M. Medical aspects of cerebral palsy. In W. M. Cruickshank & G. M. Raus (Eds.), *Cerebral palsy: Its individual and community problems*. Syracuse, N.Y.: Syracuse University Press, 1963.

Polani, P. E. Chromosome aberrations and birth defects. In M. Fishbein (Ed.), *Birth defects*. Philadelphia: J. B. Lippincott, 1963.

President's Panel on Mental Retardation. *National action to combat mental retardation*. Washington, D.C.: U.S. Government Printing Office, 1962.

Ransohoff, J., & Shulman, K. Hydrocephalus and spina bifida. In M. Fishbein (Ed.), *Birth defects*. Philadelphia: J. B. Lippincott, 1963.

Robinson, H. B., & Robinson N. M. *The mentally retarded child, a psychological approach*. New York: McGraw-Hill, 1965.

Rossmiller, R. A., Hale, J. A., & Frohreich, L. E. *Educational programs for exceptional children: Resource configuration and costs* (National Educational Finance Project Special Study No. 2). Madison, Wis.: University of Wisconsin, 1970.

Rubenstein, J. H. Cranial abnormalities. In C. H. Carter (Ed.), *Medical aspects of mental retardation*. Springfield, Ill.: Charles C. Thomas, 1965.

Silverstein, A. B. An empirical test of the mongoloid stereotype. *American Journal of Mental Deficiency*, 1964, *68*, 493–497.

Silverstein, A. B. Note on prevalence. *American Journal of Mental Deficiency*, 1973, *77*, 380–382.

Stevens, G. D., & Birch, J. W. A proposal for clarification of the terminology used to describe brain-injured children. *Exceptional Children*, 1957, *23*, 346–349.

Strauss, A. A., & Kephart, N. C. *Psychopathology and education of the brain injured child: Vol. II, Progress in clinic and theory*. New York: Grune & Stratton, 1955.

Terman, L. *The measurement of intelligence*. Boston: Houghton Mifflin, 1916.

Thorndike, R. L. *Stanford-Binet intelligence scale 1972 norm tables*. Boston: Houghton Mifflin, 1973.

Tredgold, A. F. *A textbook of mental deficiency*. London: Bailliere, Tindall, & Cox, 1952.

Warkany, J. Etiology of mongolism. *Journal of Pediatrics*, 1960, *56*, 412–419.

Weaver, E. N. Hydrocephalus, intercranial anurysms, intercranial vascular malformations, cerebral cysts, intracranial tumors, premature craniosynostosis. In C. H. Carter (Ed.), *Medical aspects of mental retardation*. Springfield, Ill.: Charles C. Thomas, 1965.

Williams, H. M. *Education of the severely retarded child*. Washington, D.C.: U.S. Government Printing Office, 1963.

Wolfensberger, W. Counseling the parents of the retarded. In A. A. Baumeister (Ed.), *Mental retardation appraisal education rehabilitation*. Chicago: Aldine, 1967.

Reference Note

1. Woo-Sam, J. M. Psychoeducational assessment in the seventies—A look at concepts and measures, The Stanford-Binet LM. Paper presented at the meeting of the American Psychological Association, New Orleans, 1974.

Chapter 2

Development of a Training Program

Historical Perspectives

Any historical review of the care and treatment of the mentally retarded would show a progression of "movements" analogous to the movement of a pendulum. As Davies and Ecob (1962) stated, there was "here reverence there persecution" (p. 9). There have been significant periods in time that had a specific impact on retardates and their circumstances.

The early history of mental retardation, although it has no significant impact on developing a modern program, does serve to illustrate the insidious influence of superstition and the lack of knowledge and understanding. The more observable forms of retardation were often equated with other circumstances, such as mental illness, birth defects, and other forms of handicapping conditions. The quality of life for this population of "unfortunates" was usually in direct proportion to the prevailing superstitions or needs (e.g., economic) of the existing society.

Early superstitions usually involved divination, and these "unusual creatures" were thought to represent the playful antics of the gods or—more importantly—omens of the Gods used to foretell the future. The omens series of *Summa Izbu*, an ancient Babylonian tablet written about 600 B.C., lists birth defects from head to foot, and diviners consulted works such as this to determine the meaning of a particular defect (Leichty, 1968). A sampling of these prophecies from the *Summa Izbu* tells us that "If a woman gives birth and the right ear of the child is withered—a moron will be born in the house of the man," or "If a woman gives birth, and the child has no lips—hard times will seize the land; the house of the man will be scattered," and finally, perhaps an ancient answer for urban renewal, "If a woman gives birth and the abdomen of the child is open—there will be a dwindling of the suburbs."

Divination continued to play a role in the superstitions of the early Greek and Roman city-states. However, as their societies became increasingly complex and greater demands were being placed on individual contributions and productivity, the position of reverence of the mentally retarded shifted to persecution and the employment of the sternest of eugenic measures. The most noteworthy policies produced the systematic destruction of handicapped offspring in Sparta and Rome.

31

The advent of Christianity precipitated a change in attitude toward the "less fortunate" members of society. A more humanitarian approach was advocated, and the church became instrumental in the establishment of institutions to provide care and sanctuary for handicapped persons.

During the Middle Ages, a minor evolution in the status of the retarded occurred. The cretins and mongoloids were often employed during this time as fools or jesters to amuse the household. However, the greater number of the retarded, although unharmed, were still subject to the whims and superstitions of the time.

During the period of enlightenment, the church—although it continued to play a significant role in the maintenance of asylums—was also instrumental in effecting a change in the status of the retarded. The Reformation precipitated a serious change in the public attitude toward the retarded. Men like Luther and Calvin subscribed to the belief that the retarded were "Godless beings" possessed by demons. Once again superstition—this time in the name of the church—had a significant impact on the social status of the retarded, and they were persecuted, tortured, or in many instances, put to death.

It was not until the beginning of the nineteenth century that men of science began to take an interest in the retarded. As Kanner (1967) has noted, there were few references to mental retardation in the scientific literature before the end of the eighteenth century, and a compilation of pertinent writings reflected "not one, however faint, allusion to mental deficiency, except for the evidence of sporadic interest in cretinism toward the end of the Middle Ages" (p. 8).

Scientific interest in retardation was sparked as a result of a sequence of events beginning in 1798, in the forest of Aveyron, France. Here a band of hunters came upon and captured a feral child roaming the woods. The boy was diagnosed by Pinel, the famous psychiatrist, as an "incurable idiot." Had a physician by the name of Jean M. G. Itard not taken an interest in the boy, the incident would have long been forgotten.

Dr. Itard was Chief Medical Officer at the National Institute for the Deaf and Dumb in Paris. He did not ascribe to the philosophy of hereditary "hopeless idiocy." Rather, he was of the sensationalist school and reasoned that through social experiences and training of the senses, he could ameliorate, if not cure, the "Wild Boy of Aveyron" of his idiocy.

Itard developed a systematic program of training, intellectual training and social experiences, and began to work with Victor, as the boy was now called. He published his first report in 1801, describing the progress of his work with Victor. His second and final report was published in 1806. Itard deemed his experiment with Victor a failure. However, the French Academy acknowledged in their official opinion of his

Jean Marie Gaspard Itard
1775–1838

work "that it was impossible for the institutor [Itard] to put in his lessons, exercises, and experiments more intelligence, sagacity, patience, courage; and that he has not obtained a greater success, it must be attributed, not to any lack of zeal or talent, but to the imperfection of the organs of the subject upon which he worked" (Davies & Ecob, 1962, p. 15).

Although Itard did, in despair, abandon Victor and the project of education, his experiment represented the first scientific attempt at educating a retarded child. Moreover, his experiment with Victor served to indicate for the first time that the retarded could learn, although to a limited extent. In addition, Itard's efforts contributed to an undertaking of almost crusader proportions in the interest of "idiot education" which were in later years to have near-cataclysmic results.

Itard's work with Victor had a profound influence on Edouard Seguin, a physician and psychologist. Seguin studied Itard's work, and he felt he saw in the methodology the secret for the cure of retardation. As a result of his interpretation of Itard's work with Victor, Seguin has since been recognized as the first great teacher-leader in mental retardation (Davies & Ecob, 1962).

Initially, Seguin followed Itard's procedures and operated in close association with him until Itard's death in 1838. Ultimately, however, Seguin made his own adaptations of the Itard methodology. These adaptations became a "physiological method" incorporating diagnosis and a "promotion of the harmonious physical, intellectual and moral development of the child" (Talbot, 1966, p. 46). The Seguin methodology was ultimately used with a group of children at the Bicetre, an institution in France. Seguin's success at the Bicetre credits him with the first viable institutional program. In addition, the Paris Academy of Science stated that he had evidently solved the problem of idiot education.

While Seguin was enjoying international acclaim for his efforts with the retarded, another physician, in Switzerland, was becoming interested in the problems of cretinism. Johann Jacob Guggenbuhl, through a series of events, abandoned his private practice and opened an institution for cretins on the Abendberg in Switzerland. It was the intention of Guggenbuhl to "awaken the souls" of his patients through a program of sense training, diet, medication and physical regimen. His program represented a major departure from current attitudes towards cretinism, and his methods were considered by many to be applicable to all the mentally retarded. His success spread rapidly throughout the world, and as Kanner (1967) noted, "he helped matters along . . . by propagating his ideas in extensive travels and publicizing the Abendberg in many pamphlets" (p. 24). The Abendberg received glowing reports from all those who visited it, and it was soon destined to become the criterion for subsequent institutions designed for the care and treatment of the retarded.

Among those who recognized the success of the Abendberg was Samuel G. Howe, an American physician who was interested in the establishment of an institution for "idiots" in the United States. Prior to this time, no conscious effort had been made to provide for the education and training of the retarded in America. Various states had enacted legislation in the interest of the retarded, the earliest being enacted in 1793 by the Commonwealth of Kentucky. This bill, as did subsequent legislation, provided for a stipend for the maintenance of the retardate in the home. However, for the most part the retarded were merely languishing in the homes and communities or in almshouses and jails (Best, 1965).

Howe felt that the various states had a responsibility to educate or train the retarded. As a result of his efforts, a committee was appointed by the Massachusetts legislature in 1846 to determine the efficacy of a program for the "relief" of the retarded in that state. As a result of this inquiry, the first public institution for the retarded was opened in South Boston on October 1, 1848. In this same year, Edouard Seguin came to

Edouard Seguin
1812—1880

America, and at Dr. Howe's invitation worked at America's first institution in an advisory capacity for a short period of time. Seguin remained in America until his death, playing a major role in the promulgation of services for the retarded in this country.

To this point, the early programs of Itard, Seguin, Guggenbuhl, and Howe, as well as others, were as Davies and Ecob (1962) stated, "organized in the hope of largely overcoming, if not entirely curing, mental retardation by the application of the physiological method" (p. 23). It was a noble venture doomed to failure.

These early workers became knights-errant. Rather than following a prudent course, they promised in their zeal more than they could ever accomplish. Seguin's catechism of a new educational model did not prove effective in the amelioration or "cure of idiots," and the existing institutions and programs founded on this model began to seek a higher level retardate in an effort to show results. Subsequently, the more severe forms of retardation (that is, TMR and below) were merely "warehoused" in the institutions, and the custodial approach prevailed for this population. In addition, the institutional model provided by Guggenbuhl came under closer scrutiny, and Guggenbuhl's early adulation deteriorated into a condemnation of his efforts. Support for the Abendberg program was withdrawn, and as Kanner (1967) stated, "its founder . . . was described as a swindler, a quack, a charlatan, an embezzler and a bigot . . . Too much had been promised" (p. 30).

This obvious failure to "cure" the retarded could perhaps be attributed to two factors: the early workers assumed that they were dealing with an intact organism, and the condition of retardation was treated as a homogeneous entity (that is, there was no appreciation or knowledge of degrees of retardation). Regardless of the reasons, their failures had a far-reaching impact on programs for the TMR. This population became a pariah, and was ultimately considered a "menace to society." From this point in time, programs for the more severe forms of retardation consisted of lifetime institutional care, and the institutions were considered "asylums for the incurable."

There was some experimentation with alternative programs within the institution in an effort to relieve the burden of total care. Various efforts were made at an attempt to train and rehabilitate the institutional population. The most noteworthy of these efforts was the colony plan, designed to train farm laborers. This plan began around the turn of the century, reached its apex around the 1920s, and decreased after 1935 (Davies & Ecob, 1962). Once again, though, the effort was futile in the training of the more severe forms of retardation, and the program proved to be beneficial only to the more mildly retarded. Programs for the TMR population continued to be one of containment in institutions, or maintenance by the family in the home and community.

For practical purposes at this point in time, the institution represented a total program for trainable people. However, occasional attempts were made to establish community-based services. These services were usually restricted to isolated parent-sponsored programs where the parents "met together to set up their own classes . . . hiring their own teachers (often not adequately qualified), procuring their own supplies, and organizing classes in homes, in basements, in churches, or wherever they could find space" (Kirk, 1962, p. 136). In addition to these parent-sponsored classes, there were also occasional attempts by the public schools to make provisions for the TMR. Hewett (1974) cites an account of one such class in the Cleveland Public Schools in 1918:

> About 14 of the most serious cases of imbecility . . . were gathered together and a superior, conscientious teacher placed in charge. The good folks responsible for this inauguration were united in their belief that the pupils would soon become as normal children, once they were properly taught. The teacher heroically attacked the problem, but before the close of the school year, all were aware that their experi-

ment was doomed to failure. At the close of the term, the class was disbanded—the imbeciles returned to their homes, probably not much the worse for this "schooling" but the poor teacher suffered a mental collapse which necessitated a sojourn at our Capitol State Hospital. [p. 46]

As humorous as this poignant account may seem, it is still remarkable to note that "cure" or making the TMR children into "normal children" persisted in the minds of those committed to working with this population.

The advent of World War II precipitated a renewed public interest in the handicapped and increased the development of services for this population as an expression of concern for the handicapped veteran. As a result of this interest, increased services also became available to the trainable mentally retarded.

The decade of the 1950s witnessed a significant change in the status of the TMR. Dunn and Capobianco (1959) reported that from 1953 forward, there was a remarkable growth in special classes for the TMR. Dunn (1963) attributes this, in part, to the founding of the National Association for Retarded Children (NARC) in 1950 (currently designated the National Association for Retarded Citizens). The founding of the NARC had a three-fold impact: (1) it stimulated new interest among parents in programs, (2) it provided a national voice and cohesiveness to the previously isolated parent-sponsored programs in the various states, and (3) it stimulated federal interest along with subsequent legislation enacted in the interest of the retarded. By 1956, every state in the United States had established some sort of legal provision for special education programs, and by 1960, it was estimated that 12,000 trainable children were enrolled in public school classes (Rhodes & Head, 1974; Rothstein, 1965).

Greater impetus was given to programs in the 1960s as a result of deeper federal involvement in funding. President Kennedy formed a panel to prescribe a program of action, and in 1963, the panel's report (President's Panel on Mental Retardation, 1962) resulted in a request being delivered to the 88th Congress for massive and far-reaching legislation (U.S. House of Representatives, 1963). The legislation called for a concerted attack, at the federal and state level, on the problems of mental retardation. To administer these programs, a Division of Handicapped Children and Youth was established, and federal support monies grew from $1,000,000 in 1958, to $15,348,000 in 1964. Ultimately, by Fiscal Year 1971, federal monies were to provide an expenditure of $27,050,007 under Title III, ESEA, and the Vocational Education Act to serve 122,760 trainable mentally retarded (U.S. Department of Health, Education and Welfare, 1973).

The legislative impetus of the 1960s and 1970s has resulted in unprecedented action in program development, and the position of the TMR population in society has shifted from pariah to prodigy. However, the proliferation of services has failed to solve, and in some instances compounded, problems that have confounded professionals for years. What constitutes an appropriate program, the appropriate sponsorship or responsibility for services, and basic human rights for the TMR are all, as yet, unresolved.

Current Trends and Issues

The current issues lacking resolution all have historical precedent. The initial emphasis in programs for the TMR population was cure-oriented. Consequently, the appropriate program of training for these "unfortunates" was to teach conformity or to rid them of their "idiocy" and have them take their place in society as "normal" individuals. The early workers were unwilling to accept the unalterable circumstances of retardation, and were so committed to the concept of cure that they ultimately abandoned the lower level retardate. Subsequently, they redirected their efforts toward the higher level retardate in order to gain the desired results. Concern for the "incurable" retardate waned, professionals became increasingly parsimonious in their efforts, and the optimistic intentions of the educational institutions deteriorated into custodial care (Davies & Ecob, 1962).

The passing of time has dimmed these early failures and their cataclysmic results. Renewed interest in the TMR has been confounded by the same failures and frustrations of the nineteenth century. The current trend is toward a change in intellectual categories and a renewed optimism toward the learning potential of the trainable. This time, the intention is not to cure, although the contention is that the "defeatist" approach of the 1950s must give way to the "normalization" of the 1970s. The current approach entails a redirection of emphasis away from the nonacademic curriculum to a concern for a more traditional program of academics and independence for the trainable mentally retarded.

Educable or Trainable?

Early program efforts were usually parent-sponsored and were concerned with quantity (that is, more services for more children) than quality (Kirk, 1962). In addition, they often reflected parental aspirations for what they wished the TMR child to be, rather than what in reality the child was. Thus, these programs often turned to academic programming as the principal component of "training" in an effort to "fix-up" the trainable.

In some lay and professional circles, there has always been a conviction that the trainable are capable of profiting from academic instruction. As Burton (1974) stated: "workers are often inclined to dismiss the nonacademic approach as too pessimistic. They feel that the trainable can and *should* be a productive member of society. To many members of our society, a non-productive member is an anathema. We would like for everyone to be consistent with the 'work ethic.' Therefore, there is a felt need to educate the trainable retardate to the level where he can become a productive member of our society" (p. 428).

There is a comparable group that contends that an academic program is inappropriate and emphasizes the term "trainable" as opposed to "educable." The term "trainable" has been a functional category used to define program and prognosis for this particular level of retardation. As Williams and Wallin (1965) noted, "the word 'trainable' . . . represented an attempt to bridge the gap between the terms 'educable' and 'uneducable' " (p. 336). Therefore, the educational experiences of the past have indicated that the trainable will not be educable, and that a traditional academic program is unwarranted for this population.

The current controversy over the educability of the trainable population is neologistic as well as philosophical. Dunn (1973) states that "trainable retardates, as contrasted with educable retardates . . . were considered to be uneducable in terms of the 3 R's. Only recently has this term been changed from trainable to moderately retarded and more academic instruction, including cognitive development added to the curriculum" (p. 92). Dunn (1973) also advocates a redefinition and upward extension of the IQ range to 35 ± 5 to 60 ± 5, "dropping out the lower end of the 'trainable' category and adding the lower end of the former 'educable' category who have been found to be nonadaptive to an academic school program" (p. 114). D'Amelio (1971) further contends that if special methods are used, the severely retarded can learn the fundamentals of academics. He specifically avoids the use of the term "trainable" for children whose IQ is below 50, because his contention is that it "does the severely mentally retarded child an injustice. The term trainable is both offensive and inaccurate. The severely retarded child is not only capable of training; he is also capable of learning" (p. vii).

These two authors are representative of the new knights-errant who are advocating a greater concern for cognitive development and academic instruction for the trainable. Attempts to raise the academic level of the trainable have been advocated on the basis of unusual cognitive abilities such as those illustrated in Figure One, or on other isolated instances such as that reported by Butterfield (1961) or evidenced by Nigel Hunt (1967).

Dear mother
I like to tell you how
I am enjoying my self with
Danny and phcillis and the
girls is everything all right
with you i am having
a wonderful time.
the girls are so adoorabel.
I just love them.
is euslie taking real
good care of you.
my beautiful sister en law
brought me to work with her
at the shore drive inn
I hope that euslie will have
a wonderful trip to dimtur.
and when the come home
I want they should tell me
all about her self.
So mother dear i love you
So much.
with best wishes to all of
you with love from
your charming daughter.

Figure One

Correspondence from a 32-year-old woman with Down's syndrome

Demonstrated performance in a given area by an individual child who is classified TMR often creates a spuriously high aspiration for the entire TMR population's abilities and achievements. Further credence is also given to the advocacy of increased emphasis on cognitive training and academics, because the TMR have already demonstrated by their performance in various controlled, systematic programs that they can "learn." However, there is a current lack of knowledge and understanding of how much and how well they learn.

How much the TMR can learn is not as critical as how well they utilize what they have learned. "Trainable" is not determined by whether they can read or write; rather it is a composite of deficits in intellectual and social development which precludes their ability to manage their affairs independently. Therefore, the extent of their retardation is determined, in a broader sense, by severe deficits in adaptive behavior. The illiterate may not be trainable, but the trainable may be illiterate—one of many factors used to determine the level of retardation.

Learning is also not the question; rather it is the extent to which the TMR child may learn as dictated by his or her optimum mental age. Usually, the TMR child does not reach the minimum mental age to permit learning at a level of functional literacy. In the future, we must exercise caution in evaluating the performance of an individual TMR in an academic area as justification for the introduction of academics into the curriculum.

Perhaps the most critical caution is expressed in a need to determine what constitutes an appropriate curriculum which would be consistent with the extant deficits of the TMR population. This issue continues to confound those who work with the TMR. The current wave of optimism notwithstanding, one must reflect on the past failures to "educate" the trainable mentally retarded and remain cognizant of the existing data which tend to indicate that an academic program is not warranted for the general TMR population.

From a historical reference, the failures of early workers (such as Itard, Seguin, and Guggenbuhl) to cure the retarded precipitated a defeatist attitude toward the lower levels of retardation. Hopes were at their nadir, and professionals were content to assume that the TMR could not profit from an academic curriculum such as that provided the EMR. The reemergence of interest in programs for the TMR in recent years has not substantially altered this assumption. Warren (1963) noted that "it has been generally accepted . . . that the trainable child is unlikely to profit from academic instruction" (p. 75). She further concluded from a study of 177 pupils with IQ's between 35 and 59, that the trainable can master a few fundamentals, but she questioned the meaningfulnes and usefulness of their level of attainment. The principal implications of Warren's study were that the limited gains came at a high cost, particularly in the price paid by the parents in terms of "false hopes, great efforts with little gains, and relatively useless skills" (p. 85). Her conclusion was that the trainable cannot profit from an academic program, but a "curriculum designed to teach trainables useful concepts . . . seems to be well warranted" (p. 85).

Various authors (Cruickshank, 1956; Kirk, 1957; Kirk, 1964; Reynolds & Kirkland, 1953) have further substantiated the "trainability" as opposed to "educability" of the TMR population. Kirk (1964) even questioned the efficacy of programs. His finding was that any program is of limited benefit to the TMR child, the implication being that programs were probably of greater benefit to the family as a means of providing relief from the constant maintenance and care of the child and developing more realistic aspirations on the part of the family for the child's future. Farber (1968) also noted that program provisions for the TMR child may serve to relieve the burden of the family, but they do not solve the problem. In view of this evidence, Burton (1974) has questioned the renewed emphasis on academics in the TMR program and called for a realignment of priorities, with major emphasis on the stabilization of the family by assisting them in coping with the developmental problems of the TMR child.

The inherent difficulty in supporting or refuting the position of increased emphasis on academics and other cognitive skills is the clear lack of longitudinal data to determine the temporal stability of the skills obtained in the academic areas and the actual relationship of these skills to the TMR person's persistent life situations and ultimate adult prognosis. Existing evidence tends to support the exclusion of academics in a training program on the basis of what the priorities are and what operates in the best interest of the TMR child and the family. However, Warren (1963) has indicated that it is going to be difficult to get parents and some classroom teachers to accept the fact of trainability as opposed to educability. This lack of acceptance was attributed to a number of factors:

1. The teacher is often reluctant to admit failure.
2. Parents are seeking every reasonable opportunity for their child.
3. Teachers and parents are often reinforced by occasional success—however "minute"—and they continue to hope for more gains.
4. There is often wishful thinking of both parties that the child can be what the parents and teachers want him to be rather than what he is.
5. The heterogeneity of the trainable population presents varied learning abilities and, consequently, some trainables at higher levels can handle academics.

Further acceptance of the "trainability" concept may be thwarted by the inclusion, in trainable programs, of a population of what Dunn (1973) refers to as "nonadaptive educables." Here academics may be warranted, but the inclusion of this population could result in a Pyrrhic victory of sorts. Academics may be deemed appropriate for the "trainable" erstwhile "nonadaptive educable" at the expense or exclusion of the population previously identified as trainable (that is, the Down's syndrome and brain-damaged population scoring within the 25 to 50 IQ range with severe deficits in adaptive behavior). This could be the new prototype of "cure" in that it will show results by once again gravitating to the higher level retardate, but it will be a policy of catastrophe for the present trainable population.

The ultimate fruition of the proposed optimistic approach to trainable programs has been erroneously expounded in the concept of "normalization." The principle of normalization was originally proposed as a formula for assisting the institutionalized mentally retarded population to obtain a life style as close as possible to normal. This was defined by Nirje (1969) as a principle that will "make a normalization of the life situation of individual retardates quite feasible . . . a great number will be helped in developing relative independence though they may always need various kinds of assistance to varying degrees; even the relatively few who are severely or profoundly retarded . . . will no matter how dependent . . . have life conditions, facilities and services that follow the normal patterns of society" (pp. 185–86).

Essentially, the normalization principle was an appeal for an improvement in the quality of life of the mentally retarded *as* mentally retarded children and adults and was directed towards the "deinstitutionalization" of this population. However, this term inspired a passion in some circles to interpret it according to the dictionary definition. This created a semantic, if not ideological, dispute. As Daniels (1974) has noted, the term "normal" or "normalization" is defined by most dictionaries as "being of normal intelligence." However, she felt that the term was more an expression of a concern for socialization or the welfare of other persons in groups. Subsequently, she cautioned that the concern should not be interpreted to mean that the retarded may become more "normal," but that they should become more "social."

The optimism generated out of a renewed interest in academic programs for the trainable and the application of the normalization principle merit some serious reflections and caution in their implementation. As Vitello (1974) has stated, there have been periodic attempts at normalization and as result of their failure, "optimism turned to pessimism . . . the push for integration became a push for segregation" (p. 39). He offered additional cautions to this current optimism, and summed them up by stating, "It is not suggested to stop or yield to arguments that we should not move forward to educate all retarded children, but that we recognize some of the cautions which, if not heeded, may turn the road of normalization into a dead end street" (p. 40).

It is obvious that the "educability" of the trainable will continue to create a serious philosophical schism in the development of programs.

We look back at our previous failures, and we look forward with great expectations. But, as Dingman (1974) so succinctly stated:

> The really important question, then, is what is to be taught as "social competence." The skills crucial for independent living—getting along with people and utilizing social abilities—are not attained in programs for the retarded designed to provide an academic education. I am afraid the current emphasis on academic achievement is not what is needed by the retarded to develop their lives. [p. 9]

The resolution of the problem of independent living or total life development will be contingent upon the comprehensiveness of the program's delivery system. A construct as broad as "social competence" cannot be met through programming in isolation. However, by providing an educational delivery system with major emphasis on academic achievement, we are doing just that—programming in isolation. The trend in service models was to assign responsibility for community programs for the TMR to the existing state agency that had a close relationship to the problems of mental retardation. However, the various related disciplines were not enthusiastic about programs for the trainable; or, in certain instances, professionals in nonretardation services (such as the behaviorial sciences) and workers in mental retardation were vying for controlling interest in program development (Doyle, 1966; Stedman, 1966). Therefore, we have not only failed to define appropriate programs, but we have also failed to define the appropriate locus of programs or responsibility for sponsoring services.

Responsibility for Program

Historically, many disciplines looked upon the retarded as uninteresting and unworthy of the concerns of the behaviorial sciences (Garrison, 1959). Kanner (1941) well illustrated this attitude when he stated that "Some child guidance clinics with a haughty let-George-do-it attitude refused to be bothered with feebleminded children, whom they mistakenly regarded as uninteresting material. The behaviorist wished feeblemindedness out of existence by the simple expedient of ignoring it completely" (p. 225). As a result of these attitudes, lifelong workers in retardation and the parents of retarded children have "held on to what was theirs," and maintained an attitude reflected by Dybwad (1964), who feels that after many years of neglect, the older agencies are hardly in a position to give adequate attention to the problem now.

A struggle for location of "ownership" has created a lack of total coordination in the development of services and has contributed significantly to the impact of program emphasis. The various disciplines or interest groups dealing with the TMR have often moved in a discretely circumscribed role and defined the program in terms of their area of expertise. Gardner and Nisonger (1962) have indicated that appropriate programs for the retarded demand a wide array of services, and that the range and diversity of the problem makes coordinated planning of fundamental importance. Therefore, a comprehensive program should include prevention, research, care, education and training, treatment, rehabilitation, and public education (Begab, 1963). However, the problem has been one of coordination of these efforts and the assignment of leadership responsibility, administrative structure, and authority for service (Nisonger, 1963).

The President's Panel on Mental Retardation (1962) called for assumption of responsibility by the local community in stating that "the challenge . . . is how to accelerate the change from large isolated facilities to smaller units close to the homes of the patients and to the health education and social resources of the community" (p. 134). The problem then became one of identifying the community resources that could best provide appropriate services. In instances, the various state departments of mental health were defined as the appropriate locus for services. It was felt that mental health represented the existing department in state government that had a broad organization of facilities and services with a close relationship to the problems of mental retardation (Gardner & Nisonger, 1962; President's Panel on Mental Retardation, 1962; Rockefeller, 1966). This locus for service was further emphasized in President Kennedy's message to the 88th Congress (House of Representatives, 1963), when he stated that mental illness and mental retardation are "among our most critical health problems. Services to both the mentally ill and mentally retarded must . . . provide a range of services to meet community needs" (n.p.). Several aspects of community needs were outlined in his message. Important among them were comprehensive mental health centers designed to provide services for the mentally ill *and* the mentally retarded. Subsequently, many of the states assigned program responsibility for the mentally retarded to state mental health directors (The National Association of State Directors of Mental Health Programs, 1965), and PL 88–156 provided the various states with federal monies to organize a comprehensive state plan for community-based mental health and mental retardation services.

From its early inception, there was serious question raised about single-agency responsibility in general, and mental health responsibility specifically, in the provision of community-based services for the retarded. Gardner and Nisonger (1962) cautioned against this lack of comprehensive planning, which they felt would lend itself to inadequate service and gaps in overall programs. In addition, the President's Panel on Mental Retardation (1962), while defining the community mental health clinic as an appropriate locus for consultation, cautioned that services should emanate from an administrative base free from identification with a single agency. Weingold (1966) also expressed a concern that the psychiatrist and the psychiatric approach might come to dominate mental retardation services. The actual limitation of mental health services to the retarded was reflected in an investigation of one state's mental health program. In this study, Burton (1971) concluded that services to the retarded were usually limited to evaluation and diagnosis without referral, and when other services were rendered, they principally involved persons identified as educable mentally retarded.

Attempts to provide community-based services for TMR were not limited to mental health programs. As other appropriate delivery systems for service were being sought, the school, as the largest child-serving agency, also felt increased demands being placed upon it to provide services for school-age TMR children. As Rothstein (1965) stated:

> The phenomenal growth of public school programs for trainable mentally retarded children is the outgrowth of three factors: (1) an awareness on the part of the parents of these children that psychologically it is better for the child and the family unit to avoid or delay institutionalization, (2) the questionable programs and the crowded conditions at many institutions, and (3) financial data which tend to show that it is more economical for society to keep retarded children in the community. [p. 332]

In addition, Kirk (1962) has stated:

> The parents have argued that they, as taxpayers, have helped to pay for the public schools and that their children should not be deprived of the benefits because they were born or have become less fortunate. They have pointed out that the statutes in many states provide that all children are entitled to an education and that school districts are required by law to supply schools for all children, not just a certain segment of the children. [p. 136]

This attitude toward the school's responsibility for the TMR also generated considerable controversy. This controversy is most aptly illustrated in what now represents a near-classic argument over the efficacy of placing TMR children within the public school, or under its sponsorship. The debate from Goldberg and Cruickshank (1958) is summarized by Kirk (1962) as follows:

Yes!

By I. Ignacy Goldberg

> There is growing recognition that children who are characterized as "trainable mentally retarded" are individuals with potentialities that deserve to be developed to the fullest extent.

Whether or not the public schools should provide training for this type of school age child is a rather academic question, since many school systems have already introduced services for these children.

It was estimated that in the Fall of 1956, there were about 7,000 trainable children receiving education (or training) in over 600 public school day classes.

In the Fall of 1958, 10 states had mandatory legislation and 15 had permissive legislation for the inclusion in the public schools of the trainable mentally retarded. Four additional states interpreted the existing statutes for exceptional children to include the trainable without further legislation . . .

Ongoing programs for trainable children are still in such an early stage of development that it is difficult to evaluate their full success. However, several research projects initiated and financed by the U.S. Office of Education and other state, local, and private agencies are investigating the effects of school training on the subsequent adjustment of these children.

In a democracy, such children have a right to be trained to the maximum of their ability, regardless of whether they live at home or in the institution. Thus, they should be: (1) educationally diagnosed; (2) placed in the best educational environment; (3) trained by qualified personnel; (4) periodically evaluated to determine progress; (5) recommended for further training and placement after "graduation" from the special class; and (6) followed up to assure optimal placement and adjustment.

What agency in our society is better qualified and equipped to assume leadership and coordination of the above mentioned services than the public school? And what agency is better qualified to initiate and conduct parent-education programs, educational research, and curriculum development or to regulate professional standards of teachers who work with these children?

In my opinion, there is no doubt that the public school has a responsibility to extend these programs further and, through concerted effort over a period of years, to decide what contribution it can make to the growth and welfare of trainable children. [p. 137]

No!
By William M. Cruickshank

For a number of reasons, I do not believe that the responsibility for severely retarded children should be assigned to the public schools.

First of all, public schools were established to educate those who have the ability to learn, and the severely retarded are unable to benefit from education (as distinguished from training).

Education, as defined by Dewey and others, demands the ability to generalize; to reason and make judgements; to remember and to form new concepts out of previous learning; to solve problems; to abstract and to deal with abstractions; to utilize language concepts. Obviously the severely retarded lack these abilities.

Secondly, public education in the United States has been seen as a medium through which citizens could be prepared to reach a level of effective understanding of and participation in civic matters and thus return something tangible or intangible to the state.

Only by the broadest stretch of the imagination can the severely retarded child be regarded as capable of returning anything to the community.

Public education is also based on the belief that as a result of learning, the individual will be able to assume a self-directed role in society and that he will probably assume responsibility for others — his wife and children or parents.

This goal is unobtainable by the severely retarded, who throughout his life will be dependent upon others, even when they have had optimum training opportunities.

Thirdly, when the severely retarded are placed in the public schools, it is only natural that both parents and community infer that such children are going to learn to do what most other pupils do in school. Such placement carries false implications of normalcy that can result only in disillusionment. There is no real advancement possible either for individual children or for society as a whole in providing public school education for the severely retarded. [p. 138]

A resolution of the merits of public school responsibility for TMR programs has not, as yet, been resolved philosophically. There is still some contention that school programs are of limited value to the TMR and their parents (Kirk, 1964) and that the inclusion of TMR children in the school is analogous to programming in a mental health setting. As Burton (1974) noted, the program becomes a reflection of the discipline, and the use of an educational delivery system is tantamount to "an emphasis on skills attendant upon education—reading, writing and arithmetic" (p. 46).

Whatever the various merits of the location of responsibility for program, the issue is rapidly becoming academic as a result of litigation that is specifying certain rights to care, treatment, and education for the TMR child or adult. These rights are interpreted to encompass institutional as well as community-based programs and are precipitating a dramatic change in the various states' approaches to comprehensive programs for the TMR.

Legal Perspectives in Program

Early litigation was very harsh in nature and was enacted against the better interest of the retarded. Provisions in these laws involved measures to control the "menace" of retardation, denying the basic human rights—extending even to the right to life.

The eugenic alarms of the early part of the twentieth century resulted in a wave of sterilization legislation enacted as a means of legally controlling mental retardation. The United States Supreme Court established the constitutionality of this measure in 1927, and the then Justice Holmes delivered the majority opinion upholding the Virginia statute as being in the best interest of the public welfare. He stated that, "Three generations of imbeciles are enough" (Davies & Ecob, 1962, p. 58). Ultimately, though, the statutes permitting sterilization became inoperative, and the civil rights legislation of the 1950s and 1960s sounded their death knell. Various states began to strike the statutes from their books.

Although there was considerable disagreement as to the efficacy of sterilization, it was generally agreed that the alternative of segregation was probably the most palatable means of controlling the mentally retarded. It was intended that the existing institutional facilities be greatly expanded to segregate all of the mentally retarded for their lifetimes. Subsequently, a retardate could be placed in an institution without the right of due process and enjoyed fewer rights than a criminal incarcerated in a penal institution.

Basic human rights notwithstanding, segregation also failed to meet the expectations of the general public. This failure is best illustrated by Gardner and Nisonger (1962) who reported that "after 150 years of experience less than 5% of the mentally retarded population are in residential institutions. The remaining 95% are living in communities" (p. 21).

As a result of mandatory legislation, the early 1950s witnessed a remarkable growth in school programs for the TMR. Although it was a controversial policy, increasing numbers of TMR children were becoming the responsibility of the public schools.

The controversy over the appropriateness of including or excluding TMR children from public school programs is still not resolved philosophically, but it is a moot point legally. In 1971, the United States District Court, Eastern District of Pennsylvania, found in the interest of the plaintiff and declared unconstitutional certain Pennsylvania statutes that denied equal right to education (*Pennsylvania Association for Retarded Children* v. *Commonwealth of Pennsylvania*, 1971). Under this court order:

> Every retarded person between the ages of six and twenty-one . . . shall be provided access to a free public education and training appropriate to his capacities . . . wherever defendants provide a preschool program of education and training for children less than six years of age, whether kindergarten or howsoever called, every mentally retarded child of the same age . . . shall be provided access to a free public program of education and training appropriate to his capacities . . . to implement the aforementioned relief and to insure it is extended to all members entitled to it Dr. Herbert Goldstein and Dennis E. Haggerty, Esquire are appointed Masters for the purpose of overseeing a process of identification, notification and compliance. [334 F. Supp. 1266]

In instances where the retardate was determined uneducable or untrainable in the public schools, the court ordered that:

Any child who is reported by a person who is certified as a public school psychologist as being uneducable and untrainable with public schools . . . shall be certified to the department of public welfare as a child who is uneducable and untrainable in the public schools. When a child is thus certified, the public schools shall be relieved of the obligation of providing education or training for such child in a manner not inconsistent with the laws governing mentally defective individuals. [334 F. Supp. 1264]

If a retardate is placed under the aegis of the Department of Public Welfare, the court ordered that they must be reevaluated no less than every two years, and a determination made as to whether the retardate is to remain a responsibility of the Department of Public Welfare or whether she or he can be maintained by the Department of Education. By this landmark decision, the courts have put to rest the controversy over the responsibility of education, wherever appropriate, in programs for the TMR. The philosophical issue (that is, appropriate curriculum) is yet to be resolved.

In addition to the availability of programs, care, treatment, and education—where programs already exist—have also precipitated litigation. In recent years, the public has become increasingly aware of the deleterious and dehumanizing effects of institutions. As a result of lack of care, inappropriate care, and overcrowded conditions, the patients in institutions often decrease in intellectual functioning and are denied certain rights enjoyed by "normal" citizens, including denial of the right to life (Rivera, 1972; White & Wolfensberger, 1969).

In 1971, a class action suit was initiated by the guardian of a patient at Bryce Hospital (Partlow State School) in Tuscaloosa, Alabama, against the Commissioner of Mental Health in that state (*Wyatt* v. *Stickney*, 1971). The plaintiff in this action contended that services in the hospital were inadequate and that the treatment failed to conform to minimum standards. The court in this action held that "programs of treatment . . . were scientifically and medically inadequate and deprived patients of their constitutional rights" (325 F. Supp. 781). The court further stated that:

For the most part (the patients) were involuntarily committed . . . without the constitutional protections that are afforded defendants in criminal proceedings . . . they unquestionably have a constitutional right to receive individual treatment. . . . Adequate and effective treatment is constitutionally required because absent treatment, the hospital is transformed into a penitentiary where one could be held indefinitely for no convicted offense. The purpose of involuntary hospitalization for treatment purposes is *treatment* and not mere custodial care or punishment. [325 F. Supp. 784]

The court, in finding in favor of the plaintiff in this case, reserved ruling until such time as a panel of experts could determine what standards would be required.

The hearing in the *Wyatt* v. *Stickney* decision precipitated an unprecedented expression by the courts in the interest of the retarded. The relief ordered by the courts as a result of these hearings was summarized in the Special Report by the American Association on Mental Deficiency (1972). The order included:

> Hiring 300 additional resident care workers, including professionals, within thirty days, on a temporary basis;
> Initiating an immediate survey of the entire Partlow population to determine those residents whose parents, guardians or kin no longer reside in Alabama, in order that such residents be relocated in facilities in the appropriate state, or discharged to the care of their guardians;
> Within ten days, engaging a team of physicians to conduct appropriate immunizations of all residents;
> Within fifteen days, engaging a team of physicians to examine every resident as to the appropriateness of any anticonvulsive and/or behavior modifying drugs, and with a view to "immediately . . . revamping (Partlow's) entire drug program;"
> Within fifteen days, completely eliminating all fire and safety hazards; installing an emergency lighting system and developing and initiating written plans and procedures for emergency evacuation from all facilities at Partlow;
> Within fifteen days, surveying the sanitation conditions related to the preparation and service of food and correcting those conditions creating immediate health hazards;
> Within fourteen days, receiving nominations of all parties for master, expert advisory panel, and court-appointed Human Rights Committee. [p. 51]

Although the *Wyatt* v. *Stickney* decision represented a landmark decision on rights to care, treatment, and education, the courts were soon in conflict over determination of the constitutionality of these rights. The conflict was precipitated by another class action suit which asked relief from inadequate diagnosis, care, and treatment to the plaintiffs on constitutional grounds (*Burnam* v. *The Department of Public Health of the State of Georgia*, 1972). However, in this instance, the court found in favor of the defendants. The court stated in a preliminary discussion that "on moral grounds the proposition that the nation's mentally ill should be provided the best possible diagnosis, care and treatment is commendable" (349 F. Supp. 1337). In rendering their decision, the court took notice of the Alabama decision but stated that:

> This court is of the opinion that plaintiffs have failed to demonstrate or sufficiently allege the deprivation of a *federally* protected right. . . . This court respectfully disagrees with the conclusion reached by that (Alabama) court in finding an affirmative federal right to treatment absent a statute so requiring. [349 F. Supp. 1340]

The *Wyatt* v. *Stickney* (under appeal as *Wyatt* v. *Aderholt*, 1974) and *Burnam* v. *Georgia* decisions were appealed to the United States Court of Appeals (5th Circuit), and a decision was rendered upholding the Alabama court. The upholding of the Alabama court decision was influenced by a previous decision on appeal (*Donaldson* v. *O'Connor*, 1974) where the court had already decided in the affirmative that the patient had been involuntarily committed to an institution in Florida and deprived of his constitutional rights to receive treatment or to be released from the hospital. In the Florida decision, the court held "that evidence supported finding that attending physicians had acted in bad faith with respect to their treatment of patient and were personally liable for his injuries or deprivations of his constitutional rights" (493 F. 2nd 508). In this case, the jury held that the defendants-appellants were personally and individually libel and awarded compensatory and punitive damages. Although the patient had been held in the hospital for fourteen years without receiving care of treatment, the appellants argued that a constitutional right to treatment could not be governed. Although they relied heavily upon the *Burnam* v. *Georgia* decision, the courts still held "that where a nondangerous patient is civilly committed to a state mental hospital, the only permissible purpose of confinement is to provide treatment, and that such a patient has a constitutional right to such treatment as will help him to be cured or to improve his mental condition" (493 F. 2nd 527).

By the nature of this decision in *Donaldson* v. *O'Connor*, the court in *Wyatt* v. *Aderholt* affirmed the right to treatment and stated that "society had to pay the price of the extra safety it derived from the denial of individuals' liberty" (43 LW 2208). The terms of this decision took cognizance of the plea of the State of Alabama when they argued that their compliance with this decision would entail "a sum equal to 60% of the state budget, excluding school financing, and a capital improvements outlay of $75 million" (43 LW 2209). However, the district court made it clear that if the state did not fully implement the standards they prescribed, that they would take steps to appoint a special master to insure proper funding and implementation of treatment at Partlow State

School. The decision indicated that the special master could oversee "selling or incumbering state lands to finance these standards, or . . . enjoining certain state officials from authorizing expenditures for non-essential state functions, and thereby alter the state budget" (43 LW 2209). These measures were deferred by the court to the state legislature and state mental health board, but the court ordered that a plan be submitted within six months for the implementation of the proposed standards.

The cited cases are only representative of the myriad of important court actions in the interest of the retarded that are currently under consideration. Whatever the outcome of future litigation, it is obvious that those interested in the welfare of the retarded will now turn to the courts to insure that the retarded will finally be elevated to the status of "citizen" rather than that of "children" who are at the mercy and whims of "adult" society. As Haggerty, Kane, and Udall (1974) so clearly point out:

> It is time for all of us . . . to realize that the retarded person pays his horrible price in legal, social and human deprivation through no fault of his own. He didn't do anything to bring about the loss of rights; for him it was pure accident. He didn't commit a heinous crime that caused him to lose the protection of the 5th and 14th Amendments, didn't become a traitor or threaten sedition, nor did he overindulge in alcohol or take narcotic drugs. He didn't turn his back on his country, but his country turned her back on him. When she said "we deem these truths to be self-evident," she forgot that he was unable to understand. To the mentally retarded person hardly anything good is "self-evident." If it is true that all men are created equal, the mentally retarded person must be the least equal of all. [pp. 149–50]

The courts may, out of necessity, provide us with a Procrustean decision for the problem. However, the designs for programs and appropriate care, treatment, and education are available, and current emphasis in program places compliance within reach. Structure for both institutional and community programs have already been defined—they need only to be implemented.

Current Emphasis in Program

The President's Panel on Mental Retardation (1962) noted the need for community-based services when they called for a decentralization of the state institutions and directed that the patients be moved to facilities closer to their homes and the resources of the community. Various authors (Blatt & Kaplan, 1966; Rivera, 1972) have also commented on the failure of the institutions to provide adequate programs, and Kugel (1969) stated that "the problems of . . . overcrowded institutions can only be solved by giving simultaneous attention to community resources" (p. 5). Therefore, in the last two decades, the institution has no longer been recognized as "total program," and program responsibility for the TMR has gradually shifted from the isolated institutions to the community. Although aegis of responsibility has not been resolved to the satisfaction of all, the various states have attempted to structure program models designed to provide a multi-agency approach to the development of a wide array of services at the community level to meet the needs of the TMR and their families.

The Joint Commission on Accreditation of Hospitals (1973) stated that any community facility serving the mentally retarded should be (1) responsive to the needs of the community, (2) available to serve a wide array of needs, (3) accessible to those who need them, and (4) individually focused on the person in need. They further noted that the service facility should keep useful records for information transmittal and continuity in program, provide quality service, and provide accountability for their services when necessary. The commission cautioned that this type of service should be designed to avoid "the duplication and splintering of effort that have long concerned workers in the field of mental retardation and other developmental disabilities" (p. vii). They finally designated that the delivery system "should be so organized that each client has services available at the time of need, and in close proximity to his home . . . services must reflect a systematic coordination of effort (and) . . . one agency in the service delivery system should be responsible for implementing a systematic method of collecting data useful for planning and coordinating activities" (p. 71).

Various service models have been proposed to meet the criteria of comprehensive community-based services. Figure Two illustrates one multi-agency approach to a program which calls upon the resources of numerous agencies in the community to provide for all levels of retardation.

The program model represented in Figure Two reflects the optimum effort for total program at the community level, providing a balance of services between the community and the institution. However, it is also apparent that every community could not support such a program, and population densities may dictate a regionalization of services. Prevalence figures would serve to indicate that in many communities there would not be a sufficient population to justify a total program. Figure Three represents a type of regional organization which could be used to provide appropriate mental health and mental retardation services over a larger geographical area.

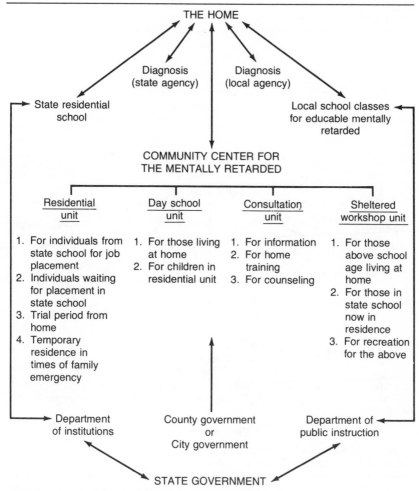

THE HOME

Diagnosis
(state agency)

Diagnosis
(local agency)

State residential
school

Local school classes
for educable mentally
retarded

COMMUNITY CENTER FOR
THE MENTALLY RETARDED

Residential unit	Day school unit	Consultation unit	Sheltered workshop unit
1. For individuals from state school for job placement 2. Individuals waiting for placement in state school 3. Trial period from home 4. Temporary residence in times of family emergency	1. For those living at home 2. For children in residential unit	1. For information 2. For home training 3. For counseling	1. For those above school age living at home 2. For those in state school now in residence 3. For recreation for the above

Department
of institutions

County government
or
City government

Department of
public instruction

STATE GOVERNMENT

NOTE: Reproduced from S. A. Kirk, M. B. Karnes, and W. D. Kirk, *You and your retarded child: A manual for parents of retarded children*, 2nd ed. (Palo Alto, Calif.: Pacific Books, 1968), p. 149.

Figure Two

A total program for the retarded

It may be noted that within this structure services emanate from a professional, lay, and governmental advisory council. This would resolve the problem of single aegis of responsibility for services and provides for input from professional workers, parents, and other lay persons and government agencies. Services handled under such a regional structure would be capable of providing a "cradle to grave" program. This would entail services as early as crib care for retarded

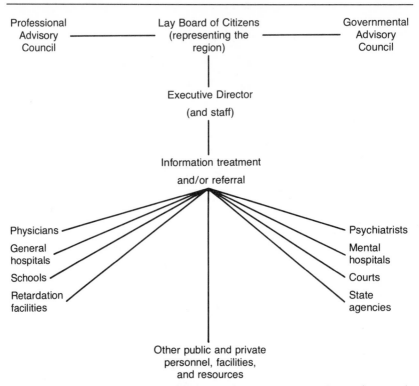

Professional Advisory Council —————— Lay Board of Citizens (representing the region) —————— Governmental Advisory Council

Executive Director
(and staff)

Information treatment
and/or referral

Physicians

General hospitals

Schools

Retardation facilities

Psychiatrists

Mental hospitals

Courts

State agencies

Other public and private
personnel, facilities,
and resources

NOTE: Reproduced from Kentucky Retardation Planning Commission, *Pattern for mental retardation programs and services* (Frankfort, Kentucky: Kentucky Department of Mental Health, 1965).

Figure Three

Regional mental health —mental retardation board and coordination network

infants on a day program basis, to sheltered workshops and other relevant adult activities. Another advantage to this type of program would be the availability of multiple agencies that could be called upon to act at the appropriate time in the best interest of the TMR person and the family at any point.

Resolution of the organizational problems for the delivery of services will not be a solution of the total problem. Additional concerns about program emphasis have evolved out of such a multidisciplinary approach. The frequently expressed fear is that this approach is vulnerable to fragmentation of services which deteriorates into no service at all or that a single discipline emerges as the *sine qua non* for service. In dealing with this contention, Shotick and Rhoden (1973) have described a "unitary approach," where emphasis is placed upon a program focusing upon the child, with the necessary resources or disciplines used to obtain the desired results (that is, a meaningful program) without being distracted by professional chauvinism. The treatment and training program they described involved thirteen areas or disciplines. These included (1) child development, (2) counseling, (3) health, (4) physical education and recreation, (5) music therapy, (6) pharmacy, (7) psychology, (8) reading, (9) school psychology, (10) social work, (11) sociology, (12) speech and hearing, (13) special education, and (14) vocational rehabilitation. These areas were all used to provide direct services to the mentally retarded at any time that the service was deemed appropriate. The program varied in emphasis which was dictated by level of disability and its relationship to the individual's programs.

The current concern for program appears to reflect a need for the various disciplines and interest groups to act in concert toward what benefits the TMR individual. An implementation of this model for services precludes the mistakes of earlier programs and will resolve many of the previous controversies which resulted in rather penurious efforts toward the training and habilitation of the TMR population.

Summary

The development of programs for the TMR have been as diverse as the history of man. The early period, although lacking in specific programs, represents a point in time when the care and treatment of the TMR, as well as other "unfortunates" in society, was dictated by the superstitions or whims of the existing culture. It was not until the early 1800s that superstition gave way to scientific method, and attempts were made to ameliorate, if not cure, the condition of retardation. The ensuing failures of these early attempts at education and cure precipitated a period of waning interest and concern for the TMR population. Other than institutionalization, programs for the TMR population nearly ceased to exist.

It was not until the 1950s that there was an increased interest in the trainable, and a remarkable increase in provisions for these people in the public schools. Although significant, this inclusion in public school programs did not represent a panacea for a problem long neglected. Moreover the legislative impetus of the 1960s did not resolve the problems of aegis of responsibility for programs, appropriate program emphasis, and rights to appropriate programs. In spite of the public reawakening to the problem, the TMR in many ways remained a conundrum.

The 1970s have witnessed a plethora of action in the courts which are attempting to resolve the question of the right to care, treatment, and education.

Although the courts have, to date, resolved in the affirmative on the rights of the trainable population, the appropriate means for implementation of this mandate is yet to be determined.

References

Begab, M. J. Some elements and principles in community planning. *Mental Retardation*, 1963, *1*, 262–266.

Best, H. *Public provisions for the mentally retarded in the United States.* Worcester, Mass.: Heffernon Press, 1965.

Blatt, B., & Kaplan, F. *Christmas in purgatory.* Boston, Mass.: Allyn & Bacon, 1966.

Burnam v The Department of Public Health of the State of Georgia, 349 F. Supp. 1335 (1972).

Burton, T. A. Mental health clinic services to the retarded. *Mental Retardation*, 1971, *9*, 38–40.

Burton, T. A. Education for trainables: An impossible dream? *Mental Retardation*, 1974, *12*, 45–46.

Burton, T. A. The trainable mentally retarded. In N. G. Haring (Ed.), *Behavior of exceptional children: An introduction to special education.* Columbus, Oh.: Charles E. Merrill, 1974.

Butterfield, E. C. A provocative case of over achievement by a mongoloid. *American Journal of Mental Deficiency*, 1961, *66*, 444.

Cruickshank, W. M. Planning for the severely retarded child. *American Journal of Mental Deficiency*, 1956, *61*, 3–9.

D'Amelio, D. *Severely retarded children: Wider horizons.* Columbus, Oh.: Charles E. Merrill, 1971.

Daniels, J. Y. Letters to the editor. *Mental Retardation*, 1974, *12*, 52.

Davies, S. P., & Ecob, K. G. *The mentally retarded in society.* New York: Columbia University Press, 1962.

Dingman, H. F. Distinguished lectures in special education, 1965. Quote without comment. *Mental Retardation*, 1974, *12*, 9.

Donaldson v O'Connor, 493 F. 2nd 507, 5th Cir. (1974).

Doyle, P. J. Mental retardation—need for the holistic approach. *Mental Retardation*, 1966, *4*, 2–3.

Dunn, L. M. Trainable mentally retarded children. In L. M. Dunn (Ed.), *Exceptional children in the schools.* New York: Holt, Rinehart, & Winston, 1963.

Dunn, L. M. Children with moderate and severe general learning disabilities. In L. M. Dunn (Ed.), *Exceptional children in the schools: Special education in transition* (2nd ed.). New York: Holt, Rinehart, & Winston, 1973.

Dunn, L. M., & Capobianco, R. J. Mental retardation. *Review of Educational Research*, 1959, *29*, 451–470.

Dybwad, G. *Challenges in mental retardation*. New York: Columbia University Press, 1964.

Farber, B. *Mental retardation: Its social context and social consequences*. Boston: Houghton-Mifflin, 1968.

Gardner, W. I., & Nisonger, H. W. *A manual on program development in mental retardation*. American Association on Mental Deficiency, Monograph Supplement No. 4, Vol. 66, January 1962.

Garrison, M. Research trends in mental deficiency. *Children*. 1959, *6*, 64–66.

Goldberg, I., & Cruickshank, W. M. Trainable but not educable. *National Education Association Journal*, 1958, *47*, 622–623.

Grossman, H. J. *Manual on terminology and classification in mental retardation*. American Association on Mental Deficiency Special Publication, 1973 (Series No. 2).

Haggerty, D. E., Kane, L. A., & Udall, D. K. An essay on the legal rights of the mentally retarded. In K. N. Sanford (Ed.), *The youngest minority*. American Bar Association Press, 1974.

Hewett, F. M. *Education of exceptional learners*. Boston: Allyn & Bacon, 1974.

Hunt, N. *The world of Nigel Hunt: The diary of a mongoloid youth*. New York: Garrett, 1967.

Joint Commission on Accreditation of Hospitals. *Standards for community agencies serving persons with mental retardation and other developmental disabilities*. Chicago: Accreditation Council for Facilities for the Mentally Retarded, 1973.

Kanner, L. Child psychiatry and the study of mental deficiency. *American Journal of Mental Deficiency*, 1941, *6*, 225–226.

Kanner, L. *A history of the care and study of the mentally retarded*. Springfield, Ill.: Charles C. Thomas, 1967.

Kirk, S. A. *Public school provisions for severely retarded children: A survey of practices in the United States*. Albany, New York: Special Report to the New York State Interdepartmental Health Resources Board, 1957.

Kirk, S. A. *Educating exceptional children*. Boston: Houghton Mifflin, 1962.

Kirk, S. A. Research in education. In R. Heber & H. A. Stevens (Eds.), *Mental retardation: A review of research*. Chicago: University of Chicago Press, 1964.

Kugel, R. B. Why innovative action? In R. B. Kugel & W. Wolfensberger (Eds.), *Changing patterns in residential services for the mentally retarded*. Washington, D.C.: President's Committee on Mental Retardation, 1969.

Leichty, E. The omen series *Summa Izbu*. Insert in L. S. Hurley, The consequences of fetal impoverishment. *Nutrition Today*, 1968, *3*, 3–10.

The National Association of State Mental Health Program Directors. *Authority in state agencies for administration of facilities for the mentally retarded*. Washington, D.C.: Bulletin 25, 1965.

Nirje, B. The normalization principle and its human management implications. In R. B. Kugel & W. Wolfensberger (Eds.), *Changing patterns in residential services for the mentally retarded*. Washington, D.C.: President's Committee on Mental Retardation, 1969.

Nisonger, H. W. State planning on mental retardation. *Mental Retardation*, 1963, *1*, 330–332.

Pennsylvania Association for Retarded Children, Nancy Beth Bowman v Commonwealth of Pennsylvania, David H. Kurtzman, 334 F. Supp. 1257, (3-Judge Court, E. D. Pennsylvania, 1971).

President's Panel on Mental Retardation. *A proposed program for national action to combat mental retardation*. Washington, D.C.: U.S. Government Printing Office, 1962.

Reynolds, M. C., & Kirkland, J. R. *A study of public school children with severe mental retardation*. Minnesota State Department of Education, 1953.

Rhodes, W. C., & Head, S. *A study of child variance: Vol. 3, Service and delivery systems*. Ann Arbor, Mi.: Institute for the Study of Mental Retardation and Related Disabilities, The University of Michigan, 1974.

Rivera, G. *Willowbrook*. New York: Vantage Books, 1972.

Rockefeller, W. Conflict or cooperation? *Mental Retardation*, 1966, *4*, 40–41.

Rothstein, J. H. *Mental retardation: Readings and resources*. New York: Holt, Rinehart, & Winston, 1965.

Shotick, A. L., & Rhoden, J. O. A unitary approach: Programming for the mentally retarded. *Mental Retardation*, 1973, *11*, 35–38.

Special Report, Re: AAMD's Recent Participation in Alabama Right to Treatment Case (*Wyatt v Stickney*). *Mental Retardation*, 1972, *10*, 51.

Stedman, D. Changing concepts for programs for the retarded. In I. Phillips (Ed.), *Prevention and treatment in mental retardation*. New York: Basic Books, 1966.

Talbot, M. E. *Edouard Seguin: A study of an educational approach to the treatment of mentally defective children*. New York: Teachers College Press, Columbia University, 1966.

U.S. Department of Health, Education and Welfare. *Basic Education Rights for the Handicapped*. Washington, D.C.: Annual Report of the National Advisory Committee on Handicapped Children, U.S. Government Printing Office, 1973.

U.S. House of Representatives. *Message from the President of the United States relative to mental illness and mental retardation* (88th Congress, Document No. 58). Washington, D.C.: U.S. Government Printing Office, 1963.

Vitello, S. J. Cautions on the road to normalization. *Mental Retardation*, 1974, *12*, 39–40.

Warren, S. A. Academic achievement of trainable pupils with five or more years of schooling. *Training School Bulletin*, 1963, *2*, 75–86.

Weingold, J. T. Letter to the editor. *Mental Retardation*, 1966, *4*, 46.

White, W. D., & Wolfensberger, W. The evolution of dehumanizing in our institutions. *Mental Retardation*, 1969, 7, 5—9.

Williams, H. M., & Wallin, J. E. W. Education of the severely retarded child. In J. H. Rothstein (Ed.), *Mental retardation: Readings and resources*. New York: Holt, Rinehart, & Winston, 1965.

Wyatt v Aderholt, 43 LW 2209 (November 19, 1974).

Wyatt v Stickney, 325 F. Supp. 781 (M.D. Alabama, 1971), Civil Action No. 3195—N.

Chapter 3

Assessment in the Development of Program

General Considerations

Daly (1966) has noted that inappropriate instructional programs for the trainable mentally retarded are principally the result of "the clear lack of guiding purposes [and] . . . lack of systematized instructional program" (pp. 117−118). A systematic process of assessment can be a step toward resolution of these problems. The process of assessment presents a predictive statement about the levels of expectancy for performance in a given area and should be the antecedent to program development. The inherent value of an assessment is the development of an appropriate program that accurately reflects individual and group characteristics and defines observable and identifiable purposes and priorities. It must be emphasized that, as Jordan (1972) has indicated, "the initial choice of what to gather and how to gather is quite crucial" (p. 307).

Assessment is usually stated in terms of a "psychological evaluation," and the "evaluation" is usually restricted to determination of an IQ score. However, for purposes of an instructional program, we must look beyond the information that is often summed up in a statement such as "based upon his IQ, the child is functioning within the trainable range." It must be remembered that to be classified "trainable," the individual must manifest severe deficits in intellectual development *and* adaptive behavior (Grossman, 1973). Therefore, we must not only seek answers to "What is he?" but we must determine the locus and extent of the deficits in a number of areas that preclude normal intelligence and adaptive behavior.

A major problem in the assessment of the trainable population is the limited number of devices that are useful for assessment (Delp, 1959). Cain and Levine (1963) noted that one of the principal difficulties encountered by teachers of the trainable is the lack of appropriate procedures and devices to determine the effectiveness of program, to assess the children's progress, and to assess the learning potential of the TMR and their social competence.

The recognized limitation in the number of devices has resulted in an incredible proliferation of instruments of assessment. However, Van Hattum (1974) has voiced a concern over this and called for a moratorium on the development of new instruments. He supports the

63

use of "well conceived, well standardized, well administered and well interpreted tests" (p. 38). However, he cautions against the continued proliferation of meaningless tests that are developed without a theoretical basis or research support. Therein lies the problem. The tests that are currently being used with the TMR population often do not meet minimum criteria of reliability and validity or are frequently not standardized or representative of the level of expectancy for this population. Thus, many of the instruments that are used to assess the TMR are either a product of a "proliferation of meaningless tests" or represent the application of an existing instrument on a population for which it was never intended.

An additional problem in the assessment of the TMR is that assessment has often been relegated to the psychologist, psychometrist, or physician, for whom the standardized instrument has been the quintessential tool. Therefore, assessment is often characterized by the administration of one or more tests which purport to quantify or measure a behavior or a construct. The measurements of these dimensions are then relegated to the "secrets" or statistics of psychometrics or medicine.

The TMR population poses a unique and complex set of problems which will obviously necessitate a comprehensive evaluation that extends beyond the administration of a single test. The teacher cannot develop a program based upon limited information such as the expression of an IQ or Social Quotient. The program must be based upon a consideration of a number of relevant facts which reflect a cognizance of the full range of assets and liabilities of the individual. The simple "discovery" via a standardized instrument that the TMR child has severe intellectual and social deficits is of limited use. It is also obvious that we cannot resolve a complex, dynamic sequence of life situations with a single administration of a battery of tests. We often find that frequent changes in the TMR child's status in any number of areas makes repeated and varied evaluations necessary. We must also be sensitive to appropriate timing in assessment and realize that certain inventories or tests must be used at the most propitious moment in the TMR child's life cycle in order to insure that the information extracted will be meaningful, useful, and appropriate in ongoing curriculum planning (Grossman, 1969).

The need for a comprehensive evaluation is often simpler in rhetoric than in actual practice. It is distressing to note that many teachers of the trainable are content to structure a program on the basis of an assigned IQ score, which merely classifies the individual as "trainable." The limitations of this practice are obvious, but Silverstein (1963) reported that, in instances, the IQ test is used as the sole criterion for program planning. In fairness to the construct, the test is often not at fault. Rather, it is the teacher's abuse of the end product (that is, the score) which is unfair. This kind of abuse is not limited to IQ tests but is true in any area of assessment when the test or its score is used for a purpose other than that for which it was intended.

A comprehensive evaluation places considerable responsibility upon the teacher to obtain and interpret information. The Professional Standards for Personnel in the Education of Exceptional Children (Council for Exceptional Children, 1966) clearly abrogated the role of the psychologist in program planning when it directed that:

> The prospective teacher of the mentally retarded needs to develop functional competence in: (a) the use of various formal and informal methods of appraising and communicating pupils' educational status and progress, both in traditional academic areas and in other areas of school responsibility, such as screening for identification of children with special problems or disabilities in cognitive, motor, sensory, language, social, or emotional growth; (b) the utilization of various types of clinical data which are relevant to special educational requirements; (c) the utilization of a wide array of data for appraisal and educational planning for the mentally retarded; (d) the evaluation of methods and materials to determine their effectiveness in meeting the instructional goals; and (e) the utilization and participation in research. [p. 32]

The implication of this statement is that teachers can no longer ignore the responsibility for teacher-directed assessment. Nor can they ignore the diagnostic information obtained from other professional sources by relegating them to some mystical order of psychometric data which is unrelated to the class program. The teacher must accept the responsibility for diagnosis, assessment, and interpretation as critical components of the decision-making process relative to what constitutes an appropriate program. Then, and only then, does assessment become a teaching tool, rather than an exercise in categorization and classification.

The teacher seeks the answer to two questions in the process of assessment: first, "What do I teach?" and second, "How well am I teaching it?" Determination of what to teach is usually accomplished by the administration of a number of psychodiagnostic instruments designed to quantify a skill or ability (such as intelligence, motor performance). How well the skill is taught is usually determined by repeated measures on a given instrument or through informal observation and anecdotal records.

There are two types of psychodiagnostic instruments—normative-based and criteria-based. The normative-based instrument compares the individual's functioning or performance on a test with a representative group or standardization sample. These are frequently referred to as "standardized tests."

The concept of criteria-based tests is a relatively recent innovation in the assessment of the TMR. The distinctive difference between criteria-based and normative-based testing is that normative-based tests involve a determination of an individual's performance in relation to the performance of other individuals in a specific population; the interpretation of a criteria-based test involves behaviorial statements that relate only to the individual without consideration of the performance of others (Glaser, 1963). Thus, criteria-based tests are concerned with what the individual can and cannot do, rather than a comparison of performance in a given population. The criteria-based instrument is similar to an aptitude or achievement test. Although it takes into consideration prior learning and may serve as a predictor of future learning, its principal use is to determine individual attainment or performance in a given area. The criteria-based instrument is best regarded as a tool rather than a goal in program.

Both types of psychodiagnostic instruments have their distinct assets and liabilities when used in a program for the TMR. A standardized test (such as an intelligence test) is useful in classification and placement. However, training objectives are not often amenable to standardized testing, and standardized tests usually demand that the examiner have extensive training in the use of the instrument. The criteria-based instrument is, however, useful in providing meaningful information for program planning, the determination of immediate priorities of need, and the establishment of long-range training goals. In addition, the criteria-based instrument usually demands limited if any sophistication in test administration.

Psychodiagnostic Instruments in a Training Program

It would be impractical, if not impossible to discuss every psychodiagnostic instrument that has been developed to measure a given dimension of behavior. Therefore, the function or use of these tests discussed here will be limited to those that enjoy the greater popularity and use with the TMR population. In addition, we will discuss the new or innovative assessment techniques that appear to have particular application or use with the TMR.

Intellectual Assessment

The IQ test, or a determination of intellectual deficit, is usually the genesis of any process of assessment. This has often been considered to be the quintessential part of any assessment. However, this approach is rapidly becoming an anacronism—particularly when used in isolation—and in general, the IQ is considered to have exceeded its usefulness (Robinson & Robinson, 1965).

The history of the objective measurement of intelligence began in 1904, when the Minister of Public Instruction in the Republic of France appointed a commission to study procedures for evaluating mentally retarded children in Paris. To meet this demand, Alfred Binet and Theodore Simon collaborated in the development of the first Binet-Simon Scale (Anastasi, 1961).

The early Binet-Simon Scale attracted wide attention. It was brought to the United States by Dr. Henry Goddard, and was warmly received by American psychologists. A number of early revisions were made in this country—the most noteworthy being the Terman revision in 1916. This revision resulted in the test being designated the Stanford-Binet (Terman, 1916), and the concept of the IQ was first presented in this revision. The test provided, for the first time, a means of measuring intelligence objectively, and Kirk (1964) stated that, "American psychologists and educators reacted enthusiastically to the testing movement initiated by Binet. Few, however, followed Binet's ideas on the educability of intelligence. Instead there arose a pessimistic attitude towards the training of intelligence" (p. 68).

The clear implication in the early period of testing was that the IQ was considered to be an unalterable constant. Later studies (Schmidt, 1946; Skeels, Updegraff, Wellman, & Williams, 1938; Skodak & Skeels, 1949; Wellman, 1932) attempted to refute this fatalistic posture of American psychologists. However, these studies were found to be fraught with error (Kirk, 1948; McNemar, 1940), and adulation of the IQ prevailed. It was not until 1958 that evidence began to emerge that the IQ was alterable through education and environmental stimulation (Kirk, 1958). However, the results of the Kirk study did indicate that the more severely retarded children (that is, those with extant organicity) demonstrated significantly smaller gains than those with no organic problems.

The decade of the 1960s witnessed a continued deterioration in attitude towards the omnipotency of the IQ score as the panacea for all diagnostic problems. The limitations of the IQ score were recognized, and psychologists and educators began to seek other means to obtain a more comprehensive or differential diagnosis.

The assessment of intelligence within the TMR population is principally conducted for classification rather than diagnostic purposes. Their intelligence is usually assessed with an individual instrument of evaluation. The efficacy or limitations of group tests or pencil and paper tests for this purpose is obvious. Thus, the Stanford-Binet, 1960 Revision (Terman & Merrill, 1960) is usually employed. The Wechsler Intelligence Scale for Children (Wechsler, 1949)—the WISC— is occasionally used, even though it was never designed to test severely retarded children (Baumeister, 1964).

Stanford-Binet

The Stanford-Binet (Terman & Merrill, 1960) appears to be the most desirable and most frequently used individual measure of intelligence with the TMR. Although there is a distinct liability in the instrument's demand for verbal skills, the floor or basal age extends down to two years, and the instrument yields a mental age. The mental age component is often considered to be useful in the determination of the timing of curricular concerns. The IQ is useful only to the extent that it classifies the individual as trainable.

Woo-Sam (Note 3) has investigated the new normative data (Thorndike, 1973), and pointed to problems that may serve to confound the practice of classification according to a Binet score. The restandardization is based upon population characteristics of the 1970s. The 1960 Binet reflects the 1937 normative data (that is, there was no change in the normative data in the 1960 revision). These new norms indicate that there will be a comparative loss of IQ points between the 1960 and 1972 normative data, particularily among younger subjects. The gradient of loss is reflected in the comparison of the two sets of data in Table Four.

As Woo-Sam (Note 3) stated, "It is readily apparent that until the age of about seven or eight, a child would lose as much as 11 IQ points when the 1972, as opposed to the 1937 norms, are applied. The same effect can be observed for all IQ ranges except that the two norms become equivalent earlier in the mentally retarded child" (p. 9). He further indicated that, "A still to be resolved problem with the 1972 norms is the change in the meaning of mental age. Since the new norms result in changes in IQ for mental ages established in the 1930s, examiners must currently report such anachronisms as the child of four, mental age of four, who now has an IQ of 88 instead of 100" (p. 11). In the case of the mentally retarded, generally, the conclusions were that there will be more young children classified as mentally retarded, and the lower IQ score will result in the "identification" of an increased number of children as trainable.

Wechsler Scales

The particular problem with the use of the WISC with a trainable population is that its basal age is five years. Consequently, it would be inappropriate to use this test with a population like the TMR who would not ordinarily be expected ever to obtain a mental age of five. A recent revision of the WISC (Wechsler, 1974) may, in part, remedy this prob-

Table Four

The mental age and IQ differences
(1960 and 1972 Binet norms at the average level)

C.A.	1960 M.A. For 1960 IQ of 100	1972 M.A. For 1972 IQ of 100	IQ equivalent 1972 IQ for 1960 M.A.s 1960 IQ = 100	IQ differences with 1972 norms
2−0	2−0	2−3	90	−10
2−6	2−7	2−11	89	−11
3−0	3−2	3−2	89	−11
3−6	3−7	4−0	89	−11
4−0	4−1	4−6	89	−11
4−6	4−6	5−0	90	−10
5−0	5−0	5−6	91	− 9
5−6	5−6	5−10	93	− 7
6−0	6−0	6−4	93	− 7
6−6	6−6	6−10	94	− 6
7−0	7−1	7−4	96	− 4
7−6	7−7	7−10	97	− 3
8−0	8−2	8−5	97	− 3
8−6	8−8	8−11	97	− 3
9−0	9−3	9−5	98	− 2
9−6	9−9	9−11	98	− 2
10−0	10−3	10−6	98	− 2
10−6	10−9	11−6	98	− 2
11−0	11−3	11−6	98	− 2
11−6	11−8	12−0	97	− 3
12−0	12−2	12−6	97	− 3
12−6	12−8	13−0	98	− 2
13−0	13−1	13−5	97	− 3
13−6	13−5	13−10	97	− 3
14−0	13−10	14−3	97	− 3
14−6	14−2	14−8	97	− 3
15−0	14−6	15−0	96	− 4
15−6	15−0	15−7	96	− 4
16−0	15−5	16−2	96	− 4
16−6	15−6	16−3	95	− 5
17	15−7	16−4	95	− 5
18	15−9	16−8	94	− 4

NOTE: Reproduced from J. M. Woo-Sam, Psychoeducational assessment in the seventies—A look at concepts and measures the Stanford-Binet LM. Unpublished manuscript, 1974.

lem, but this research is not currently available. Wechsler has also developed the Wechsler Preschool and Primary Scale of Intelligence (WPPSI), which represents a downward extension of the WISC. The WPPSI may be used with four to six year olds, but at this point Wechsler cautions that it should not be used with young children with IQs below 75. Therefore, an inadequate floor or basal age in all of the Wechsler scales appears to preclude its use with the trainable population.

Peabody Picture Vocabulary Scale

An instrument that has proven quite useful in the measurement of intelligence among the TMR population is the Peabody Picture Vocabulary Scale (Dunn, 1959)—the PPVT. The PPVT has been subjected to considerable empirical scrutiny and found to be a particularly reliable measure of intelligence with the TMR. The evidence indicates that correlations between the Stanford-Binet and the PPVT range from .22 to .92. The median correlation among all groups of mentally retarded is .66 (Sattler, 1974).

In a study of 220 TMR children (Dunn & Hottel, 1961), the PPVT mental age scores, when compared with the Stanford-Binet, yielded a correlation of .66. The authors concluded that "the PPVT measures (to some extent) whatever it is that the . . . [Stanford-Binet] measures in trainable children . . . Furthermore since the Stanford-Binet requires approximately one hour for administration while the PPVT requires only about fifteen minutes, it measures more quickly" (p. 452).

Mein (1962) also found that the PPVT correlates highly with the Stanford-Binet, and that it is of value in the assessment of intelligence where prolonged testing is impracticable. Furthermore, Budoff and Purseglove (1963) found that the PPVT correlated better with the Stanford-Binet at lower ability levels, and they indicated that the test is much more reliable with a TMR population than an educable one.

The research on the PPVT appears to point to several factors which would benefit the teacher in the determination of the intellectual abilities of the TMR individual. Certainly, time in administration is a factor. So is the type of instrument that a classroom teacher, with a minimum of training in psychometric evaluation, can administer and score. Finally, this test can be used with some assurance that the score will compare favorably with the more sophisticated forms of intellectual assessment (such as the Stanford-Binet) (Shotwell, O'Connor, Gabet, & Dingman, 1969).

There are, of course, other instruments that may be useful in the assessment of the intellectual level of the TMR. However, the instruments we have commented on represent those most often used in the determination or categorization of individuals as "trainable" by the statement of an obtained IQ score. Baumeister (1965) in his reference to this "ubiquitous IQ score" has offered a final word of caution in the process of intellectual evaluation among the lower levels of retardation who are also limited in adaptive behavior. He stated, "The point is that low IQ should not be equated with mental retardation for the reason that the intelligence test measures only a narrow band of adaptive behaviors . . . they are often inappropriately used to the exclusion of other and perhaps more relevant data concerning the function of an individual" (p. 881). He further emphasized that within the severely retarded population, the IQ score does not provide information relative to appropriate program and questioned the utility of an IQ score with this population.

As one reviews the many instruments of evaluation available and the complex problems that the TMR present in the development of programs appropriate to their needs, certainly an *in situ* definition of their intellectual capacity is of limited use. It represents only one criterion necessary to determine their level of retardation. Perhaps the most logical and useful area of assessment in the determination of level of retardation and development of program would be a consideration of the social competence or adaptive behavior of the individual. The concern for this second dimension in assessment is based upon evidence that a measure of adaptive behavior or social competence provides additional, different, and more useful information in the development of a training program than that which is measured by an IQ test (Leland, Shellhaas, Nihira, & Foster, 1967). Furthermore, as Heber (1962) has noted, "Social adjustment is the most important qualifying condition of mental retardation at the adult level" (p. 73).

Measurement of Adaptive Behavior

The concept of social competence in mental retardation was the antecedent to the construct of adaptive behavior. Various authors (Doll, 1941; Sarason, 1955; Tredgold, 1947) have discussed the historical criterion of social competency in defining mental retardation. In the early part of this century, the "moron" was much maligned for the creation of social problems. This crisis reached its apex in this country with the publication of Goddard's study of the Kallikak family in 1912 (Davies & Ecob, 1962). The social problems of "these incompetents" were elaborated on indiscriminately. Sarason (1955) later made a distinction between the social problems of "mental retardation" (EMR) and "mental deficiency (TMR), when he stated:

> The term mental deficiency refers to individuals who are socially inadequate as a result of an intellectual defect which is a reflection of an impairment of the central nervous system which is essentially incura-

ble . . . The mentally defective individual will always be in need of supervision and assistance . . . it is not expected that they will be able to fend for themselves socially and vocationally. Whereas the mentally retarded may require *temporary* specialized assistance, the mentally defective will *always* require it. [p. 442]

An early concern for the social problems of the mentally retarded was expressed by Doll (1935), and he proposed a rating scale for determining social age and social competence. This scale was the precursor to the Vineland Social Maturity Scale (Doll, 1965) and was considered to be useful in differentiating between mental retardation with and without social competence or by degree of retardation, highlighting the difference between educable and trainable mentally retarded.

The concept of social inadequacy and its relationship to degree of retardation was redefined by Heber (1959) in terms of adaptive behavior. He stated that "The dimensions of *Adaptive Behavior* . . . [are] a composite of many aspects of the behavior and function [which] . . . all contribute to and are part of total adaptation to the environment [and that] . . . the *Measured Intelligence* dimensions will correlate with level of *Adaptive Behavior*" (p. 61). The implication is that the lower the intelligence, the more we can expect severe deficits in adaptive behavior. Grossman (1973) placed such importance on the concept of adaptive behavior that he considered it a necessary criterion for defining mental retardation and indicated that a deficit in this area must occur concurrently with an intellectual deficit before retardation is extant.

The Vineland Scale of Social Maturity

From its inception to present day, the Vineland Scale of Social Maturity (Doll, 1965)—VSSM—has been considered to be the best single instrument available for the measure of social competence or, more recently, adaptive behavior (Grossman, 1973; Heber, 1959). The scale is designed to measure social competence through a determination of personal social maturation. It is an interview scale that requires someone other than the subject to serve as respondent (such as the retardate's parent or teacher). The categories involved in the evaluation are (1) self-help general, (2) self-help eating, (3) self-help dressing, (4) self-direction, (5) occupation, (6) communication, (7) locomotion, and (8) socialization. The VSSM is essentially a normative-based instrument. The categories are scored by age levels, and the total score may be converted into a social age or social quotient (SQ). In the use of this scale, Doll (1965) emphasizes that "this is not a rating scale and that a major difficulty in its use is its illusory simplicity. Adequate use of the scale requires sophisticated skill in interview technique" (p. iii). Thus, the VSSM, like many other standardized instruments of assessment, requires a well-trained and qualified examiner. However, because of its universal acceptance and comprehensiveness, the VSSM is often adapted by teachers of the TMR as a check sheet that becomes a part of the permanent record on a pupil or a part of a reporting form.

The efficacy of the VSSM, particularily in its relationship to IQ, has been subjected to exhaustive research. Leland *et al.* (1967) have reported correlations of SQ and IQ ranging from .90 to .00. The variance was dependent upon the intelligence test used or the subjects and the variability of the sample. However, within the studies using mentally retarded subjects, Heber (1962) reported that there was a "moderate" correlation between IQ and SQ. The "moderateness" of this correlation could be attributed to the fact that the two scores (IQ and SQ) measure different parameters of an individual. The discrepancy would, then, be greater among the EMR who may have intellectual deficits but an acceptable level of adaptive behavior, and less among the TMR who would be expected to manifest severe deficits in intellectual ability and adaptive behavior. Leland *et al.* (1967) also indicated that the discrepancies between IQ and SQ are the result of poor methodology and that "To compare IQ and SQ scores directly would require that the mean of the IQ and SQ distributions be the same and that they have the same standard deviation (which they do not)" (p. 368).

Despite the obvious statistical limitations of the comparison of the two scores, the practical dimension of a measure of adaptive behavior will provide more meaningful information for identification and program purposes than reliance upon a single measure of intelligence. For this purpose, the VSSM is still considered to be the best measure available.

The Adaptive Behavior Scales

The interest in adaptive behavior, as in any other dimension of behavior, has precipitated the development of several other scales which purport to measure this construct. The Adaptive Behavior Scales (Nihira, Foster, Shellhaas, & Leland, 1969)—the ABS—are probably the most recent instruments developed to measure adaptive and maladaptive behavior in children and adults. These scales were principally designed for use with institutional populations to determine the individual's level of independence and means of coping with the environment. They assess adaptive behavior within ten areas of concern. Within these ten areas, there are twenty-three subareas to be assessed. The ten major areas of adaptive behavior are:

1. Independent functioning
2. Physical development
3. Economic activity

4. Language development
5. Number & time concept
6. Occupation—domestic
7. Occupation—general
8. Self-direction
9. Responsibilities
10. Socialization

As mentioned previously, the scales also provide for a measure of maladaptive behavior. The difference between adaptive and maladaptive behavior "depends upon the way that behavior is perceived and interpreted by people in our society" (Nihira et al., 1969, p. 7). The maladaptive behavior is rated in fourteen areas of personality and behavior. These are:

1. Violent and destructive behavior
2. Antisocial behavior
3. Rebellious behavior
4. Untrustworthy behavior
5. Withdrawal
6. Stereotyped behavior and odd mannerisms
7. Inappropriate interpersonal manners
8. Inappropriate vocal habits
9. Unacceptable or eccentric habits
10. Self-abusive behavior
11. Hyperactive tendencies
12. Sexually aberrant behavior
13. Psychological disturbances
14. Use of medications

The examiner is the respondent on the scales, and consequently must be well acquainted with the individual who is to be rated. The scales can be used with all levels of retardation and all ages, from three years of age to adulthood. The scales appear to be most appropriate for children under twelve, and with the lower levels of retardation (Miller, 1972). However, they appear to have limited use with the more profoundly retarded (Congdon, 1973). They have been found to relate well to IQ and to be useful with institutional populations in determining programs or training level placement (Malone & Christian, 1975; Schwartz & Allen, 1975).

Current evidence notwithstanding, the ABS are still in experimental form. Certain refinements have been proposed (Bhattacharya, 1973; Congdon, 1973), and additional research is needed to determine the efficacy of the instrument—particularly with noninstitutionalized retardates. Until the normative data is extended to a more representative sample, their use with a noninstitutionalized population is still subject to serious question. In view of their newness and limited research with the ABS, it would appear that their indiscriminate use at this point in community-based programs would not be warranted.

Other Scales of Social Competence

There are other measures of social skills that are designed for use with the trainable population. The Balthazar Scales of Adaptive Behavior (BSAB), Section 1 (Balthazar, 1971) and Section 2 (Balthazar, 1973), is a recently developed scale that is designed for use with the profoundly and severely mentally retarded. Section 1 provides a scale for determining functional independence which involves eight ratings in the areas of (1) dependent feeding, (2) finger foods, (3) spoon usage, (4) fork usage, (5) drinking, (6) total eating skills, (7) total dressing, and (8) total toileting. Section 2 is concerned with social adaptations and provides for a rating of: (1) unadaptive self-directed behaviors, (2) unadaptive interpersonal behaviors, (3) adaptive self-directed behaviors, (4) adaptive interpersonal behaviors, (5) communication, (6) play activities, (7) response to instructions, and (8) a checklist of personal care and other behaviors.

Because of the newness of the instrument, research on the BSAB is limited. One of the principal limitations appears to be that the research and development of the scales were conducted with an institutional population. Therefore, its efficacy in community programs may be questionable.

The Cain-Levine Social Competency Scale (Cain, Levine, & Elzey, 1963) was standardized on 716 noninstitutionalized TMR children living in California. It identifies 188 behaviors that are organized into four areas: (1) self-help, (2) initiative, (3) social skills, and (4) communication. The Cain-Levine has been found to be useful as a measure of the TMR child's progress in a program (Burnes & Hassol, 1966; Levine, Elzey, & Paulson, 1966), and it appears to correlate well ($r = .77$) with the VSSM (Congdon, 1969). However, there is limited research on this scale, and its use with an institutional population is questionable.

The Progress Assessment Chart of Social Development (Gunzburg, 1963) also appears to have some merit in evaluating social skills and deficiencies. The chart is specifically designed for the mentally retarded and provides for assessment at primary, intermediate, and senior stages. The author (Gunzburg, 1963) feels that it is of value in assisting in the development of an individualized remedial program by diagnosing specific weaknesses in self-help, communication, socialization, and occupation. Within these areas, there are 120 scoring possibilities. In addition, the chart provides for an evaluation of various aspects of personality. Again, there is a paucity of research on this instrument that would assist in determining its efficacy, but it, as well as the Cain-Levine, may at some future date prove to be useful. At the present time, however, the practical limitations of the necessity for lengthy contact with the individual, evaluation based on observed behaviors, and the complex scoring process, has produced a reluctance to use the multidimensional measures of adaptive behavior, and the VSSM has retained its position for no other reason than convenience (Adams, 1973).

A final note of caution on the use of any measure of social competence or adaptive behavior. The examiner or teacher must always remember that social competence or adaptive behavior is subjective and must be seen as relative to the social or cultural milieu within which the TMR person lives. "Appropriate" behavior is also subject to change. What is coping or adaptive in one situation may be maladaptive in another. Also, variables such as teacher expectation, chronological age, etiology, and experiences in social interaction will all have an impact on the social adaptability of the TMR (Newman & Doby, 1973). For this reason, many programs develop their own checklists which reflect the unique circumstances of their population and program, because, as Silverstein (1973) has noted, there is no entirely suitable measure of adaptive behavior.

Regardless of the manner in which it is done, an evaluation of the individual's adaptive behavior is a critical component of a comprehensive diagnosis. This information, along with other pertinent information, will contribute significantly to the decision-making process leading to an appropriate program.

Concurrent with intellectual and social behavior, the developmental progress is often considered as a separate dimension of assessment and program planning. However, it is frequently difficult to separate these dimensions of behavior and development, since they are often closely interrelated. Grossman (1973) discussed the variability of deficits of adaptive behavior in young children and incorporated developmental aspects within this framework. Also, the problem of isolating developmental progress was identified by Jordan (1972) when he stated that "The cognitive functions of man are related to his development and growth. As he grows older, his abilities increase; as he matures his cognitive skills also mature. Clearly intellect is a correlate of organic growth. The use of the word *correlate* is deliberate, because it suggests the probability that the two phenomena will occur together frequently" (p. 416).

Assessment of Developmental Progress

The actual assessment of developmental progress as a single construct poses several additional problems. The use of certain instruments to determine the developmental patterns of a trainable population is often tantamount to equating the TMR with a "normal" population, since most developmental scales have been standardized on a normal preschool population. Secondly, the few attempts that have been made to structure developmental scales for the TMR have succumbed to the indeterminate abyss of a multidimensional assessment. These instruments are often global, to the extent that they lack definition. As a result, in view of the vagueness of the construct and the normative data (or lack of it), the use of developmental scales is often limited. However, as Robinson and Robinson (1965) have noted, the practical need often forces us to use instruments that are less than satisfactory.

Denver Developmental Screening Test

The Denver Developmental Screening Test (Frankenburg, Dodds, & Fandal, 1970)—the DDST—is a normative-based instrument that enjoys considerable popularity in TMR programs. The DDST is a composite of 105 tasks for children in the age range of birth to six years. The items are grouped under four major subheadings: (1) personal-social, (2) fine motor-adaptive, (3) language, and (4) gross motor. The normative data indicates that the instrument was standardized on normal children living in Denver, Colorado. Handicapped children were selectively excluded. The expressed purpose of the scale is to diagnose developmental problems as early as possible. The attractiveness of the DDST is probably related to its simplicity in administration and scoring. The limitations of the scale with any handicapped population would be dictated by the normative sample. However, one distinct value in its use with the TMR or any other handicapped population is that it provides a range for each of the items giving a basis for comparison with normal expectancy.

Bayley Scales of Infant Development

The Bayley Scales of Infant Development (Bayley, 1969) are designed to determine the developmental status of infants ranging in ages from two months to thirty months. The scales are divided into three parts: (1) the mental scale, which is designed to yield a mental development index, (2) the motor scale, which yields a psychomotor development index, and (3) the infant behavior record, which assesses the child's orientation towards the environment. The total scale has been found to have some predictive validity with children who are developmentally or intellectually abnormal, particularly within the first three years of life (Erickson, Johnson, & Campbell, 1970). The limitations of this scale are again determined by the normative sample. Additional limitations appear to be the time required for administration, and perhaps most important, the requirement by author definition that demands a well-trained examiner.

Although the use of these scales may provide some useful information relative to the developmental status of the trainable, there is limited research evidence to support this assumption. The information obtained must be interpreted in terms of the normative data. Also, the rapid changes that often take place in developmental status and the discrepancy between chronological age and developmental age in most TMR people may serve to confound further the use of these scales. It is also obvious that the DDST and the Bayley will have limited, if any, prognostic value for the individual TMR child enrolled in a program.

TMR Performance Profile

Although not specifically defined as a developmental scale, the TMR Performance Profile (DiNola, Kaminsky, & Sternfeld, 1963) has been designed as a multidimensional type of developmental inventory to be used with a TMR population. The profile is a criteria-based instrument that reflects the individual's achievement as a result of school program, rather than ability that may be determined by IQ score (Sellin, 1967). It evaluates pupil performance based upon teacher observation in six major areas: (1) social behavior, (2) self-care, (3) communication, (4) basic knowledge, (5) practical skills, and (6) body usage. These major areas are subdivided, and the total profile identifies 240 different behaviors. The pupil performance is rated by the teacher on a continuum of zero to four. The levels of performance are:

0   Negative or nonperformance
1   Minimal performance
2   Limited acceptability
3   A realistic goal
4   Performance above the goal

The authors are careful to indicate that the scale is not a psychometric instrument. They emphasize that it is for the use of the classroom teacher in rating pupil performance.

The profile has excellent face validity, and the items reflect abilities well within the range of the TMR. However, one cannot ignore the lack of research connected with the instrument, and it has frequently been criticized for lack of standardization. An additional, though not serious, problem is the subjective nature of the instrument. With the teacher serving as respondent, the profile will reflect individual teacher biases, which precludes interchangeability of the information from teacher to teacher, program to program (that is, with each new teacher, a new profile must be done). These liabilities notwithstanding, the TMR Profile appears to represent, at present, the best comprehensive effort at determining the TMR person's level of functioning and evaluating progress in the program.

Learning Accomplishment Profile

Sanford (1973) has recently developed a criteria-based instrument that relies heavily upon child development data from other existing instruments. The Learning Accomplishment Profile (LAP) is an experimental instrument which purports to provide a record of the handicapped child's existing skills in the areas of (1) self-help, (2) social, (3) cognitive, (4) gross motor, and (5) language. The author states that the LAP is designed to "enable the teacher to: identify developmentally appropriate learning objectives for each individual child; measure progress through changes in rate of development; and provide specific information relative to pupil learning" (n.p.). The LAP is divided into three sections: Section I provides the developmental data, Section II provides a task level hierarchy, and Section III provides an outline for forty-four weeks of curriculum units appropriate for the developmental behaviors. As with the TMR Profile, the author is careful to indicate that the LAP is not a psychological test. It does not classify a child according to level of ability. It is designed to identify appropriate learning objectives for individual children as illustrated in Figure Four.

The face validity of the LAP is quite good. However, it lacks research or field testing. Since the various tasks are assigned by developmental age, it would appear critical that the inventory be subjected to some form of research scrutiny to determine the appropriateness of the positioning of the tasks within the hierarchy. In addition, the length of the inventory, which provides for 486 scoring possibilities, precludes rapid administration. However, there is a condensation of the LAP which provides for 160 scoring possibilities. The condensation may be useful as a screening device to determine the need of a complete administration of the LAP.

The real strength of the LAP may prove to be in the provision of a task level hierachy (Section II) and the curriculum units (Section III) which offer a program supplement for the TMR's existing skills. This added dimension in the LAP resolves the frequent criticism of pupil inventories or tests, that after determining the existing status of the child's skills, there is little if any information provided for increasing these skills.

With or without assessment devices, there are considerable limitations on determining the developmental level of a TMR individual. As Grossman (1973) noted, "Individuals . . . with the same level of measured intelligence and of adaptive behavior may still differ widely in patterns of ability" (p. 6). Further, the paucity of research in this area is indicative of its practical limitations. The assessment of an individual's development is by nature multidimensional and encompasses the cognitive, social, and developmental domains. The principal value in con-

Bibliog. Source	Behavior	Age (dev.)	Assessment date	Date of achievement	Comments (criteria, materials), problems, etc.
3	Manipulates egg beater	27 mos.			
9	Enjoys finger painting	30–35 mos.			
9	Makes mud and sand pies	30–35 mos.			
13	Paints strokes, dots, and circular shapes on easel	30–35 mos.			
6	Cuts with scissors	35 mos.			
13	Picks up pins, thread, etc., with each eye separately covered				
7	Drives nails and pegs	36–48 mos.			
13	Builds tower of 9 cubes	36–48 mos.			
7	Holds crayon with fingers	36–48 mos.			
3	Strings 4 beads	36–48 mos.			
13	Can close fist and wiggle thumb in imitation, R & L	36–48 mos.			
11	Puts 6 round pegs in round holes on pegboard	36–48 mos.			

Mark + for positive demonstration of skill
Mark − for negative demonstration of skill
NOTE: Reproduced from A. R. Sanford *The learning accomplishment profile* (Chapel Hill, North Carolina: Chapel Hill Training—Outreach Project, 1973).

Figure Four

Sample sheet for scoring the developmental level of fine motor skills on the Learning Accomplishment Profile (LAP) tinuing to attempt to assess the global concept of developmental progress is more curricular than prognostic, and should not take on the aura of the assessment of intelligence.

A recent concern in programs for the trainable mentally retarded has been directed towards evaluating and programming for deficits in communication skills, or more specifically language development. Limited communication skills represents one of the many deficits in adaptive behavior which contributes to the determination of mental retardation (Grossman, 1973), and Farber (1968) has noted that the limited communication skills of the TMR are often the principal criteria which precludes their participation as responsible individuals.

It has long been generally accepted that intellectual and linguistic deficits are mutually debilitating and that there is a causal relationship between the two. It has only been in recent years, though, that any interest has been generated in the investigation of language development and its impact on the retarded (McCarthy, 1964).

Harrison (1958) reported that there was an increased interest in the problems of linguistic deficits during the 1950s, but concluded that there was an apparent lack of scales for diagnosis and evaluation of linguistic deficits among the mentally retarded. The implication was that the lack of scales was in part related to the extant problems of developing such instruments.

Assessment of Communication Skills

The growth of interest in language development for the mentally retarded has resulted in a new wave of enthusiasm for remediation of the retardates' language deficits. McCarthy (1964) has pointed out that there was always a recognition of a need for speech and linguistic training for the retarded, but that the efficacy of this type of training has only recently been determined. He did caution though, that this enthusiasm may not be the result of improved techniques, but rather a result of abandoning the TMR population in favor of a higher level retardate. The TMR have long been considered a poor risk for linguistic training because of multiple organic problems. Therefore, the gravitation to a higher level retardate (EMR) lacking the severe organic problems was tantamount to measurable success. Obviously, though, participants in TMR programs have not given up. An example of their tenacity was reported in a survey by Hudson (1960), which indicated that content emphasis according to her rating scale reflected 29%, or almost one-third of the class time being devoted to language development. This type of interest in language development for the mentally retarded has produced the usual plethora of instruments for assessment.

Illinois Test of Psycholinguistic Abilities

The Illinois Test of Psycholinguistic Abilities (Kirk, McCarthy, & Kirk, 1968)—the ITPA—has enjoyed considerable notoriety in the past decade. The ITPA was developed as a diagnostic rather than classification instrument. According to the authors, it is principally designed to provide effective remediation and "provides (a) a framework within which tests of discrete and educationally significant abilities have been generated; (b) a base for the development of instructional programs for children. With this dual purpose the diagnostic/teaching model serves not only as a model for evaluating learning problems but also as a model for selecting and programming remedial procedures" (p. 5).

The ITPA normative data were obtained from approximately 1,000 average children between the ages of two and ten. The "averageness" of the children was determined from IQ tests, school achievement, socioeconomic status and absence of problems in sensory and motor development. According to the authors, the administration of the ITPA demands the same sophistication on the part of the examiner that would be expected for administration of any psychometric instrument (such as the Stanford-Binet Intelligence Scale).

The ITPA has generated considerable controversy. It has been hailed as a significant instrument of assessment and severely criticized, particularly in its use with retarded children. Although recognized for having made significant contributions to the study of language, the remediation aspects of the ITPA have been questioned (Spradlin, 1967). Further, the research with a retarded population has been principally devoted to the educable mentally retarded, and the results of this research are not conclusive because of limited information on the performance gains when language training ceased (Batemen, 1965).

The limited research on the ITPA with a TMR population has been equally inconclusive. It has been indicated that the educational prognosis of mongoloids as a group was more promising than the nonmongoloid group (McCarthy, 1965). However, further evidence indicates that the effect of a language development program with TMR subjects was insignificant (Blue, 1970).

In comparing the efficacy of the ITPA with educable and trainable populations, Wiseman (1965) speculated that "the more retarded the less response can be expected . . . and the unknown language and learning characteristics of the mongoloid child make program planning and analysis of the results difficult" (p. 17). He further indicated that "educable mentally retarded children seemed to benefit more from psycholinguistic training than trainable mentally retarded children" (p. 22).

Whatever the assets and liabilities of the ITPA, it will need to be subjected to further research scrutiny before its usefulness is determined. It may be useful in defining some practical aspects of language behavior among the trainable, but its efficacy with this population appears to be limited. It would seem sufficient at this point to accept the authors' own conclusion that the ITPA is not infallible and that it is only a tool to be used along with other information as an aid to diagnosis (Kirk, McCarthy, & Kirk, 1968).

Parsons Language Sample

Spradlin (1963) designed an instrument for language assessment that has been specifically standardized on a retarded population. The Parsons Language Sample (PLS) was developed to sample language according to the Skinnerian system. It is intended to sample both vocal and nonvocal responses. The empirical evaluation of the PLS was conducted on 275 mentally retarded children between the ages of seven years eleven months and fifteen years eight months residing at Parsons State Hospital and Training Center, Parsons, Kansas. The PLS does not require extensive training or background to administer, and it appears to be a reasonably valid instrument for predicting nonspeech communication behavior of retarded children (Travis, 1971). There is further evidence to indicate that it compares favorably with the ITPA (Horner, 1967), and that the statistical characteristics are sufficient to indicate that the PLS appears to be quite useful in determining expressive language ability (McCarthy, 1964).

There was some initial enthusiasm generated for the use of the PLS in assessing the speech and language of the mentally retarded (McCarthy, 1964). However, one cannot ignore that it was developed with a select group of educable mentally retarded in an institutional setting (Schiefelbusch, 1963), and the paucity of studies on the use of the PLS would serve to indicate that it has not generated much interest among professionals in the last decade.

Other Language Scales

There are several other instruments that are, at present, in experimental form that may later prove to be useful in the assessment of language abilities among the TMR.

The Preschool Language Scale (Zimmerman, Steiner, & Evatt, 1969) is designed to diagnose strengths and weaknesses in the language of any child functioning at the preschool level. The initial edition of this scale (D'Asaro, Lehrhoff, Zimmerman, & Jones, 1956) was developed exclusively for cerebral-palsied infants and children. The original scale represented a global assessment of language skills. The present preschool scale provides for a bifurcation of auditory comprehension and verbal ability and is designed to measure maturational and developmental aspects of language. The empirical data are based upon the average attainment of preschool and primary-level children, and the authors stress that in its present form the Preschool Scale is not a test but an instrument of evaluation in experimental form.

Another interesting experimental dimension to the assessment of language is the Telediagnostic Protocol (Curtis & Donlon, 1972). This is a criteria-based instrument developed to assess low functioning multi-sensory disabled children, when traditional instruments of evaluation prove impractical. The experimental protocol was originally designed to assess deaf-blind children between the ages of three and eight years. By definition, it is to be used with the child who shows a low level of response on traditional instruments of assessment and with difficult-to-test populations. It is unique in that it employs the use of video tape to assess skill by situation in three major areas: (1) communication, (2) adjustment, and (3) learning. Eight situations related to the child's daily living are structured within these major areas and videotaped. The situations are then rated by psychoeducational personnel. However, Tweedie (1974) has found that teachers, or even less trained personnel, may be effective raters of the videotaped performance in the specific area of communication. The ultimate goal of this protocol is to give information that may be unobtainable via traditional assessment techniques or to supplement existing information. The principal value of such a protocol appears to be twofold: (1) it provides assessment of performance in structured life-like situations, and (2) the video tape provides a permanent record of behavior which may be retrieved at any time to evaluate change through comparison of repeated measures on the same instrument.

The growth in the number of instruments for assessing communication disorders among the mentally retarded is considered to be encouraging (McCarthy, 1964). The efficacy of these assessment devices with a TMR population is yet to be determined. The renewed enthusiasm for speech and language programs appears to focus more on assessment and remediation of communication deficits among the EMR population. Many of the instruments of assessment were not designed with the TMR population in mind, and their application to a TMR population is after-the-fact and ignores the original intention of the instrument. The relationship between language and intelligence continues to mark the TMR as a poor risk for measurable gains in communication skills, and there is little to no conclusive evidence to support the indiscriminate use of many of the available language inventories with this population.

The development or remediation of motor skills ranks, in instances, second only to language development activities in training programs

(Hudson, 1960). The research is unequivocal in indicating that the retarded, in general, are below expected norms in motor and physical characteristics (Francis & Rarick, 1959), but there is equal evidence to indicate that these characteristics can be improved (McCarthy & Scheerenberger, 1966).

Assessment of Motor Abilities

The trainable mentally retarded are measurably inferior to the EMR in motor abilities and as a group show greater variability in performance on a given test. Motor deficits in the TMR are related to a number of learning factors, organic factors, structural impairments, and impairments of perceptual modalities. Definitive norms for evaluating motor proficiency in the TMR is seriously lacking (Cratty, 1974).

The evaluation of motor performance of the TMR population is further confounded by a lack of agreement on the dimensions of the construct. The interrelationship of perceptual and motor performance was first defined in the methodologies of Itard and Seguin. Strauss and Lehtinen (1947) discussed the interrelationship in terms of visuo-motor and auditory-motor performance, and Kephart (1971) stated that "we cannot think of perceptual activities and motor activities as two different items; we must think of the hyphenated term *perceptual-motor*" (p. 115). Thus, perceptual-motor, as a single construct, has been generally accepted as an area of performance. However, the lack of precision in this category and the broadness of the construct makes it difficult to assess.

Malpass (1963), in a discussion of etiological considerations in motor disability, suggests that there are multiple factors which interfere with motor skills, and that even though the effect on sensory-motor function is well known, the methodology employed to study this among the retarded has been subject to serious question. He further noted that "A great deal has been written about perceptual-motor abilities. Until better means of separating these functions is available, it seems only confusing to discuss them together" (p. 607).

Mann (1970) has relegated the perceptual-motor concept to the level of "educational fad" which he feels is unwarranted. He contends that perceptual improvement can be accomplished by traditional means but states that specific perceptual training leads to "emphasis upon the irrelevant" (p. 35).

There has been a preoccupation with the efficacy of the hyphenation of perceptual-motor and its role in development. It is a broad and little-understood process involving heredity and environment (Noble, 1970). However, the components of perceptual and/or motor abilities are included in the daily program of training, and this training, in some ways, has proven beneficial. The enthusiasm generated from evidence of improvement has resulted in new attempts at assessment. In some instances, existing assessment techniques are used interchangeably to determine motor skills, motor fitness, or the perceptual-motor abilities of TMR children and adults. The problem is that there is often an indiscriminate use of the assessment devices without discerning the applicability of the information to the individual's program (that is, the teacher is often not sure of what has been evaluated, and once evaluated, what to do with the information). Consequently, extant motor deficits are often identified and then ignored, or the tests become curriculum guides. The teacher teaches the test, and motor development activities become endless hours of scribbling on the chalkboard, walking 2 × 4's, or filling out reams of ditto sheets.

Regardless of the problems in identification and measurement of motor abilities, the practice of assessment of gross motor and fine motor skills persists in training programs.

Oseretsky Motor Development Scale

The Oseretsky Motor Development Scale (Sloan, 1955) has enjoyed considerable popularity in TMR programs. It was first published in 1923 and has undergone a number of revisions for use with specific populations. It is designed to test motor aptitude or maturation and is administered individually. The administration requires about forty-five minutes, but Kershner and Dusewicz (1970) have developed a new revision which employs group techniques in an effort to reduce the time of administration.

The use of the Oseretsky is considered to be quite restrictive. Oseretsky admitted to discrepancies in the diagnostic value of certain items which appeared to be associated with acquired skills, and to date there is no evidence to indicate that the scale has any diagnostic value. It appears to be more descriptive of motor performance (Morris & Whiting, 1971).

In spite of its limitations, the Oseretsky is frequently used to determine the motor development of the mentally retarded and to compare retardates with normals. The Sloan revision (Lincoln-Oseretsky, 1955) is still considered to be the best standardized motor development scale available (Malpass, 1963). However, Sloan (1955), in recognition of the complex process of motor development, cautioned against its use in isolation.

Purdue Perceptual Motor Survey

The Purdue Perceptual Motor Survey (Roach & Kephart, 1966) is designed to identify the multiple factors of the hyphenated construct desibed by Kephart (1971) as perceptual-motor deficits which are necessary to acquire motor skills. Although frequently used as a test of motor development, the authors emphasize that the Purdue is not a test or diagnostic instrument. It is designed to provide a qualitative synthesis of development in three major areas: (1) laterality, (2) directionality, and (3) perceptual-motor matching. These are assessed in order to determine areas of necessary remediation.

The Purdue is restrictive in the sense that the normative data were developed with normal children in grades one through four. Known retarded and physically handicapped children were selectively excluded. The authors further caution against misinterpretation of the information obtained from the survey and appeal for judicious use of the instrument in determining its value. In view of these restrictions, Hammill and Bartel (1975) stated that, "It is likely that the Purdue was never intended for use as a standardized instrument and that it is better employed as a structured informal device" (p. 210). Cratty (1974) further noted that it is principally a screening device that allows the teacher to observe the child in a variety of movement tasks and has little value as an instrument of evaluation for the retarded.

Developmental Test of Visual Perception

The Developmental Test of Visual Perception (Frostig, Maslow, Lefever, & Whittlesey, 1963)—the DTVP—is another instrument that incorporates a perceptual-visual-motor construct that is frequently used as a motor assessment/program with the TMR population. The DTVP is not, by definition, a motor test but incorporates what Malpass (1963) determined as the "confusing" hyphenated construct of perceptual-motor abilities. The DTVP is designed to detect perceptual disabilities in comparison with the norm of such activity. The current standardization is based upon 2,100 children between the ages of three years and nine years of a generally white, middle-class population in Southern California. The test contains five subtests which are designed to assess (1) eye-motor coordination, (2) perception of figure/ground, (3) perception of form constancy, (4) perception of position in space, and (5) perception of spatial relationships. The test is a pencil and paper instrument and may be administered individually or in groups. It yields a deviation score (perception quotient) which is used to serve as a total prognostic indicator. The time of administration is about thirty to forty-five minutes. The authors state that the DTVP is a useful screening tool for identification of young children who may need perceptual training. An additional dimension to the DTVP is that Frostig and Horn (1964) provide related program materials designed to increase perceptual skills.

The DTVP and the program materials designed to supplement the test have been used most effectively with the educable mentally retarded. The literature provides some empirical evidence that the use of this material does, to some extent, evaluate and contribute to the improvement of the EMR's visual and auditory perceptual skills (Allen, Dickman, & Haupt, 1966; Alley, 1968; Sabatino, Ysseldyke, & Woolston, 1973). However, there is a conspicuous lack of literature that would provide empirical support for the use of the Frostig Test or the program materials with the TMR population. Hall and Deacon (1970) conducted an evaluation and program study with sixty institutionalized TMR people and found that the Frostig material is an effective method to assist the TMR in attaining visual-perceptual skills in specific areas. However, the findings in this instance represent a statement of the obvious. Children who receive training on the Frostig program will obviously test higher on the DTVP, because the training exercises teach the test. The real issue, in this case, would be the temporal stability of those gains.

The limited use of the DTVP with a TMR population could also be the result of the instrument's expressed focus towards factors which contribute to school performance or educational progress (that is, reading and writing skills). The anticipated lack of progress in academic skills and the limited evidence of gains in related areas as a result of the Frostig program requires caution in its use with a TMR population. The expectations of improvement of perceptual-motor skills in the TMR without empirical evidence to support such expectations leaves considerable doubt as to whether perceptual-motor skills can be measured and trained with this population. In terms of the complex problems of the TMR, Mann (1970) may be correct when he says, "We cannot train perception . . . How can we train what isn't there?" (p. 32).

The assessment of motor development is frequently ancillary to a concern for the general health and physical fitness of the TMR population. There has been an increased interest in this area of program, and a number of instruments have recently been developed or adapted to identify the constants and variables in the physical functioning and general health of the TMR.

Assessment of General Fitness

The American Association on Health, Physical Education, and Recreation (AAHPER) developed a list of a number of tests and scales that can be used to determine the physical fitness of the mentally retarded (Information Center Recreation for the Handicapped, 1971). Most of these are adaptations of existing instruments, experimental instruments, or instruments that represent traditional approaches to evaluating fitness of the general population.

Special Fitness Test for the Mentally Retarded

The Special Fitness Test for the Mentally Retarded (AAHPER, 1968) has probably enjoyed the greatest popularity of any of the instruments of assessment in this area. The test is composed of seven items: (1) flexed arm hang, (2) sit-ups, (3) shuttle run, (4) standing broad jump, (5) 50-yard dash, (6) softball throw for distance, and (7) 300-yard run/walk. It is used to provide information on the physical fitness of the individual, and norms are provided by sex and chronological age from eight to eighteen years. The norms were developed on a population of 4,200 educable mentally retarded boys and girls in public school programs. However, there is an adaptation of the test for the TMR which is designed to be a "challenge so each individual has a feeling of accomplishment and personal fulfillment" (n.p.).

The expressed purposes of the test are:

1. To provide teachers, supervisors and parents with a test battery appropriate for assessing the physical fitness of mentally retarded children.
2. To assess progress of the individual child and serve as a diagnosis for specific strengths and weaknesses.
3. To give mentally retarded children an incentive to improve their physical fitness and levels of motor performance.
4. To serve as stimulation to teachers of the retarded and to schools which serve the retarded to upgrade physical education and recreation programs for these children. [p. 4]

Perhaps the greatest incentive for this testing program is that there is an award system for those who have attained certain levels of physical fitness. The awards are emblems of various colors and types that the child can wear on a jacket or sweater.

Thus far we have discussed a number of objective measures or inventories which are frequently used to determine the TMR child's motor development and general fitness. However, the Wetzel Grid (Wetzel, 1948) may provide the simplest and most efficient method for the teacher to evaluate and maintain a record of the TMR's general physical status. The Wetzel Grid is a screening device that represents an ongoing evaluation of physical status as determined by the child's height, weight, and age. These data are interpreted into a "physique channel" which designates body build according to (1) obese and stocky types, (2) good or medium, and (3) fair, borderline, and poor physiques. These data are recorded at three-month intervals, and if a child remains in his or her "physique channel," his or her growth pattern is determined normal. If the child deviates into an adjacent channel, this may be interpreted as a warning sign. The warning sign does not have diagnostic implications but indicates that a further evaluation may be warranted to determine the reason for change of status. The Wetzel is not meant to replace a formal or detailed evaluation of physical status. It is a simple, objective method of data collecting for picking up clues or early warning signs of deviations in a child's growth.

Assessment of Perceptual Modalities

A final area of concern within the complex of handicapping conditions in the TMR population is problems in auditory and visual deficits. Kodman (1963) has noted that the prevalence of hearing loss in this population is higher than that expected for public school children by a factor of three or four to one. He further speculated that the prevalence of visual pathology or impaired vision would also be higher among the retarded. The extant pathologies usually found among the TMR population would further contribute to a speculation that auditory and visual deficits among this population would be quite high.

The assessment of these deficits usually requires a clinical competence in excess of that anticipated among teachers. Therefore, the role of the teacher becomes that of observer. The teacher would be expected to note difficulties or suspect pathologies in the auditory or visual mechanisms and make appropriate referral for assessment by a competent clinician or physician.

Further Implications for Assessment

The various psychodiagnostic instruments that have been discussed are not inclusive, but they do represent the means that are frequently used to evaluate the various dimensions of the assets and liabilities of the TMR. Certainly, the data obtained from these tests are often useful but should not be considered as indispensable, nor in isolation.

The emphasis on the use of psychodiagnostic tests has generated much controversy and has cast a pall of criticism over the formal testing process. The efficacy of the various instruments has been subjected to serious scrutiny. Bersoff (1973) has pointed to a number of problems in relying on psychological tests. Critical among these are problems in validity and the normative use of testing which ignores individual behavior in a natural setting.

Wolfensberger (1965) views the total diagnostic process as "contradictions and inefficiencies, thoughtless cliches and bankrupt practices" (p. 29). He elaborated on his position by citing specific "embarrassments" where "program" is often limited to diagnosis, endless cross-referrals, and inadequate feedback counseling.

It is perhaps these very factors which have contributed to the depressing state of the available instruments and their use, or abuse, with a TMR population. What we are attempting to test or assess are the characteristics of the TMR that will have an impact on programs. This should involve the identification of target behaviors for training and/or remediation. Unfortunately, most of the available psychodiagnostic tests were not designed for use with a TMR population and are consequently considered to be of little value in determining programs (DiNola *et al.*, 1963).

It is difficult to obtain useful test data that can be interpreted into meaningful recommendations for programs. For this reason, the process of assessment should reach beyond the administration of a test or a battery of tests. Newland (1963) has noted that testing and assessment are different activities. He stated that testing is "exposure of a client to any given device . . . [while assessment represents] both this quantitative depiction of the client, and the qualitative and integrated characterization of the client as a dynamic, ongoing total organism functioning in a social setting" (p. 54).

It would be well to remember that psychodiagnostic tests constitute only one component of a comprehensive evaluation of diagnosis. However, we would be loathe to totally reject the use of tests because they provide limited information. Tests are neither all bad, nor all good. A structured comprehensive assessment can be a vital component in the determination of an effective and meaningful program, if we recognize the limitations of a given instrument and interpret the data appropriately (Cabanski, 1969).

The testing of intelligence or other ability factors is often useful for selection, classification, and prediction of performance. However, there are other phases of assessment which are teacher-oriented and entail evaluation of daily progress and means of reporting this progress (Bijou, 1973).

Perhaps the most remarkable observation in this total area of assessment is that teachers often cling tenaciously to the structure of standardized instruments as the quintessential part of any decision-making process. They often legitimize the instrument because it is there, even when it represents an anachronism or gives empty claim to a construct. As indicated throughout this chapter, we are often using the instruments without the benefit of empirical data to support their use, or the test is used for purposes other than that for which it was intended. Thus, standardized data often provide limited or meaningless information until they are interpreted in terms of the individual and her or his program. The "passing" or "failing" of a test does not provide an instant formula for curriculum. The determination of IQ, Social Quotient, language age, and so on, only represents the status of the individual as measured on a given instrument. It is incumbent upon the teacher to interpret this information in terms of program.

There are also several areas of behavior that the teacher must assess. This information is obtained by informal ongoing diagnosis that the teacher conducts in order to (1) supplement existing information derived from psychodiagnostic instruments, (2) make decisions about the day-to-day progress of the TMR individual in the program, and (3) interpret the person's progress to parents.

Interpretation of Psychodiagnostic Information

The results of performance on psychodiagnostic instruments often provide a basis for determining learning readiness or timing of curricular concerns (Williams, 1963). The psychodiagnostic information provides a sound basis for determining curriculum objectives and developing a systematic process of instruction. The translation of this information into appropriate classroom activities is the responsibility of the teacher. The psychodiagnostic data assist in defining behaviorial objectives. The teacher must then determine what prerequisites or tasks are necessary for the successful attainment of the objective. The prerequisite tasks are arranged by the teacher in a systematic hierarchy or sequence in order of difficulty, and the teacher must identify on the basis of available data the appropriate instructional level of the child on this continuum. For example, based upon available objective information reinforced by teacher observation, the child is determined to be ready to participate in toilet training. This becomes the target behavior. The teacher then identifies a series of prerequisite skills for the successful attainment of toilet training. For the sake of example, the teacher identifies six prerequisite skills:

1. Locating the toileting area
2. Pulling down his/her pants
3. Sitting on toilet
4. Eliminating
5. Using toilet tissue
6. Pulling up pants

The teacher evaluation indicates that the child is able to perform prerequisite skills one and two but will not sit on the toilet and attend. Thus, the instruction begins at level three (sitting on toilet). In this example, the use of psychodiagnostic data provides information on entering behaviors, identification of behaviorial objectives, and assists the teacher in task analysis.*

In summary, the available data assists the teacher in determining when the TMR child is "ready" to learn, what he or she is "ready" to learn, and where the child is "ready" to learn. The systematic organization of these readiness factors assists in determining (1) that the trainable child has reached the intellectual or social developmental level to begin to resolve certain objectives in the curriculum, (2) what of these objectives are realistic goals, and (3) where within the task hierarchy

---

*The further dimensions of task analysis will be discussed in detail in later chapters.

she or he is ready to work. In addition, the teacher may interpret quantitative and qualitative aspects of the data in other behaviorial terms which may have an impact on the instructional process. Quantitative information, such as mental age scores, may assist in determining the level of the TMR child's psychosocial development which is considered to be consistent with mental age (Begab, 1966). Also, the qualitative information may provide insights into the child's ability to deal with stress, the presentation of novel situations, and so on.

Assessment of Progress in Program

The assessment of the TMR child's progress in an ongoing program is principally concerned with how well the individual is learning, and if learning is not taking place, what adjustments are necessary to improve the process. Initial decisions relative to appropriate levels of training are frequently "subject to change without notice." Therefore, Ginglend (1957) has noted that "Every teacher needs a basis from which to evaluate her [his] own expenditure of energy and planning in terms of the child's growth" (p. 35).

In the ongoing program, the teacher must make frequent assessments which determine the individual's program or curriculum emphasis. Hofmann (Note 2) suggests that the objective of teacher assessment is to determine, "what we have done," and "how well we have done it." In order to determine this, the evaluation process would have as objectives:

1. To see if the child has learned what we have tried to teach him.
2. To advise parents of their child's growth and to encourage a coordination of home and school training.
3. To determine whether the curriculum is appropriate.
4. To appraise the teacher of the adequacy of her [his] techniques and to decide whether a change in methodology is indicated. [Hoff, 1969, p. 108]

The teacher would also be expected to maintain a level of awareness of factors which insure success and growth in the program. The growth curve of a TMR person is not a smooth elliptic line. We often find frequent long-term plateaus, and in instances, regression in skills previously obtained. An ongoing assessment of the program will equip the teacher with the precise means of initiating change and determining appropriateness of various activities according to developmental progress.

The assessment of the program is teacher-oriented as well as child-oriented. Teachers must also evaluate their forms of presentation or methodology and appropriateness of the materials being used.

If the teaching process is to be exacting, the assessment process must be equally as exacting. The assessment process must involve reporting and record keeping rather than incidental judgments. Although anecdotal in nature, program assessment should be a reflection of detailed progress and "failures" in the teaching process and provide a complete description of behaviors at each level of instruction.

Connor and Talbot (1964) defined a structure for teacher evaluation that may be used for rating the child's progress in the curriculum, determining progress towards long-term training goals, and reporting progress to parents. Their structure involved "a running account of individual and group activity [and] . . . events relevant to the planned program [which] . . . provided the framework; supplementary happenings and incidents which referred to continuing problems were also included. Teacher observations were focused directly on individual children" (p. 279).

A log of anecdotal records is useful for short-term evaluation of program progress, changes in objectives, and changes in methods and materials. However, the teacher will need to translate this information into some form of checklist of behaviorial observations for ready reference and information on long-term goals.

Modification of the program based upon teacher assessment has further implications for the original determination of appropriate behaviorial objectives. Figure Five is an illustration of the relationship between planning and the assessment process.

The cyclic structure of this process involves:

1. Planning objectives which define the behavior to be achieved
2. Determining methods or training techniques
3. Observing entering behaviors relevant to the objectives
4. Recording behaviors in the training process
5. Testing of performance in desired behavior
6. Evaluation of performance and repetition of the planning cycle on the basis of progress towards desired behavior (Hofmann, Note 2).

The teacher assessment program becomes a continuous act which insures appropriateness of program and building of skills in the TMR as an interrelated and ongoing process.

Reporting Progress to Parents

The final process of teacher assessment is home-oriented as well as school-oriented. The teacher must evaluate and interpret progress to parents in meaningful terms and assist the parents in adjusting their level of expectation and understanding of their TMR child. Although Ginglend (1957) noted that "The parents of severely retarded children

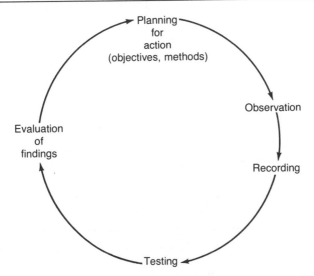

NOTE: Reproduced from H. Hofmann, Evaluation, the teachers tool. Unpublished manuscript.

Figure Five

The cycle of program evaluation and planning

generally are well informed and painfully and emotionally aware of the child's inability to perform in academic activities like other children. They are also aware that their child can be helped and that he can exhibit progress and growth, no matter how small, under the right direction and training" (p. 35), the acceptance of the program is another dimension. Many parents are unhappy with the program and its impact on their child. Some feel that the curriculum reflects a defeatist attitude and subsequent meaningless babysitting. Teachers are often criticized for not providing what the parents deem an appropriate program (that is, reading, writing, and other traditional "school" tasks). These parents do not often have a fully objective understanding of their child's abilities and disabilities. This lack of common understanding of the TMR child and the child's program often precludes cooperative home-school planning and often engenders parental reaction ranging from false hopes of normalcy to hostility.

A common understanding of the child's progress may eliminate the fury of a belated reaction on the part of the parents about the quality of the child's program and contribute significantly to cooperation between the home and school. A meaningful and understandable interpretation of program may reduce conflict and assist the parent in developing a better understanding of the teacher's determination of what constitutes an appropriate program.

Reporting to parents begins when the child enters the program. The parent should have an early understanding of the philosophy of the program and the objectives established for their child. Periodic appraisals through meetings and written reports should also be provided the parents. The teacher should also encourage an interchange of information between the teacher and parent in order to determine effectiveness of the program in the home and to insure home-school cooperation and coordination (Baumgartner, 1960).

No single rating scale can provide the parents with all of the necessary information. The teacher must make use of all available information (such as, psychometric data, anecdotal records, check lists) in providing the parents with a realistic appraisal of their child's progress. The information should then be interpreted in a manner that the parents can understand and in realistic task specifics (that is, in phrases like "the child can do this but cannot do that"). The parent should also be helped to understand the developmental problems of the child, and that the TMR child can be expected to stay much longer at a given level of development. This understanding should emphasize that noticeable progress does not represent the antecedent to learning and ultimately normal behavior. The interpretation, like the evaluation, should be an ongoing process, if the teacher is to insure a realistic acceptance of the child and the program.

Summary

The process of assessment is considered the antecedent to defining appropriate structure and guidelines for the program. The use of standardized instruments is steeped in controversy, and current focus is directed towards a more extensive use of criteria-based instruments and teacher evaluation for assessment and program development.

Assessment should reflect a comprehensive evaluation of the various dimensions of the TMR population. These data should reflect a composite of factors, such as measured intelligence, adaptive behavior, developmental levels, language development, development of motor skills, and general fitness. In addition, informal teacher-directed assessment should be conducted to determine the effectiveness of the ongoing program and to provide information on the TMR child's progress in the program.

References

Adams, J. Adaptive behavior and measured intelligence in the classification of mental retardation. *American Journal of Mental Deficiency*, 1973, *78*, 77–81.

Allen, R. M., Dickman, I., & Haupt, T. D. A pilot study of the immediate effectiveness of the Frostig-Horne training program with educable retardates. *Exceptional Children*, 1966, *33*, 41–42.

Alley, G. R. Perceptual-motor performance of mentally retarded children after systematic visual perceptual training. *American Journal of Mental Deficiency*, 1968, *73*, 247–250.

American Association on Health, Physical Education and Recreation. *Special fitness test for the mentally retarded.* Washington, D.C.: NEA Publications, 1968.

Anastasi, A. *Psychological testing* (2nd ed.). New York: Macmillan, 1961.

Balthazar, E. E. *Balthazar scales of adaptive behavior for the profoundly and severely retarded: Section 1.* Champaign, Ill.: Research Press, 1971.

Balthazar, E. E. *Balthazar scales of adaptive behavior for the profoundly and severely retarded: Section 2.* Champaign, Ill.: Research Press, 1973.

Bateman, B. Role of the ITPA in the differential diagnosis and program planning for the mentally retarded. *American Journal of Orthopsychiatry*, 1965, *35*, 465–472.

Bhattacharya, S. Adaptive behavior scale refinement. *Mental Retardation*, 1973, *11*, 27.

Baumeister, A. A. Use of the WISC with mental retardates: A review. *American Journal of Mental Deficiency*, 1964, *69*, 183–194.

Baumeister, A. A. The usefulness of the IQ with severely retarded individuals: A reply to MacAndrew and Edgerton. *American Journal of Mental Deficiency*, 1965, *69*, 881–882.

Baumgartner, B. B. *Helping the trainable mentally retarded child.* New York: Columbia University Press, 1960.

Bayley, N. *The Bayley scales of infant development.* New York: The Psychological Corporation, 1969.

Begab, M. J. Emotional impact of mental retardation. In I. Phillips (Ed.), *Prevention and treatment of mental retardation.* New York: Basic Books, 1966.

Bersoff, D. N. Silk purses into sow's ears: The decline of psychological testing and a suggestion for its redemption. *American Psychologist*, 1973, *28*, 892–899.

Bijou, S. W. Behavior modification in teaching the retarded child. In C. E. Thoresen (Ed.), *Behavior Modification.* Chicago, Ill.: The National Society for the Study of Education, 1973.

Blue, C. M. The effectiveness of a group language program with trainable mentally retarded children. *Education and Training of the Mentally Retarded*, 1970, *5*, 109–112.

Budoff, M., & Purseglove, E. M. Peabody picture vocabulary test performance of non-institutionalized mentally retarded adolescents. *American Journal of Mental Deficiency,* 1963, *67,* 756–760.

Burnes, A. J., & Hassol, L. A pilot study in evaluating camping experiences for the mentally retarded. *Mental Retardation,* 1966, *4,* 15–16.

Cabanski, S. Psychological diagnosis and evaluation of the severely retarded: A pragmatic approach. In R. C. Scheerenberger (Ed.), *Mental retardation, selected conference papers.* Springfield, Ill.: Illinois Department of Mental Health, 1969.

Cain, L. F., & Levine, S. *Effects of community and institutional programs on trainable mentally retarded children.* Research Monograph (Series B), The Council for Exceptional Children, 1963.

Cain, L. F., Levine, S., & Elzey, F. F. *Manual for the Cain-Levine social competency scale.* Palo Alto, Ca.: Consulting Psychologist Press, 1963.

Congdon, D. M. The Vineland and Cain-Levine: A correlational study and program evaluation. *American Journal of Mental Deficiency,* 1969, *74,* 231–234.

Congdon, D. M. The adaptive behavior scale modified for the profoundly retarded. *Mental Retardation,* 1973, *11,* 20–21.

Connor, F. P., & Talbot, M. E. *An experimental curriculum for young mentally retarded children.* New York: Columbia University Press, 1964.

The Council for Exceptional Children. *Professional standards for personnel in the education of exceptional children.* Washington, D.C.: Council for Exceptional Children, 1966.

Cratty, B. J. *Motor activity and the education of retardates* (2nd ed.). Philadelphia: Lea & Febiger, 1974.

D'Asaro, M., Lehrhoff, I., Zimmerman, I. L., & Jones, M. H. A rating scale for the evaluation of language development in the preschool cerebral palsied child. Chicago, Ill.: American Academy for Cerebral Palsy, 10th Annual Session, 1956.

Daly, F. M. The program for trainable mentally retarded pupils in the public schools of California. *Education and Training of the Mentally Retarded,* 1966, *3,* 109–118.

Davies, S. P., & Ecob, K. G. *The mentally retarded in society.* New York: Columbia University Press, 1962.

Delp, H. A. Psychological evaluation: Some problems and suggestions. *Training School Bulletin,* 1959, *56,* 79–84.

DiNola, A. J., Kaminsky, B. P., & Sternfeld, A. E. *TMR performance profile for the severely and moderately retarded.* Ridgefield, N.J.: Reporting Service for Exceptional Children, 1963.

Doll, E. A. A genetic scale of social maturity. *American Journal of Orthopsychiatry,* 1935, *5,* 180–188.

Doll, E. A. The essential of an inclusive concept of mental deficiency. *American Journal of Mental Deficiency,* 1941, *46,* 214–219.

Doll, E. A. *Vineland social maturity scale.* Circle Pines, Minn.: American Guidance Service, 1965.

Dunn, L. M. *Peabody picture vocabulary test.* Circle Pines, Minn.: American Guidance Service, 1959.

Dunn, L. M., & Hottel, J. V. Peabody picture vocabulary performance of trainable mentally retarded children. *American Journal of Mental Deficiency,* 1961, *65,* 448–452.

Erickson, M. T., Johnson, N. M., & Campbell, F. A. Relationship among scores on infant tests for children with developmental problems. *American Journal of Mental Deficiency,* 1970, *75,* 102–104.

Farber, B. *Mental retardation: Its social context and social consequences.* Boston, Mass.: Houghton Mifflin, 1968.

Francis, R. J., & Rarick, G. L. Motor characteristics of the mentally retarded. *American Journal of Mental Deficiency,* 1959, *63,* 292–311.

Frankenburg, W. K., Dodds, J. B., & Fandal, A. W. *Denver developmental screening test.* Denver, Colo.: University of Colorado Medical Center, 1970.

Frostig, M., & Horne, D. *The Frostig program for the development of visual perceptions.* Chicago, Ill.: Follett, 1964.

Frostig, M., Maslow, P., Lefever, W. D., & Whittlesey, J. R. B. *The Marianne Frostig developmental test of visual perception.* Palo Alto, Ca.: Consulting Psychologist Press, 1963.

Ginglend, D. R. Some observations on evaluating the progress of severely retarded or "trainable" children in school program. *American Journal of Mental Deficiency,* 1957, *62,* 35–38.

Glaser, R. Instructional technology and the measurement of learning outcomes. *American Psychologist,* 1963, *18,* 519–521.

Grossman, H. J. Comprehensive diagnostic services in mental retardation. In R. C. Scheerenberger (Ed.), *Mental retardation: Selected conference papers.* Springfield, Ill.: Illinois Department of Mental Health, 1969.

Grossman, H. J. *Manual on terminology and classification in mental retardation* (Special Publication No. 2). Washington, D.C.: American Association on Mental Deficiency, 1973.

Gunzburg, H. C. *Progress assessment chart of social development.* London: National Association for Mental Health, 1963.

Hall, S. L., & Deacon, K. F. Effects noted from the use of the Frostig training program with trainable retardates. *Training School Bulletin,* 1970, *67,* 20–24.

Hammill, D. D., & Bartel, N. R. *Teaching children with learning and behavior problems.* Boston, Mass.: Allyn & Bacon, 1975.

Harrison, S. A. A review of research in speech and language development of the mentally retarded child. *American Journal of Mental Deficiency,* 1958, *63,* 236–240.

Heber, R. *A manual on terminology and classification in mental retardation* (Monograph Supplement). Washington, D.C.: American Association on Mental Deficiency, 1959.

Heber, R. Mental retardation: Concept and classification. In E. P. Trapp & P. Himmelstein (Eds.), *Readings on the exceptional child.* New York: Appleton-Century-Crofts, 1962.

Hoff, E. M. Education evaluation of the child in a day care center for the mentally retarded. In R. C. Scheerenberger (Ed.), *Mental retardation: Selected conference papers.* Springfield, Ill.: Illinois Department of Mental Health, 1969.

Horner, D. R. A factor analysis comparison of the ITPA and PLS with mentally retarded children. *Exceptional Children,* 1967, *34,* 183–189.

Hudson, M. Lesson areas for the trainable child. *Exceptional Children,* 1960, *27,* 224–229.

Information Center Recreation for the Handicapped. *Newsletter.* Carbondale, Ill.: Southern Illinois University, 1971, *5,* 3.

Jordan, T. E. *The mentally retarded* (3rd ed.). Columbus, Oh.: Charles E. Merrill, 1972.

Kephart, N. C. *The slow learner in the classroom* (2nd ed.). Columbus, Oh.: Charles E. Merrill, 1971.

Kershner, K. M., & Dusewicz, R. S. K.D.K.-Oseretsky tests of motor development. *Perceptual Motor Skills,* 1970, *30,* 202.

Kirk, S. A. An evaluation of the study by Bernadine Schmidt entitled: Changes in personal, social and intellectual behavior of children originally classified as feebleminded. *Psychological Bulletin,* 1948, *45,* 321–333.

Kirk, S. A. *Early education of the mentally retarded.* Urbana, Ill.: University of Illinois Press, 1958.

Kirk, S. A. Research in education. In H. A. Stevens & R. Heber (Eds.), *Mental retardation: A review of research.* Chicago, Ill.: University of Chicago Press, 1964.

Kirk, S. A., McCarthy, J. J., & Kirk, W. *The Illinois test of psycholinguistic abilities.* Champain-Urbana, Ill.: University of Illinois, 1968.

Kodman, F. Sensory processes and mental deficiency. In N. Ellis (Ed.), *Handbook of mental deficiency.* New York: McGraw-Hill, 1963.

Leland, H., Shellhaas, M., Nihira, K., & Foster, R. Adaptive behavior: A new dimension in the classification of the mentally retarded. *Mental Retardation Abstracts.* Washington, D.C.: U.S. Government Printing Office, 1967.

Levine, S., Elzey, F. F., & Paulson, F. L. Social competence of school and non-school trainable mentally retarded. *American Journal of Mental Deficiency,* 1966, *71,* 112–115.

Malone, D. R., & Christian, W. P., Jr. Adaptive behavior scale as a screening measure for special-education placement. *American Journal of Mental Deficiency,* 1975, *79,* 367–371.

Malpass, L. F. Motor skills in mental deficiency. In N. Ellis (Ed.), *Handbook of mental deficiency.* New York: McGraw-Hill, 1963.

Mann, L. Perceptual training: Misdirections and redirections. *American Journal of Orthopsychiatry,* 1970, *40,* 30–38.

McCarthy, J. J. Linguistic problems of the retarded. *Mental Retardation Abstracts.* Washington, D.C.: U.S. Government Printing Office, 1964.

McCarthy, J. M. *Patterns of psycholinguistic development of mongoloid and non-mongoloid severely retarded children.* Unpublished doctoral dissertation, University of Illinois, 1965.

McCarthy, J. J., & Scheerenberger, R. C. A decade of research on the education of the mentally retarded. *Mental Retardation Abstracts.* Washington, D.C.: U.S. Government Printing Office, 1966.

McNemar, Q. A critical examination of the University of Iowa studies of environmental influence. *Psychological Bulletin,* 1940, *37,* 63−92.

Mein, R. Use of the Peabody picture vocabulary test with severely subnormal patients. *American Journal of Mental Deficiency,* 1962, *67,* 296−273.

Miller, L. C. Adaptive behavior scales. In O. K. Buros (Ed.), *The seventh mental measurements yearbook, vol. I.* Highland Park, N.J.: Gryphon Press, 1972.

Morris, P. R., & Whiting, H. T. A. *Motor impairment and compensatory education.* Philadelphia: Lea & Febiger, 1971.

Newland, T. E. Psychological assessment of exceptional children and youth. In W. M. Cruickshank (Ed.), *Psychology of exceptional children and youth* (2nd ed.). Englewood Cliffs, N.J.: Prentice-Hall, 1963.

Newman, H. G., & Doby, J. T. Correlates of social competence among trainable mentally retarded children. *American Journal of Mental Deficiency,* 1973, *77,* 722−732.

Nihira, K., Foster, R., Shellhaas, M., & Leland, H. *Adaptive behavior scales. Washington, D.C.: American Association on Mental Deficiency,* 1969.

Noble, C. E. Research on the learning of psychomotor skills in children and adults. Proceedings of the New York State Conference on Models and Methods in Research on Compensatory Education, 1970. (Summary)

Roach, E. G., & Kephart, N. C. *The Purdue perceptual-motor survey.* Columbus, Oh.: Charles E. Merrill, 1966.

Robinson, H. B., & Robinson, N. M. *The mentally retarded child: A psychological approach.* New York: McGraw-Hill, 1965.

Sabatino, D. A., Ysseldyke, J. E., & Woolston, J. Diagnostic-prescriptive perceptual training with mentally retarded children. *American Journal of Mental Deficiency,* 1973, *78,* 7−14.

Sanford, A. R. *The learning accomplishment profile.* Chapel Hill, N.C.: Chapel Hill Training-Outreach Project, University of North Carolina, 1973.

Sarason, S. B. Mental retarded and mental defective children: Major psychosocial problems. In W. M. Cruickshank (Ed.), *Psychology of exceptional children and youth.* Engelwood Cliffs, N.J.: Prentice-Hall, 1955.

Sattler, J. M. *Assessment of children's intelligence.* Philadelphia: W. B. Saunders, 1974.

Schiefelbusch, R. L. Introduction: Language studies of mentally retarded children. (Monograph Supplement No. 10). *Journal of Speech and Hearing Disorders,* 1963, 3−7.

Schmidt, B. Changes in personal, social and intellectual behavior in children originally classified as feebleminded. *Psychological Monographs,* 1946, *60.* (Monograph)

Schwartz, B. J., & Allen, R. M. Measuring adaptive behavior: The dynamics of a longitudinal approach. *American Journal of Mental Deficiency,* 1975, *79,* 424−433.

Sellin, D. F. The usefulness of the IQ in predicting performance of moderately retarded children. *American Journal of Mental Deficiency,* 1967, *71,* 561−562.

Shotwell, A. M., O'Connor, G., Gabet, Y., & Dingman, H. F. Relation of the Peabody picture vocabulary test IQ to the Stanford-Binet IQ. *American Journal of Mental Deficiency,* 1969, *74,* 39−42.

Silverstein, A. B. Psychological testing practices in institutions for the mentally retarded. *American Journal of Mental Deficiency,* 1963, *68,* 440−445.

Silverstein, A. B. Note on prevalence. *American Journal of Mental Deficiency,* 1973, *77,* 380−382.

Skeels, H. M., Updegraff, R., Wellman, B. L., & Williams, H. M. A study of environmental stimulation, an orphanage preschool project. *University of Iowa Studies in Child Welfare,* Vol. 15. Iowa City, Iowa: University of Iowa, 1938.

Skodak, M., & Skeels, H. M. A final follow-up study of one hundred adopted children. *Journal of Genetic Psychology,* 1949, *75,* 85−125.

Sloan, W. *The Lincoln-Oseretsky motor development scale* (Genetic Psychology Monographs). 1955, *71,* 183−252.

Spradlin, J. E. Assessment of speech and language of retarded children: The Parsons language scale. Monograph supplement No. 10, *Journal of Speech and Hearing Disorders,* 1963.

Spradlin, J. E. Procedures for evaluating processes associated with receptive and expressive language. In R. L. Schiefelbusch, R. H. Copeland, & J. O. Smith (Eds.), *Language and mental retardation: Empirical and conceptual considerations.* New York: Holt, Rinehart, & Winston, 1967.

Strauss, A. A., & Lehtinen, L. E. *Psychopathology and education of the brain-injured child.* New York: Grune & Stratton, 1947.

Terman, L. *The measurement of intelligence.* Boston: Houghton Mifflin, 1916.

Terman, L., & Merrill, M. A. *Stanford-Binet intelligence scale.* Boston: Houghton Mifflin, 1960.

Thorndike, R. L. *Stanford-Binet intelligence scale, 1972 norm tables.* Boston: Houghton Mifflin, 1973.

Travis, L. E. *Handbook of speech pathology and audiology.* New York: Appleton-Century-Crofts, 1971.

Tredgold, A. F. *A textbook of mental deficiency* (7th ed.). Baltimore: Williams & Wilkins, 1947.

Tweedie, D. Observing the communication behavior of deaf-blind children. *American Annals of the Deaf,* 1974, *119,* 342−347.

Van Hattum, R. J. Considerations of traditional views of mental retardation. *Mental Retardation,* 1974, *12,* 37−39.

Wechsler, D. *Wechsler intelligence scale for children.* New York: Psychological Corporation, 1949.

Wechsler, D. *Wechsler preschool and primary scale of intelligence.* New York: Psychological Corporation, 1967.

Wechsler, D. *Wechsler intelligence scale for children—revised.* New York: Psychological Corporation, 1974.

Wellman, B. L. The effect of preschool attendance upon the IQ. *Journal of Experimental Education,* 1932, *1,* 48–69.

Wetzel, N. C. *The Wetzel grid for evaluating physical fitness.* Cleveland, Oh.: NEA Services, Inc., 1948.

Williams, H. M. *Education of the severely retarded child.* Washington, D.C.: U.S. Government Printing Office, 1963.

Wiseman, D. E. The effects of an individualized remedial program on mentally retarded children with psycholinguistic disabilities. Unpublished doctoral dissertation, University of Illinois, 1965.

Wolfensberger, W. Embarrassments in the diagnostic process. *Mental Retardation,* 1965, *3,* 29–31.

Zimmerman, I. L., Steiner, V. G., & Evatt, R. L. *Preschool language manual.* Columbus, Oh.: Charles E. Merrill, 1969.

Reference Notes

1. Curtis, W. S., & Donlon, E. T. *The development and evaluation of a video-tape protocol for the examination of multihandicapped deaf-blind children.* Final Report, U.S. Office of Education, Grant No. OEG–0–9–422134–2764 (032), 1972.

2. Hofmann, H. Evaluation, the teacher's tool. Unpublished manuscript. Weber State College, Ogden, Utah.

3. Woo-Sam, J. M. Psychoeducational assessment in the seventies—A look at concepts and measures, the Stanford-Binet LM. Unpublished manuscript. Presented at APA, New Orleans, 1974.

Chapter 4

Trends and Issues in Curriculum Development

The choice of curriculum reflects a conscious attempt at enculturation and induction of individuals into society. The values of the society within which one lives are thus transferred from one generation to another. The sequential order of experiences that are incorporated into this induction process is curriculum, and its optimum goal is usually a responsible and productive adult life.

The interpretation of curriculum for the "normal" members of society has usually had some commonality of purpose in educational direction and objectives for adult living. However, the problem of what to teach the "abnormal" members of society (for our purposes, the trainable mentally retarded) has been omnipresent in our history. Attempts at resolving this problem are apparent in a chronology of events that began in the early part of the nineteenth century, when scientists began to design a specific curriculum for the induction of the retarded into society.

Early Curriculum: 1800 to 1950

Historically, TMR children or adults were relegated to the periphery of society. They were persecuted or permitted to languish in the home and community and were denied full membership in society. In some instances, they were removed from society and placed in asylums. In essence, society had "given up" on attempting to integrate this population. Their condition was deemed incurable and not worthy of efforts beyond rudimentary care.

A Scientific Approach to Program

In the early 1800s scientists like Itard and Seguin rejected the prevalent defeatist attitude toward the retarded and focused upon the development of a program or curriculum of amelioration and cure for this population. The concern of these people was to make the retarded "normal" members of society. With a "cure," they would be what society wanted them to be rather than what they were. Their curricular goals were unobtainable, and their experiment failed. The retardates did not learn what it was hoped they would learn, and the curricula were abandoned—at least in terms of the lower levels of retardation. Again,

105

opportunities for the lower-level retardates were ultimately reduced to institutionalization, because these people did not possess the abilities nor, consequently, the credentials for induction into normal society.

Although these early failures resulted in near-cataclysmic circumstances, the contributions of these early workers have survived as a remarkable and, in some ways, prophetic attempt at defining curriculum and program for the trainable mentally retarded. Their work possesses contemporary significance and has been little diminished by time.

Jean M. G. Itard   1775 − 1838

Itard was a disciple of John Locke and subscribed to his theory that human knowledge was obtained through experience. Locke proposed that the human mind was a *tabula rasa,* or blank slate, and commented:

> Let us suppose the mind to be . . . white paper, void of all characters, without any ideas; how comes it to be furnished? Whence comes it by that vast store, which the busy and boundless fancy of man has painted on it with an almost endless variety? Whence has it all the materials of reason and knowledge? To this I answer, in one word, from experience; in that all our knowledge is founded, and from that it ultimately derives. [Locke, 1949, pp. 25 − 26]

From this principle, Itard reasoned that human behavior or education could be modified through a program of sense training, and he was compelled to reject the prevailing theory that idiocy was hereditary and essentially incurable.

The story of Itard and Victor the Wild Boy of Aveyron merits repeating only in the sense that Itard's association with Victor was the genesis of a structured approach to the development of a curriculum and program of training for the retarded. He rejected the diagnosis of Victor as "hopelessly incurable" and declared that "the child with whom I have been concerned is not, as is generally believed, a hopeless imbecile but an interesting being" (Itard, 1962, p. xxiv). He then proceeded to design a program of "aims" or objectives for Victor's "mental and moral education." These were defined by Itard (1962) in five steps:

> 1st Aim. To interest him in social life by rendering it more pleasant to him than the one he was then leading, and above all more like the life which he had just left.
>
> 2nd Aim. To awaken his nervous sensibility by the most energetic stimulation, and occasionally by intense emotion.
>
> 3rd Aim. To extend the range of his ideas by giving him new needs and by increasing his social contacts.
>
> 4th Aim. To lead him to the use of speech by inducing the exercise of imitation through the imperious law of necessity.
>
> 5th Aim. To make him exercise the simplest mental operations upon

the objects of his physical needs over a period of time afterwards inducing the application of these mental processes to the objects of instruction. [pp. 10–11]

With these objectives in mind, Victor's training was initiated and directed towards the training of his social skills and the development of his sensory modalities and intellectual functioning. Itard (1962), in his second report to the Minister of the Interior, on November 19, 1806, defined the continuing training cycle in three sequences:

1. Development of the functions of the senses
2. Development of the intellectual functions
3. Development of emotional faculties

It soon became apparent that these global objectives could not be met, and in his final evaluation of this educational program, Itard stated "that by reason of the almost incomplete apathy of the organs of hearing and speech, the education of this young man is still incomplete and must always remain so" (p. 100). Although this first attempt at training terminated in abandonment of the program, Itard implored the government to continue to provide for Victor's care. The government complied with his wishes, and Victor died at about forty years of age in 1828.

The program developed by Itard is regarded as the first scientific or systematic approach toward the structuring of a curriculum for the training and education of idiocy. Although the first step produced only limited gains on Victor's part and was regarded as a failure by Itard, it represented the dawn of a new era of interest in idiot education. It was up to Edouard Seguin, a student of Itard, to prove conclusively that idiots could be trained and educated.

Edouard Seguin   1812–1880

The fact that Victor did develop some purposeful behavior in the five years that Itard worked with him greatly intrigued Seguin. His early work with Itard and later experimentation with "feebleminded" children resulted in the development of a broader educational philosophy and extension of Itard's early curriculum into a "physiological method." Seguin (1971) felt that "most idiots and children proximate to them, may be relieved in a more or less complete measure of their disabilities by the physiological method of education" (p. 81).

The method developed by Seguin was based on the belief that education involved an integration of concepts, and therefore the individual should be taught as a total organism. The program of physiological education involved:

1. *Training of movement:* This level of training was accomplished through exercise and activities designed to force specific movement in order to develop an integrated, educated muscular sys-

tem. This physical training was considered by Seguin (1971) to be critical to all other areas of training: "Of all the incapacities of idiocy, none are so striking and none so detrimental as those which affect motion and locomotion" (p. 98).

2. *Education of the senses:* Once the motor functions were trained, Seguin (1971) declared "those of the senses present themselves as the foremost impediment to future progress" (p. 133). He attempted to train touch, audition, vision, taste, and smell. His principal thrust in this training was toward touch training, because he considered it to be "the most general, and in fact all the senses being mere modifications of it" (p. 137). After his student learned to distinguish shape, texture, temperature, and so on, by touch, Seguin would then inaugurate training in taste and smell "as appendages to the touch, because they are senses the nearest akin to it, and their treatment once disposed of here, we shall . . . follow . . . the education of the eye and ear as far as they will carry us into the intellectual training" (p. 142). The training of taste and smell was directed towards "awakening their dull senses," and the proper choice of "good food" and "sweet air." Auditory training was conducted through the extensive use of music throughout the day because, "Music pleases the child without hurting him" (p. 149).

3. *Teaching speech:* Seguin (1971) recommended that an initial survey be made to determine whether there was any organic or physical damage to the speech mechanisms before one attempted to develop meaningful speech sounds. In this recommendation, he noted, "we are governed at first by the structure of.the organs" (p. 155). The speech program was an integral part of the total day, and the children were encouraged to vocalize at all times. As soon as the child began to imitate speech, she or he was to receive specific instruction alone and in groups. Of particular interest, Seguin discusses the training of sight in the context of speech training, because "articulation is appreciated by the look" (p. 160).

4. *Academic training:* The previously described training processes were all to be integrated into an educational program. The teaching of colors, shapes, and other "elementary notions" were considered to be antecedents to the teaching of the use of pen and pencil for drawing, writing skills, and ultimately reading. The curriculum-methodology also included instruction in the elements of numbers, memory, and imagination.

In addition to the principles involving the physiological method and academic training, the individual was also to receive "moral treatment" or training in socialization.

It is remarkable to note, that after almost 100 years the ideas of Seguin were still being recognized as sound educational practice (Kirk & Johnson, 1951), and that much of the curriculum is still being advocated today. One need only to visit many existing training programs to see a remarkable similarity between what Seguin proposed and current curricular emphasis. Recent years have witnessed a renewed focus upon movement, muscle training, and physical education. Knowledge of texture, size, weight, and temperature are still being taught through the kinesthetic senses, and music as an auditory training device is quite apparent in many programs. Speech and language development continue to be emphasized, and pre-academic skills such as recognition of colors and shapes are frequently found in current curricula. Seguin also placed a great deal of emphasis on eye-hand coordination (perceptual-motor training), and it is interesting to note that scissors, a common item in current training programs, was identified by Seguin as being "among our favorite instruments" (Seguin, 1971, p. 172).

Much of the academic training that Seguin advocated is also incorporated into current training programs, and we continue to adhere to his suggestion that:

> Individual and group reading must be alternated, beginning with the first. Individual reading may be more insisted upon in cool, mild weather, and in the morning when attention causes no effort, and is not exhausted; on stormy days and in the afternoon, dullness is prevented from settling down upon the classroom by group teachings. [Seguin, 1971, pp. 183–184]

Seguin's failure was perhaps not so much in the curriculum design, but in his concept of idiocy. Entirely too much was expected through the hope of cure. He failed to cure the retarded, and the guiding force provided by Seguin was, for all practical purposes, abandoned. As a result, a defeatist attitude toward the more severe forms of retardation reappeared.

The best efforts of Itard, Seguin, and others were effective only to the extent of minimal improvement in certain areas of behavior. Emphasis on program was lost, and the institutions once more became asylums for the incurable. Some limited effort was continued in order to provide for other alternatives, and those who continued to work in the interest of the retarded can be credited with remarkable tenacity in their efforts to develop an appropriate program model.

The Focus on Remediation

The Seguin curriculum continued to be the chief inspiration for later workers in programs for the retarded. His curriculum was expanded in other hands, and individuals like Maria Montessori, Ovide Decroly, and

Alice Descoeudres were responsible for adding dimensions to the program. Greater stress was placed on motivation, gratification, and intellectual and moral discrimination through active learning with concrete objects. The sensory-motor experiences were later complemented with occupational training in self-care and vocational pursuits (Doll, 1967).

In the later part of the nineteenth century, Maria Montessori became interested in the retarded as a pedagogical rather than a medical problem. She introduced psychological principles into her instruction and made teaching more individualized and informal. To enhance these principles, she developed specific didactic materials to be used in auto-instruction. Her results, much like Seguin's, were regarded as significant. However, she failed to maintain the interest of educators, and it was concluded that she had enhanced scientific pedagogy, but that her methods did not significantly contribute to a transfer of the training to real-life situations.

Ovide Decroly and his student Alice Descoeudres continued the effort into the twentieth century, toward developing a meaningful curriculum for the retarded. Their efforts were principally responsible for the final step in transition from the previous medical-treatment orientation to an educational program designed to prepare the retarded for living in society. Their contribution was more philosophical than that of Itard, Seguin, or Montessori. The aims of their program were less cure-oriented and more concerned with remediation. They accepted the fact that retardation was essentially incurable and focused on academic remediation directed towards making the retardate into a productive citizen (Kolstoe, 1972).

By the twentieth century, adoption of a philosophy of education for life had become a firmly established principle in educational thought, and emphasis in curriculum for the retarded shifted to "trade training" and "useful labor." However, this approach was found to be of greater benefit to the higher level retardate, and differential instruction began to be offered. The mildly retarded, those with sensory and motor defects and the "morally weak"—were provided restorative training, but the more severely retarded were retained in custodial institutions or allowed to languish in the community (Doll, 1967).

The Period of Abandonment

Society had tried and failed. The institution became the principal locus of program for the TMR, and programs became curricula of containment. The TMR, in general, were warehoused and provided only rudimentary care. Professionals were reluctant, or at best parsimonious, in their attempts to provide programs for this population.

It soon became obvious that the institutions were unable to contain all the retarded and that the greater number of these people were still residing in the community. Thus, the parents were faced with little other alternative than maintenance of the trainable in the home.

Public school classes were usually not available for the TMR, the institutions lacked space, and the cost of private schools was prohibitive. In addition, the community offered limited resources or facilities for training. Home training often became the only alternative (Ingram, 1960). As a result of these limitations, many parents sought to develop some sort of organized program for their TMR children.

Parents of the TMR ultimately began to join forces and establish programs in their own communities. The parents were usually ill-informed and untrained, and the curriculum in such programs often reflected the "education for life" principle. Therefore, efforts were often intensified to normalize the TMR children through instruction in cognitive skills. As a result of parental aspirations or a lack of other structured alternatives, the parent-class curriculum was often deeply invested in the skills attendant upon a formal education. This approach was fostered as a result of a number of influences:

1. Although the curriculum of Seguin was abandoned, his hopes for cure were not. The vehicle for cure was merely changed from medico-educational to educational.
2. The parents of the TMR sought "normal" experiences and hoped for "normal" adult life. Consequently, the focus in training became education and the skills attendant upon normal schooling (e.g. reading, writing, and arithmetic).
3. Parents and some professionals were demanding the same democratic rights for the TMR as those enjoyed by other members of society.

In addition, parental pressures were often successful in obtaining a class for the TMR in the public schools. This locus of program and its attendant orientation (that is, education) caused the TMR in the classroom to receive educational services for lack of any other curricular alternative.

While the principal focus of curriculum during this time reflected an educational model, the other alternative to curriculum in these early community programs was the "sunshine" approach, where curriculum was much more affective than cognitive. The curriculum in this type of program was based primarily upon nursery school, developmental experiences, or occasionally, sub-professional babysitting.

The parent movement continued through the 1930s and 1940s with limited concern or recognition from society. They continued to function without any significant amount of professional guidance, and curriculum was usually dictated by the whims and aspirations of the parents supporting the program.

In 1950, a national voice was given to the parent movement through the organization of the National Association for Retarded Children (NARC), and the movement toward public school provisions for the TMR began to gain momentum. Programs for the TMR began to move out of the basements of churches into the "respectability" of the public school.

As society's major child-serving agency, the public school became the principal locus for training programs. With the inclusion of the TMR population into the system of public education, a professional concern for appropriate curriculum came into focus again. However, professionals in education and the parents of the TMR were often in conflict over what kind of curricular provisions should be made for a population that was by definition "uneducable."

Toward a More "Respectable" Curriculum

The use of the word "respectable" is not a capricious choice of words. By the 1950s, the work of the previous century was, for all practical purposes, ignored by the new generation of workers in the area of mental retardation (Doll, 1967). And why not? Had not the old curriculum failed? The 1950s was a period of renewed optimism; TMR children were entering the public schools in greater numbers. However, the rapid and widespread expansion of classes for the TMR created confusion and controversy. Not only were professionals concerned with the efficacy of public school placement for this population, but there was an even greater concern over what should be done in the way of curriculum.

The literature of the 1950s is replete with differing opinions and justifications for public school placement of the TMR. This conflict rapidly became an academic issue, but Goldberg and Rooke (1967) noted that:

> In considering the confusion which has developed . . . professional workers should recognize that the fundamental problem actually has not been the development of training for the mentally deficient; the difficulty has been and still is the development of an educational philosophy which extends educational provisions and facilities to individuals who are not educable. [pp. 116–117]

Although there was, generally, a common agreement that the program needed to be something other than a traditional school program, Wirtz (1956) indicated that "programs which are not academic in nature have not been viewed by school administrators as a legitimate function of the public schools" (p. 499).

The 1950s: The New Curriculum

Although it was conceded that something other than a traditional curriculum was needed for the TMR, it was equally noted that there would be problems in applying this curriculum or program to the traditional public school.

The problem appeared to be less severe in institutional programs. Hafemeister (1951) reported on an experimental program designed to meet the needs of the institutionalized TMR which realized that the TMR could not profit from an academic instruction. This curriculum was organized around:

1. Daily training activities such as health, personal grooming, safety, and attitudes
2. Diversional activities like arts and crafts, physical activities and recreation, music and nature study
3. Number development activities which encompassed counting, recognizing coins, understanding the concepts of time, and understanding quantity and its relationship
4. Language development directed towards a means of expression, improvement of speech, and increased vocabulary

In developing this curriculum, though, the author recognized that there would be problems in its use in the public schools. He defined these as problems in:

1. Type of formal teacher training (few teachers were trained to teach this sort of nonacademic curriculum)
2. The school's view of the appropriateness of such a curriculum as a function of the public school
3. Parent expectations for such a class
4. The ultimate placement of a TMR adult in society after having received such training
5. The necessity of parent education
6. The difficulty of transportation to and from school
7. The education of professional groups about the need for such a class
8. The need for home training for the parents

These problems, although representative of the concerns of many for public school programs for the TMR, became moot and educators were caught in a wave of enthusiastic legislation which mandated the inclusion of the TMR in the public school program. By mid-1950, there was a significant increase in public school programs for the TMR, and a new curriculum, reflective of this single-agency responsibility, began to emerge.

In the beginning, the public schools did limit the amount of academic instruction in the training program. The new curriculum was frequently defined in terms of training in physical needs, coordination, independent skills, social skills, colors, and speech. The academics were limited to number concepts, like counting and telling time, and language arts instruction involving reading simple material, writing names, and making simple sentences (Ingram & Popp, 1955).

Other examples of training programs during this decade completely divested themselves of academics and focused exclusively upon a program designed to assist the TMR in achieving happiness, functioning as effectively as possible in group living, and developing as much independence as possible (Rosenzweig, 1954).

Although the direction of curriculum for the TMR continued to vacillate, the Illinois curriculum (Baumgartner, 1955) probably epitomizes the thrust in public school programs during this period. Furthermore, it became a model for many other states attempting to resolve the issue of curriculum for the TMR. The objectives of this curriculum were defined in the areas of: (1) self-care, (2) social adjustment, and (3) economic usefulness. It was the expressed opinion of the author of this curriculum that, "These objectives are sound in terms of the children's capacities. They point the way to a program that is nonacademic" (p. 2).

The skills to be developed within this curriculum were:

1. *Self-care:* Abilities in this area included personal routines like using clothing, eating and resting, health routines focused on grooming, and toilet and safety routines involving recognition of simple precautions.
2. *Social adjustment:* The principal areas of instruction in this area were defined as participation, to include an understanding of sharing, taking turns, cooperating, and appreciating, accepting responsibility in recognizing limits, following directions, respecting property, making choices and developing work habits.
3. *Economic usefulness:* This curriculum area was defined as an effort towards developing independence and good work habits. The general areas of training involved household tasks such as preparing and serving simple meals, cleaning, making beds and laundering, yard work, running errands, sewing, caring for pets and plants, and various other pre-work experiences like sorting, folding, envelope stuffing, and woodworking.

In addition, the Illinois curriculum was also designed to include activities in physical training, language development, music, arts, and crafts.

Some credence continued to be given to the need for a more academic curriculum, but the general theoretical basis for the curriculum during this period was simply that the TMR were uneducable and could not profit from traditional academics. However, discussion continued on the need for a reevaluation of the concept of education in TMR programs. This was not so much in terms of teaching skills, like counting, telling time, or reading simple materials, but more in terms of what Hudson (1955a) defined as "a problem in adapting education to the capacities of the severely retarded children, than of ignoring their need for education" (p. 584). To many, it was obvious that the TMR could respond to more than a custodial program, but they also realized that little would be accomplished until workers developed a better theoretical framework for curriculum.

Hudson (1955b) noted that a proper framework for a TMR curriculum should be developed around (1) the general goals for all children, (2) a consideration of the type of handicap, and (3) a consideration for a distinction between that which is remedial and that which is developmental in program. In this context, she defined curriculum as:

1. Social adaptation to include anything that has to do with living in a society
2. Home and community living
3. Self-help training
4. Self-entertainment or use of leisure time
5. Prevocational experience

This did not represent a significant departure from other operational curricula, but the objectives were more global and open-ended in order to accommodate a more unified curriculum theory. It was her concern that, "Without a unified curriculum theory there is a danger that this branch of special education will degenerate into a series of isolated learning experiences, if indeed, it develops at all" (p. 276).

Although lacking in resolution, the 1950s was the decade of the "happiness" curriculum. Progress was being made towards a better understanding of the needs and abilities of the TMR, but these early efforts were principally concerned with immediate needs of the TMR in adjusting to their environment. However, by the close of this decade, research (McCaw, 1958; Williams, 1963) was beginning to indicate that the parents were disillusioned and unhappy with their child's progress in the existing programs. Perhaps most devastating of all were the follow-up studies that were indicating that the existing programs were of little or no benefit to the TMR, and that the program had not had a significant impact on their circumstances (Hottel, 1958; Kirk, 1964).

Parents began to press for a more academic curriculum, and public educators who were accustomed to thinking in terms of academic training were reevaluating their curricula and gravitating towards a greater emphasis on learning skills consistent with a more traditional education. In addition, those who were invested in the experimental findings of B. F. Skinner were finding that even the most severely retarded could learn through a systematic methodology, or "precision teaching."* Therefore, by the close of this decade, the successes of the "new" methodology and the continued pressure of parents and educators resulted in a curricular focus on an increase in the cognitive abilities of the TMR population.

The 1960s: A Period of Reappraisal

By 1960, the TMR had become an integral part of the public school program. Some of the problems of learning and adjustment in the TMR population had been resolved, but as Goldstein (1963) observed:

> Our greatest deficiency . . . has been in the lack of development of a systematic program of education that is constructive in the sense that it goes beyond immediate satisfactions of the children and adults involved. [p. iii]

As our knowledge broadened, so did our aspirations for the TMR population. Various curriculum guides were developed or revised during this period, and the focus of these programs ranged from an emphasis on the curative aspects of academics to the "adjustment" curriculum which was usually more affective than cognitive in its concerns for skills and activities for daily living.

Many of the curriculum guides continued to model their program after the Illinois approach (Baumgartner, 1955), but expanded on the original global objectives of self-care, social adjustment, and economic usefulness. This expansion was reflected in a number of areas but was most remarkable in the development of experiences in intellectual growth designed to increase the cognitive abilities of the TMR. The increase in this area was largely the result of parental demands and expectations, and success in the application of behaviorial principles to training.

Hudson (1960) reviewed various programs and curriculums and identified fifteen major areas of instruction that existed in training programs. The rank order of these areas according to amount of emphasis in program was:

1. Language development
2. Motor development

---

*This teaching strategy will be defined in Chapter 5

3 and 4. Mental development and sensory training
5, 6, and 7. Music, health, safety, and social studies
8. Arithmetic
9, 10, and 11. Self-help, occupational education, and socialization
12. Arts and crafts
13. Dramatization
14. Social concepts
15. Practical arts

Areas that were principally concerned with attitudes and life adjustment began to take on a minor role in comparison to the more cognitive abilities. In fact, Hudson (1960) noted that language development, which included such activities as talking time and lessons in reading and writing, was receiving a "disproportionate" amount of time in the classroom.

Although later research (Warren, 1963) continued to indicate the questionable nature of an academic curriculum, its presence continued to emerge in the training curriculum as a note of "respectability" in the program and for the placation or edification of educators and parents (Lance, 1968).

The emphasis in program continued to vary according to the philosophy and design of the curriculum. A further summary of areas indicated that the following objectives were most frequently emphasized:

1. Self-care
2. Economic usefulness
3. Safety
4. Health
5. Motor coordination
6. Communication skills
7. Social adjustment
8. Knowledge of the world
9. Recreation and diversional activities
10. Aesthetic appreciation
11. Self-concept
12. Spiritual development
13. Emotional adjustment (Williams, 1963)

These were not arranged in any particular rank order of emphasis but are illustrative of the ever-growing curriculum. The scope of these objectives tends to substantiate the major problems in curriculum at this point in time that were defined by Daly (1966) as lack of purposes for training, lack of agreement on worthwhile objectives in curriculum, and lack of a systematized program.

The 1960s witnessed a continued increase in program provisions for the TMR, but the issue of curriculum was not resolved. Guskin and Spicker (1968) attributed the failure of special education for the TMR, at the close of this decade, to be the result of inadequate curriculum. Professionals continued to appeal for curriculum development as a top priority, along with a realignment of emphasis away from the traditional academic orientation of the school (Lance, 1968; Martinson, 1967); but the controversy continued over the major thrust of the curriculum.

A uniform curriculum for the TMR still eludes us. We still have limited knowledge of the unique circumstances of the TMR and their future needs.

Current successes in behavior modification techniques and other forms of precision teaching have resulted in an emerging technology, but this represents process rather than curriculum. The issue of educational technology in training represents process without defined goals. In reality, we have the "how to do it" without a common agreement on "what to do," beyond the more obvious priorities like toilet training or other severe maladaptive behaviors. We continue to speak in vague terms like "normalization" or "maximizing individual potential," without a clear understanding of what the maximum potential is or what it will mean to the TMR sometime in the future. In seeking "respectability," we have conceivably arrived at process without purpose.

The Future: The Past as Prologue?

A reflection on the past may be prefatory to the resolution of 150 years of dilemma in curriculum development for the TMR. We have, perhaps, made a serious error in ignoring what has already been accomplished. Since 1950, we have struggled for the "new curriculum" without gaining perspective from our predecessors' experiences. We may be attempting to rediscover procedures which are ours for the reading. It might be better to elaborate on what we have had than to struggle to "reinvent the wheel." Doll (1967) has perhaps caught the essence of the past as prologue when he stated:

> Probably no field of education has ignored its past so cavalierly as have educators of the mentally retarded . . . Even the recent revival of Montessori came to us largely from general education—and characteristically it was the disciple, Montessori, rather than the master Seguin who is revived . . . We need researchers grounded in the past. Only so duplication of effort can be avoided, with each investigator carrying the problem forward from the point where it was left by earlier studies. Building on the best of what has gone before. Only so can the mistakes, successes, and learnings of the past be winnowed and incorporated into progressive advances. [pp. 181–182]

Thus, a step forward in the development of appropriate objectives and curriculum may be a look backward to our early failures. In so doing, we may both profit from the failures and apply current knowledge and technology to the efforts of Seguin and others in order to make the "progressive advances" needed in the development of curriculum. As Kanner (1967) noted, the main difference between today and the days of Itard and Seguin "is that by now medicine, education, psychology, sociology and genetics have furnished tools more precise than existed then" (p. 169). If this be so, the past has defined the curriculum, and the present has defined the process. This may, then, be the propitious moment for some reflective thinking on our failures, and a realignment of the curriculum in a true spirit of normalization. The curative or educational thrust of the past and present has represented failure not because the curriculum was all inappropriate, but because it was designed for the edification of others without a consideration of what suited the immediate and future needs of the TMR as trainable. We now know that retardation is essentially incurable, and the curriculum should reflect that fact. The failure of Seguin and others lay in the opposite assumption. It was not that the curriculum was inappropriate; rather it was originally designed to achieve the impossible—cure. Perhaps, then, the structure of the Seguin approach, coupled with current knowledge and technology, may hold the answer to the dilemma of appropriate objectives for a curriculum designed to insure normalization, or the best quality of life for the TMR.

The Development of Appropriate Objectives

In a compatible society, beliefs and biases have a commonality, and it is not difficult to determine educational direction. However, the pluralism of the American society precludes an easy determination of educational objectives, and therefore the process of education is often controversial. Although the American society is committed to equal opportunity and total fulfillment of the individual, the social circumstances often precipitate disagreement. Oftentimes, this disagreement is reduced to a question of what the individual is, as opposed to what we wish that person to be.

In essence, the rationale for any curriculum is to "normalize" an individual, and curriculum organization is directed towards an ultimate adult performance that is compatible with the ethic of the society within which we live. Consequently, we have organized our curriculum experiences in such a way as to insure that the greater number, after training, will perform at a given level.

The "work ethic" is probably the principal criterion for adult responsibility and acceptance into our society. Everyone "pulls his weight," and dependence is an anathema. Therefore, a nonproductive individual becomes a species apart from society because, after being provided the "normalizing" experiences of the curriculum, that person has not lived up to expectancy and society either gives up or intensifies efforts towards making him or her more "normal."

In our society, an often-neglected component of the curriculum is the maximization of individual potential. The focus on adult productivity often ignores the fact that some members will neither be "adults" nor productive, and the maximizing process may never realize the goal of filling a slot in an organized society. For these members, the fulfillment of their basic human needs may never result in self-maintenance, but for the most part must be provided.

The trainable mentally retarded, will usually be semidependent upon someone for a portion of their maintenance and support throughout their lives. The TMR child will grow up to be a TMR adult, and for that person, maximum potential will represent what Farber (1968) has defined as a surplus population (that is, that population in excess of those needed to fill a slot in an organized society). Therefore, the maximizing of the individual's potential has offered and will continue to pose some unique problems. Society, to date, has not been able to come to complete agreement on the direction or appropriateness of the TMR curriculum, nor do we know what it may mean in terms of their adult potential.

The problems notwithstanding, an effective curriculum should grow out of a consideration for the individual and personal strengths *and* limitations, along with that which is consistent with the demands and expectations of the environment. What we are initially concerned with is a statement of objectives that can ultimately assist the TMR in adjusting to the environment and will prepare him for as "normal" a life as possible as a TMR adult. Therefore, to arrive at a statement of objectives, we must first consider the relationship of the curriculum to the individual and the environment within which the person lives. The efficacy or validation of these objectives is tied to two factors: the cultural milieu and the psycho-social factors which make the TMR unique. Consideration of these factors precludes a uniform curriculum. The broad objectives may be defined, but the heterogeneity of the TMR population and the pluralistic nature of our society precludes uniformity. The broad objectives, then, must frequently be defined by the individual teacher in terms of the community and the psycho-social factors that are consistent with the unique characteristics and circumstances of the particular class.

Community Validity

The criteria of community validity is concerned with the requirements and aspirations of the community for its members. The community or social system within which the TMR live is usually concerned with its members becoming socially competent and independent. Society has placed a premium on intelligence and cognitive abilities, and the schools have historically been expected to inculturate the TMR with some sort of educational experience. Although confronted with failure in these efforts, educators have been reluctant to recognize the appropriate social circumstances of the TMR population and have consistently yielded to the "respectable" facade of education.

It is remarkable to note that a nearly universal expression for curriculum for the TMR begins with something like, "To maximize the individual's potential. . . ." The curriculum then proceeds to reflect or interpret the aspirations of the society with little regard for the individual's social realities in terms of present status and maximum potential. Therefore, community validation of the curriculum has frequently been interpreted in terms of *what society wants* in maximum potential—a competent individual. However, given the social and intellectual demands of a contemporary society and the extant limitations of the TMR population, it is unrealistic to expect full competence in any society (Edgerton, 1968).

The criterion of community validity in the TMR curriculum merits reevaluation. The present needs or expectations of modern society do not insure or reflect community validity for the TMR curriculum. Meaningful community validity must be a reflection of the community in terms of the reality of the position of the TMR in that community. The first consideration in determining community validity is that the TMR will probably be dependent and will never realize a fully competent position in society. Therefore, the traditional ideas and virtues usually found in curriculum will not be appropriate nor adequately reflect the social situation.

In traditional education programs, the concern is for the future needs of the community and the position that those who are to be educated will ultimately hold. Considerable emphasis is placed on adult productivity and what the individual will return to the community as a result of and in return for being educated. Given these purposes and values, TMR *are* surplus and consequently are in conflict with our major value systems.

Farber's reflections (1968) on the mentally retarded as a problem in social reform and societal surplus place the major portion of the trainable's activity in the home, precluding his participation in normal activities, regardless of the social situation. Therefore, the determination of community validity in a TMR curriculum should be indicative of the TMR's ultimate placement in society—life-long dependence.

Further validation of the curriculum would be in terms of available resources in the community. If there is a comprehensive community program through the adult years (such as sheltered workshop or other adult activities), the curriculum should reflect preparation for adult life in a program appropriate to the person's potential. However, if community resources are limited, it would be of questionable value to prepare a child for sheltered workshop or any other adult activity when none exists. Thus, to be valid, the curriculum must reflect the limitations of the community, and the ultimate prognosis of the TMR under these circumstances. In extreme circumstances, it may even be appropriate to train the individual for institutional living when that is the obvious or only alternative for adult life.

Reasonable adherence to the principles of community validity serves to answer the often-posed question, "Training for what?" Also, it places in realistic perspective the ultimate result of a training program without the illusion of normalcy. It clearly defines normalization in the sense that a valid curriculum will be designed to assist the TMR to live as normal a life as possible, consistent with the circumstances of the environment.

While there will be certain decisions relative to the community validity of the curriculum, it is equally incumbent upon the teacher to define the curriculum in terms of psycho-social validity in order to meet unique group characteristics and individual differences.

Psycho-Social Validity

The psycho-social validity of the curriculum is related to group characteristics and individual needs for various levels or types of training. In defining this criterion, the curriculum should take into account the physical, emotional, mental, and social characteristics of the TMR. McCarthy and Scheerenberger (1966) have noted that the negative results of past programs appear to be related to a lack of information about these characteristics. In general, we have already seen that previous appraisals of a TMR person's learning characteristics indicate that a non-academic approach is most appropriate, and that greater success has been found in programs that focus upon group and individual training for adjustment to routine or persistent life situations.

More specifically, psycho-social validity entails a consideration of the specific group's and individual's characteristics which will have implications for curriculum planning. Warren (1966) listed a number of these characteristics which should be considered in curriculum planning. Most important among these were:

1. Unclear and varied needs among the TMR population.
2. May fit into a family group, but sometimes needs sheltered facilities for short- or long-term care
3. Are more likely to be physically handicapped and have speech handicaps and chronic illness
4. Have a current increased life span into middle or even old age
5. May present difficult medical and psychological diagnostic problems
6. Are mostly capable of learning care for their personal needs
7. Many can eventually learn to perform simple useful tasks
8. Cannot learn traditional academics, but may profit from a program of functional academics
9. Are generally unable to learn to the extent that they will become self-supporting or self-sufficient

In addition, Sauter (1967) pointed to several other specific problems in the general characteristics of the TMR which should also be considered in curriculum planning. These involve:

1. Short attention span and resulting distractability demanding an "engineering of their attention" through a higher quality of instruction.

2. A limited ability to learn through incidental experiences necessitating instruction in even the most rudimentary skills and knowledges
3. A difficulty in abstracting, which limits the acquisition of academic skills

Bijou (1966) has also characterized the TMR as having a limited repertoire of appropriate social responses. This single behavioral characteristic has probably contributed more to changes in the determination of psycho-social validity in the curriculum than any other characterization of the TMR as individuals or groups. Adherents to this principle have rejected the previously conservative characteristics and criteria as being counter-productive in developing the potential of the TMR, and have focused on an optimistic curriculum which provides for a systematic structuring of the environment in order to develop or enhance specific behaviors previously assumed to be unobtainable. The research in this area is not without promise, but the ultimate validity of the approach is yet to be determined.

Although there is some common agreement on individual and group characteristics, a structuring of the curriculum to meet the criterion of psycho-social validity is confounded by a lack of agreement on definition of the population. There is also a lack of agreement among parents, educators, and other professionals about the ultimate potential of the TMR. Finally, the determination of psycho-social validity is complicated by the heterogeneity of the population. The complexities of this population make the determination of psycho-social validity a problem for individual teacher decision and preclude a uniform expression of a single set of criteria in the development of a curriculum that reflects group and individual needs consistent with adult prognosis.

The maintenance of community and psycho-social validity is a dynamic factor in the curriculum and must reflect changes in the social environment and in the individual. Training should reflect relevant goals that will motivate and assist the child or adult to profit as much as possible from experiences that are realistic and appropriate. Thus, the curriculum should take a developmental approach that reflects goals consistent with the developmental progress of the individual and the changes that occur over time.

The Need for a Developmental Approach

Human development is determined by a composite of physical and intellectual behaviors that have influence in an orderly process of maturation and learning from birth to adult life. The organized sequence of interrelated events accumulating from experience constitutes milestones in the individual's development towards adulthood.

These milestones, or developmental levels, are usually defined according to age behavior or appropriate developmental task level. Havighurst (1953) has defined developmental tasks as tasks that occur at certain periods of life with successful completion being prerequisite to the completion of later tasks. He further stated that failure to complete a developmental task level usually results in societal disapproval and difficulty in subsequent developmental progress.

Developmental tasks are expressions of age-appropriate behaviors that are usually socially prescribed (for example, we are expected to walk by a certain age or talk by a certain age). Physical and mental development are closely paralleled, and the individual's progress toward physical and mental maturity is expected to increase proportionately. Therefore, the principal index for this growth is chronological age. We are expected to be or to "act" our age physically and mentally.

The TMR fail to meet this criteria expectancy in maturity and, by definition, will be delayed in the acquisition of developmental tasks and delayed physically and mentally in divergent proportions with a growing discrepancy between expectancy for performance according to physical development (chronological age) and actual ability (mental age).

Although these expectations exist, there continue to be various traditional approaches to developmental considerations in the TMR curriculum. We often repeat the mistake of determining the ability of the TMR to learn according to chronological age rather than mental age (Goldberg & Rooke, 1967). This approach has the underlying assumption that the attainment of certain developmental skills by the TMR is more a product of maturation than learning. Thus, we are frequently confounded by circumstances such as a ten year old who cannot feed herself or an eight year old who is not toilet trained. This type of discrepancy is frequently the source of considerable consternation when we attempt to define appropriate developmental tasks for the TMR curriculum.

One of the principal problems in a developmental approach to curriculum is that in a normal developmental sequence, children are expected to mature in terms of mastery of certain tasks. For example, tasks such as learning to walk, eating solid foods, talking, or toilet training are all expected to occur between birth and six years of age (Havighurst, 1953). The mastery of these tasks is an integrated process of maturation, learning, and social reinforcement or approval. These developmental milestones seem to occur in the general population as incidental learnings and appear to reflect minimal efforts at training (that is, the child just "picks them up"). The TMR, unlike their normal counterparts, will usually be unable to profit from incidental learnings. Therefore, we cannot assume that they will pick up certain skills. All aspects of development should be considered integral parts of the training curriculum.

Consideration of the developmental aspects of the curriculum should involve the use of mental age rather than chronological age as an initial index of ability. There are many objectives frequently included in the TMR curriculum that are implicit in the assumption that certain skills are more influenced by maturation, and the curriculum usually reflects terminal behaviors according to chronological age levels. Therefore, we frequently find that the developmental aspects of the curriculum are misguided or poorly structured on the basis of an *a priori* consideration of chronological age expectancy.* Furthermore, the continued use of chronological age expectancy has resulted in many of the developmental milestones being excluded from the curriculum as unrelated to school tasks. However, a consideration of ability factor, or mental age, as an index for curricular concerns makes these milestones quite germane to the TMR curriculum.

The TMR are also often expected to follow the normal sequence of development, but at a slower rate. As a consequence of this expectation, a developmental approach to curriculum is frequently a downward extension of anticipated normal readiness for various levels of instruction. This erroneously assumes that the TMR will learn about as efficiently as their normal counterparts of equivalent mental age, albeit at a slower rate, and will ultimately obtain the optimum level of development necessary for responsible adult behavior.

In defining curriculum, we must take a developmental approach to determine priorities. Ignoring this principle in planning can seriously limit the opportunities of the TMR to develop and can be the precursor to additional failures. Withholding training and reinforcement or introducing a developmental skill prematurely will further limit their ability to respond to stimuli in an age-appropriate manner and will compound the problems of retardation. Further, the failures often result in teacher despair and withdrawal of attempts at future intervention and remediation. Ultimately, the motivation of the TMR individual decreases, his or her dependency increases and the TMR's abilities are misinterpreted or ignored.

In summary, the ordering of developmental tasks must consider priorities of training according to mental age and chronological age. However, these priorities should reflect the individual and the divergent

---

*An example of this problem would be that, by age seven, normal children are expected to engage in reciprocal play. However, TMRs at age seven are still in the stage of parallel play which is consistent with their mental age development of 2 to 3½ years. Therefore, the curriculum should reflect this difference; that is, the terminal behavior of group play will have to be trained rather than assumed on the basis of maturation.

development of mental age and chronological age in order to guard against erroneous expectations, premature or inappropriate training, and subsequent failure in the program.

Cognitive and Affective Concerns

An expression of appropriate objectives in a training program is often caught in the dilemma of a cognitive vs. affective approach to content and process. These concerns are frequently separated in the curriculum, and one may operate to the exclusion of the other. The curriculum often becomes exclusively cognitive with an emphasis upon knowledge or skills without a consideration of motivation; or, the curriculum will focus on the affective concerns with a limited emphasis on content and deteriorate into a "happiness" program.

The two issues are interrelated and should not be isolated. Cognitive behavior is easier to define, quantify, instruct, and evaluate; whereas affective behavior is rather vague and elusive and much more difficult to express in terms of curriculum. However, motivation is a function of affective behavior and should be used as a vehicle to further cognitive development.

The TMR, much like all of us, are quite hedonistic. If an activity is pleasant and relevant, they will be much more interested in participating. Therefore, cognitive and affective concerns are both critical components in the identification of appropriate objectives. If the objectives are expressed in terms of relevance and the nature of the learner and taught at a level that reflects developmental readiness, the TMR will be motivated, they will learn, and they will be willing to continue to participate.

A specific definition of appropriate objectives in curriculum for the TMR must obviously be based upon multiple criteria, and a ready-made curriculum guide that incorporates all contingencies into a training program is neither available nor appropriate. However, in planning curriculum we can define operational objectives which will reflect general goals for training. These objectives can be viewed as antecedents to appropriate and feasible experiences that should reflect the unique characteristics of an individual training program.

Operational Curriculum Objectives for the TMR

The sum total of experiences afforded a TMR pupil has been the subject of some controversy centered on the content emphasis appropriate for adult life. This controversy may continue as definitions and agency responsibility change; however, at this point, the overwhelming evidence tends to recommend the continued efficacy of the nonacademic approach rather than a program of traditional education. The major operational objectives of the curriculum still appear to involve the three major areas defined by Baumgartner (1955): (1) self-care, (2) social adjustment, and (3) economic usefulness. The content emphasis within these three global objectives have changed with time and will continue to change as new evidence emerges. However, the general organization of the curriculum under these objectives most adequately reflects a program consistent with the capacity of the TMR and will contribute most effectively to adult adjustment.

Self-care

The objective of self-care is basic to all other areas of training. Essentially, the entire curriculum is a self-care curriculum directed towards maximum independence and adult participation in life. Achieving this objective is all the more crucial because dependence is an anathema to society, and lack of self-care (dependency) is often the single most important factor in parental exhaustion and the resulting desirability of institutionalization.

The initial curricular approaches to self-care were less than optimistic and reflected an estimated adult prognosis of life-long dependency. Self-care was thus limited to achievements in washing hands and face, combing hair, brushing teeth, and learning other areas of grooming and personal hygiene (Baumgartner, 1955; Williams, 1963). While these are still important achievements for the TMR, increased knowledge of higher ability levels has resulted in the dimensions of self-care being expanded to assist the TMR in obtaining a higher level of independent functioning.

The curricular areas of self-care usually involve activities in the areas of (1) grooming and personal hygiene, (2) communication skills, (3) motor skills, (4) functional academics, and (5) community living. Although representing major dimensions of the total program, these five areas have been included under self-care, since they appear to be most critical to independent functioning. A proficiency in these major areas will contribute significantly to the highest level of independence possible.

Grooming and Personal Hygiene

The normal child usually learns most of grooming and hygiene skills with a minimum of training. However, the TMR child will need specific instruction in this area. Limited skills in grooming and personal hygiene contribute to social distance between the TMR and other members of the community and to dependency status. The specific aims for instruction in grooming are to develop practical experience in caring for personal needs in areas such as dressing, undressing, and hair care along with other cosmetic concerns related to personal appearance. Activities in personal hygiene will be principally directed towards care of teeth, nails, and other hygienic concerns such as toileting, body odor, drooling, and care of nose using a handkerchief or tissue. Other personal skills, such as eating and handling food, should also be incorporated into the training for good grooming and personal hygiene.

Communication Skills

Language training has often been the major focus in the development of communication skills in a training program and is frequently considered a separate major curriculum goal. It has often been given an inordinate amount of attention in the classroom (Hudson, 1960), albeit with little success (McCarthy & Scheerenberger, 1966). It is included here as a self-care skill because language, or the broader dimension of communication skills, contributes most significantly to independence in a number of performance skills in the home and community.

The principal goal in the training of communication skills is not perfect speech. The focus of training is more appropriately placed on the development of a usable and effective means of communicating wants. Training in communication skills should be directed towards increasing the individual's ability to communicate. This entails learning, listening, or receptive language for protection (understanding concepts like no, wait, sit down, come here, or do not touch) and the production of an appropriate response or reaction. Also, expressive language, or the production of speech writing and gesture, should be developed to the optimum level of the individual's ability. It must be kept in mind, though, that negative influences such as the extant retardation, sensory defects, and other etiological factors may preclude effective or intelligible speech. Thus, acceptable expressive language could range from a primitive grunt or gesture to articulate speech.

The communication curriculum should focus on performance skills rather than specific speech therapy. Speech therapy often has limited value in a training program and is indicated only when it will assist in increasing verbal output.

Motor Skills

Motor skills are also frequently considered a separate major area of curriculum. Perceptual-motor training has received considerable attention in training programs in recent years. Emphasis has been placed on body movements and body mechanics in order to improve the scope of activities that the individual can participate in. In a training program, the optimum level of ability in motor skills will be defined by the presence or absence of organic defects. The curriculum for developing these skills should reflect a structure or sequence of tasks that incorporate gross and fine motor development directed towards increased ambulation and participation in activities where the antecedent skill is an operational level of perceptual-motor ability.

Functional Academics

While academics in the sense of "readin', writin' and 'rithmetic" are usually inappropriate for emphasis in the TMR curriculum, there are legitimate areas of academic instruction which will contribute to the person's independence.

Reading proficiency among the TMR population is usually limited to reading words for protection and information. Words such as "poison," "hot" and "cold," or "fire exit" would be included in such a protective vocabulary. Words such as men, women, entrance, and exit would be in the category of reading for information. This "survival" vocabulary would define the immediate priorities in a reading program. However, in instances where measurable gains in reading are demonstrated, the program may be expanded to include the reading of simple materials for pleasure. The critical issue, of course, is comprehension. Word calling, or a simple verbal response to stimuli, is not reading. It must be remembered that reading does not take place until a level of comprehension is reached. Therefore, the TMR must be able to recognize the word and associate it with an appropriate act or thought.

Number concepts are usually limited to a vocabulary of relationship. Words such as "big" and "little," "tall" and "short," or "high" and "low" usually represent the highest level of abstract reasoning that the TMR are capable of. The more abstract processes of addition and subtraction are usually beyond their level of comprehension. The rational use of numbers can be taught through counting and sorting, with application to other life situations involving numbers for protection (for example, knowing their address and telephone number), or time and money. Time and money, much like other number concepts, are initially taught in terms of a vocabulary of relationship. Time is taught according to the concepts of day and night, morning or afternoon, or in the more global sense in terms of the seasons of the year. Additional time-related activities would involve concepts like the understanding of late or early. The actual process of telling time, if taught at all, will probably be limited to an understanding of time by the hour. Instruction in the use of money is usually limited to an understanding of money as being something of value and recognition of various coins. As in reading, individual ability levels and comprehension will dictate the upper limits of comprehension of number concepts that are to be included in the curriculum.

Writing is a composite of skills involving cognitive as well as perceptual-motor development. It is not anticipated that the TMR will advance beyond a level of writing their name, address, and telephone number.

In any area of functional academics, the level of curriculum will depend upon the unique abilities of the group. The deficits may be so severe as to preclude the inclusion of any level of functional academics in the curriculum. However, the level of sophistication may be sufficient to advance beyond the functional aspects of academics to more abstract concepts. The limitations of this area of the curriculum are specifically related to individual ability levels, but regardless of the level, we must always weigh the emphasis on this area of curriculum against the ultimate adult prognosis and value in adult life.

Community Living

The optimum goal of self-care for the TMR is to develop a maximum level of independence in community living. Being able to live in a community is directly related to a composite of self-care skills which are placed in meaningful context in persistent life situations. Therefore, the curriculum should provide for an extension of the classroom into the community with focus upon mobility and the use of community facilities such as movies, restaurants, and other public buildings.

Social Adjustment

Social adjustment is perhaps the most elusive objective in terms of specific curricular emphasis or in the defining of specific activities. It is a pervasive objective that relates to effective participation in all other areas of the curriculum.

The focus in social adjustment is on an optimum level of what is now termed "adaptive behavior." The curricular emphasis is towards developing in the TMR individual the ability to cope with persistent life situations and to interact effectively with other children and adults in a variety of situations. This aspect of curriculum, therefore, can be taught as a component of other activities through participation, understanding of one's position in a group, and appropriate social behavior for the situation. Instruction may be conducted in the area of manners and other social amenities for specific situations involving circumstances such as greeting people, behavior in public places, or other general conduct involving good manners and acceptable social responses. However, in general, social skills will emerge as the TMR begin to accept responsibility and participate in the activities of the group. In adult life, the ability of the TMR to function in a community, or in a less open environment, will largely depend upon his degree of social adjustment.

Economic Usefulness

Economic usefulness, as opposed to the goal of economic self-sufficiency, indicates the ultimate adult prognosis of marginal dependency for the TMR. With proper training, the TMR can be taught to contribute to the family unit by assisting or carrying out various household tasks such as meal preparation, cleaning, yard work, and gardening. In addition, economic usefulness is directed towards the development of good work habits and attitudes including pride in work and successful completion of a task. The limits of economic usefulness or the extent to which the TMR may contribute to the labor force is dependent upon individual ability levels. In rare instances, the TMR adult may become gainfully employed; but the usual optimum expectancy is sheltered workshop placement with continued economic support and guidance from the family or other community agency.

Age appears to be the most critical component in training for economic usefulness. This is frequently a curriculum area where training is delayed until adolescence or early adult life, with emphasis being placed on self-care and social adjustment in the younger years. Blue (1964) has determined that this is a serious error in training, and he advocates early introduction of the TMR to the world of work in order to insure optimum success and appropriate placement in the adult years.

Ancillary Training

Within the curriculum, there should be additional experiences in diversional activities such as recreation, music, and art. This can include a range of activities, developed according to the readiness of the group, to provide opportunities for participation and self-expression through singing and listening, use of various media, and participation in recreation. Participation in these activities provides additional opportunities for meaningful expreriences in the major areas of self-care, social adjustment, and economic usefulness.

It has not been the intent of the foregoing discussion to design a specific curriculum. If such were done, it would violate one of the principles of curriculum development which demands that the curriculum reflect the individual and the cultural milieu, along with the demands or expectancies that this milieu will have for participation in adult life. In general, each teacher will have to make decisions about curriculum emphasis according to the developmental level and other characteristics of the group. Once again, the heterogeneity of the TMR population would preclude the possibility of a uniform curriculum, and the plurality of our society would make the value of such a curriculum questionable. Thus, in defining a realistic curriculum in keeping with the assets *and* liabilities of the TMR population, the ultimate goal is to insure the best quality of life for the TMR. We would surely not want less for any other member of our society.

Establishing Priorities

The typical objective of any curriculum for the TMR is to insure a maximum level of adjustment in the home, school, and neighborhood, and to provide a program that is consistent with their capacity for development (Baumgartner, 1955). This represents a rather ambiguous, global expectation. It provides little assistance in determining steps necessary for maximum adjustment in terms of immediate concerns or future situations.

A systematized approach to the establishment of various levels or priorities in the curriculum is necessary, but the teacher must also define these priorities in terms of group and individual characteristics. A TMR child's composite of entering behaviors often confounds the decision-making process of where to begin training. We are frequently overwhelmed by the myriad of behaviors that demand our attention, and we fail to see or sort out immediate and long-range objectives for the program.

Immediate, observable priorities are frequently represented by problems in self-care (such as a lack of toilet training) or social adjustment (such as physical abuse of other class members). These priorities are classified as immediate because they seriously affect the ability of the TMR to function or interact effectively in the program. The next level of priority is usually identified through assessment (for example, "cannot meet criteria expectancy for fine motor control"). This level of priority usually determines areas in need of remediation. The third level of priority represents the global objective of training ("maximum level of adjustment").

The proper sequencing of these priorities is necessary if training is going to be effective. Gorelick (1963) offers an example of how objectives may be sequenced according to four levels:

Global	To learn to get along with others.
Major	To learn good manners.
Minor	To learn to take turns.
Operational	To learn to wait in line for a drink without pushing others. (p. 213)

This arrangement of objectives from immediate to long-range goals provides a continuum for curriculum development that will lead the individual to a defined level of functioning and will enhance teacher effectiveness in the achievement of these goals.

The systematic determination of priorities ultimately leads to a statement of behavioral objectives for individual and group instruction. These objectives should be expressed in terms of the characteristics and needs of the TMR, with focus upon content, process, and product that reflect both cognitive behavior (that is, knowledge, comprehension, and application) and affective behavior (attitude, interests, and motivation).

Summary

The curriculum for the trainable mentally retarded is deeply rooted in past efforts to cure the retardation. Early curricula reflected a conscious effort towards amelioration of the retardate's circumstances through sense training and a physiological method designed to "rid society of idiocy." These early attempts at cure failed, and society abandoned the lower levels of retardation. Programs for this population were reduced to institutionalization or languishing in the home and community.

There were continued isolated efforts toward development of a meaningful program for the TMR, but it ultimately fell to the parents to provide programs in the home. Such parental efforts eventually served as catalysts for reappraisal of programs for the TMR. It was through this reappraisal that the TMR eventually became the educational responsibility of the public school. This change in responsibility for programs required the public schools to develop curricula for a population that was considered uneducable.

The placement of the TMR in public schools created a new controversy in curriculum development. The traditional role of the school was in conflict with the ultimate prognosis of the population that they were now being asked to serve. Nevertheless, professional educators attempted to develop a curriculum that was consistent with the disabilities, and the new focus was upon a nonacademic curricula designed to enhance the adjustment and general happiness of the TMR population.

Parental dissatisfaction and evidence that indicated the limitations of the existing programs resulted in a change in focus to a more traditional curriculum with a greater emphasis on academic skills. Despite its gain in popularity, the academic approach has had limited success, and the controversy of appropriate curricula is yet to be resolved.

Current technology, coupled with the efforts of the past, appear to hold the greatest promise for resolution of the issue of appropriate curricula. The development of appropriate objectives entails a validation of the social, psychological, and developmental components of the curriculum to insure proper emphasis to priorities of need and the affective and cognitive concerns of the program.

The development of appropriate objectives in terms of the population to be served still appears to support the efficacy of a nonacademic program structured around the broad objectives of self-care, social adjustment, and economic usefulness. A program developed from these objectives is more meaningful and most appropriately reflects the ultimate adult prognosis of the TMR population.

References

Baumgartner, B. B. *A curriculum guide for teacher of trainable mentally handicapped children.* Springfield, Ill: Superintendent of Public Instruction, 1955.

Bijou, S. W. A functional analysis of retarded development. In N. R. Ellis (Ed.), *International review of research in mental retardation, vol. 1.* New York: Academic Press, 1966.

Blue, C. M. Trainable mentally retarded in sheltered workshops. *Mental Retardation,* 1964, *2,* 97–104.

Daly, F. M. The program for trainable mentally retarded children in the public schools of California. *Education and Training of the Mentally Retarded,* 1966, *3,* 109–118.

Doll, E. E. Trends and problems in the education of the mentally retarded. *American Journal of Mental Deficiency,* 1967, *72,* 175–183.

Edgerton, R. B. Anthropology and mental retardation: A plea for the comparative study of incompetence. In H. J. Prehm, L. A. Hamerlynck, & J. E. Crosson (Eds.), *Behaviorial research in mental retardation.* Eugene, Ore: University of Oregon, 1968.

Farber, B. *Mental retardation: Its social context and social consequences.* Boston, Mass.: Houghton Mifflin, 1968.

Goldberg, I. I., & Rooke, M. L. Research and educational practices with mentally deficient children. In N. G. Haring & R. L. Schiefelbusch (Eds.), *Methods in special education.* New York: McGraw-Hill, 1967.

Goldstein, H. Preface. In J. S. Molloy (Ed.), *Trainable children.* New York: John Day, 1963.

Gorelick, M. C. A typology of curriculum objectives for mentally retarded: From ambiguity to precision. *Mental Retardation,* 1963, *1,* 212–215.

Guskin, S. L., & Spicker, H. H. Educational research in mental retardation. In N. R. Ellis (Ed.), *International review of research in mental retardation, vol. 3.* New York: Academic Press, 1968.

Hafemeister, N. R. Development of a curriculum for the trainable child. *American Journal of Mental Deficiency,* 1951, *55,* 495–501.

Havighurst, R. J. *Human development and education.* New York: Longmans, 1953.

Hottel, J. V. *An evaluation of the Tennessee day class program for severely retarded (trainable) children.* Nashville, Tenn.: George Peabody College for Teachers, 1958.

Hudson, M. The severely retarded child: Educable vs. trainable. *American Journal of Mental Deficiency,* 1955, *59,* 583–586. (a)

Hudson, M. Some theoretical aspects to curriculum building for the severely retarded child. *American Journal of Mental Deficiency,* 1955, *60,* 270–277. (b)

Hudson, M. Lesson areas for the trainable child. *Exceptional Children,* 1960, *27,* 224–229.

Ingram, C. P. *Education of the slow learning child* (3rd ed.). New York: Ronald Press, 1960.

Ingram, V. M., & Popp, C. E. A public school program for the severely mentally handicapped child. *American Journal of Mental Deficiency,* 1955, *60,* 285–290.

Itard, J. M. G. *The wild boy of Aveyron* (G. Humphrey & M. Humphrey trans.). New York: Appleton-Century-Crofts, 1962.

Kanner, L. Medicine in the history of mental retardation. *American Journal of Mental Deficiency,* 1967, *72,* 165–170.

Kirk, S. A. Research in education. In R. Heber & H. A. Stevens (Eds.), *Mental retardation: A review of research.* Chicago: University of Chicago Press, 1964.

Kirk, S. A., & Johnson, O. *Educating the retarded child.* Cambridge, Mass.: Riverside Press, 1951.

Kolstoe, O. P. *Mental retardation, an educational viewpoint.* New York: Holt, Rinehart, & Winston, 1972.

Lance, W. D. School programs for the trainable mentally retarded. *Education and Training of the Mentally Retarded,* 1968, *3,* 3–9.

Locke, J. *An essay concerning human understanding.* Chicago: Open Court Publishing, 1949.

Martinson, M. C. IMC network report: Education for trainable children—an opportunity. *Exceptional Children,* 1967, *34,* 293–297.

McCarthy, J. J., & Scheerenberger, R. C. A decade of research on the education of the mentally retarded. *Mental Retardation Abstracts, Vol. 3.* Washington, D.C.: U.S. Government Printing Office, 1966.

McCaw, W. R. A curriculum for the severely mentally retarded. *American Journal of Mental Deficiency,* 1958, *62,* 616–621.

Rosenzweig, L. Report of a school program for trainable mentally retarded children. *American Journal of Mental Deficiency,* 1954, *59,* 181–205.

Sauter, J. Philosophy, goals, and the curriculum. In R. C. Scheerenberger (Ed.), *Training the severely and profoundly mentally retarded.* Springfield, Ill.: Illinois Department of Mental Health, 1967.

Seguin, E. *Idiocy and its treatment by the physiological method.* New York: Augustus M. Kelley, 1971.

Warren, S. A. Academic achievement of trainable pupils with five or more years of schooling. *Training School Bulletin,* 1963, *2,* 75–86.

Warren, S. A. *Lifetime planning for the mentally retarded.* Chicago: Illinois State Pediatric Institute, 1966.

Williams, H. M. *Education of the severely retarded child.* Washington, D.C.: U.S. Government Printing Office, 1963.

Wirtz, M. A. The development of current thinking about facilities for the severely mentally retarded. *American Journal of Mental Deficiency,* 1956, *60,* 492–507.

Chapter 5

Procedures Affecting the Training Process

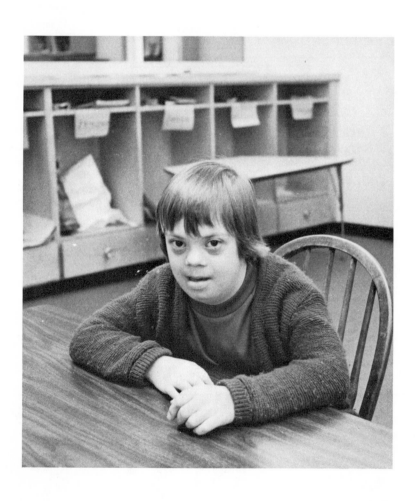

The growth of knowledge in procedures for training the more severely retarded has been most remarkable in the last fifteen years. Previous teaching strategies were usually ineffective and often dictated by the curriculum, when a number of curriculum goals were defined and improvised on by the teacher. When these goals were defined in terms of a cognitive or strongly academic orientation, they were often interpreted in a coercive, authoritarian process using pressures to learn academic subjects as the key to success in adult life.

Affective programs, another approach, were usually more *laissez-faire,* and the TMR were allowed to "do their thing," while engaging in random trial-and-error learning. The usual intent of this strategy was to "love 'em" and assist the TMR in developing good attitudes towards themselves and their environment.

There were also other instances where a more eclectic approach was taken towards training. However, this approach usually involved a vacillation from authoritarian to *laissez-faire,* depending upon the immediate crisis of the classroom or the tolerance limits of the teacher.

This early lack of appropriate or well-defined procedures for training was considered to contribute significantly to the limited impact of past efforts in training programs (Guskin & Spicker, 1968; McCarthy & Scheerenberger, 1966), and there has been an emerging and widely acknowledged concern for an instructional system that is based on some sort of educational technology.

Although reinforcement techniques were used inconsistently in many early programs, the principles of systematic reinforcement did not appear until the early part of the twentieth century. In the past ten years, there has been increasing application of the principles of behavior modification in programs for the mentally retarded. The application of behavior modification techniques and the extension of this process to a precision-teaching methodology has probably made the most significant contribution to procedures in training programs in recent years. Programs where these techniques are used have reported remarkable success, and it is the general opinion of many professionals that they will continue to increase in value as new knowledge emerges.

Behavior Modification

The behavior modification movement was generated out of the research of Pavlov (1927) and was ultimately extended to experimentation in the conditioning of humans. By the 1950s, the work of B. F. Skinner (1953) stimulated considerable research in the application of a Stimulus-Response-Reinforcement continuum to the behaviorial management of humans. The genesis of this Skinnerian approach to behavior management was "operant conditioning," a view of behavior concerned with the organism operating in its environment. The principle was that if the consequences of an operant, or behavior, are favorable, the behavior is likely to be repeated. Therefore, the operant approach attempted to identify and program for a functional relationship between stimuli and behavior.

By the 1960s, Bijou and Baer (1961; 1966) were calling attention to the relationship of the child and the environment, and behavior modification techniques were beginning to be introduced into programs for the mentally retarded. Bijou (1966) provided additional emphasis to the application of the principles of behavior modification in programs for the retarded when he suggested that "mental retardation" was a hypothetical construct that contributed to the existing random and ineffective teaching techniques. He emphasized that the environment was at fault, and that retardation was actually a developmental deficit contributing to inappropriate behavior, because appropriate behavior had not been learned. He defined a stimulus-response component to this problem in which "a retarded individual is one who has a limited repertory of behavior shaped by events that constitute his history" (p. 2). In a later publication (Bijou, 1973), Bijou discussed the means for expanding the retardate's behavior, skills, and knowledge through a behavior modification program.

The application of the principles of behavior modification in TMR programs has been so successful that the current literature is replete with studies indicating success in various aspects of training. The most successful long-range effects in behavior modification programs have been in training for self-care, and the largest category of studies in this area have been in the area of toilet training. Rentfrow and Rentfrow (1969) reviewed a number of these studies related to toilet training and indicated that the programs reported all led to significant improvements in elimination control.

In more recent studies, the factor of time was reduced in the toilet training process. Azrin and Foxx (1971) were able to train within a median of four days and a mean of six days. In a subsequent study (Azrin, Bugle, & O'Brien, 1971), the time factor in training was reduced to three days.

Other studies have reported on the improvement of personal appearance behaviors through the use of behavior modification. Hunt, Fitzburgh, and Fitzburgh (1968), using tokens as generalized reinforcers, were able to improve on-the-job appearance with "exit-ward" patients. Karen and Maxwell (1967) were successful in increasing self-dressing skills with the use of primary and secondary reinforcers, and Minge and Ball (1967), through systematic reinforcement, increased the self-help skills of dressing and undressing. The success of operant techniques in the development of self-help skills has also been demonstrated by Bensberg, Colwell, and Cassell (1965), and Roos and Oliver (1969) compared the effectiveness of operant conditioning to a "no treatment" and a "placebo" control group and found a significant increase in self-help skills in the group trained by operant conditioning procedures.

Girardeau and Spradlin (1964) demonstrated success in the improvement of multiple behaviors defined as "constructive and socially acceptable." In the course of the study, they noted that the procedures were so successful that the subjects became so highly motivated that they could not create tasks fast enough for them.

Birnbrauer and Lawler (1964) applied operant principles to the development of multiple behaviors in the classroom and were successful in training a group of retarded children to respond appropriately to the classroom environment. In this same context, Perline and Levinsky (1968) reported success in decreasing maladaptive behaviors in a classroom setting through a token-reinforcement program.

These cited studies are only representative of the growing body of literature indicating the successful application of the principles of behavior modification in training programs. Nawas and Braun (1970 a & b) provide an excellent review of additional research in this area, which continues to indicate success in the application of behavior modification techniques in a variety of situations involving training and behavioral management.

Although the early operant programs were essentially confined to institutional programs, their success began to gain the attention of educators, and the use of operant techniques began to move out of the institution and into the classroom. The extension of these programs was motivated by a determination of the effectiveness of their use in the development of more complex behaviors, and they were successful in increasing appropriate classroom behavior and participation in academic tasks (Haring & Lovitt, 1967). The operant methodology continued to be extended to the more complex processes of academic instruction (Bijou, Birnbrauer, Kidder, & Tague, 1966; Birnbrauer, Bijou, Wolf, & Kidder, 1965) and continues to contribute significantly to the development of other systematic program models for training in areas of self-help and language (Chalfant & Silikovitz, 1972; Lent, Keilitz, Foster, & McLean, 1974; Watson, 1973).

The reported success of behavior modification in training programs must be kept in proper context. The teacher must remember that this process represents a tool or effective technique that can be used to train the mentally retarded. It is not a panacea! It is a technique to be used within the broader scope of education in certain elements of program. Unfortunately, it is often misunderstood to the extent that it has grown completely out of proportion in some programs, while being so feared or resented in others that it is not used at all.

The Process

In discussing the process of behavior modification, it is not the intention of this chapter to make the student a behavior modification technician. There are several excellent texts, such as Haring and Phillips (1972), Sulzer and Mayer (1972), Watson (1973), or Neisworth and Smith (1973) that are better suited for this purpose. Actually, I agree with MacMillan (1970) in questioning whether the process, in the pure sense, can even be used by a classroom teacher. It is thus my intention to give an overview of some general principles and practices that may be useful to the prospective teacher faced with somewhat less than the controlled circumstances of a clinical setting but confronted with the problems of training in the classroom.

The essential element of behavior modification in the classroom is not what Lovitt (1970) described as "the ubiquitous M & M." As Forness (1970) pointed out, "tangible reward systems are not those aspects of behavior modification which may have the greatest impact" (p. 13). He further noted that the techniques of behavior modification which help the teacher to be more systematic may be of greater value. In this context, Bijou described behavior modification as more an issue of environmental modification when he stated that the approach involves:

> Individualization of instruction, programmed subject matter and learning sequences, explicit prompting techniques, contingency management, assessment of individual behavior repertoires, monitoring methods of evaluation, progress in academic and social learning, and systematic program modification. [1973, p. 286]

Therefore, our practical interest in behavior modification is to determine how the individual responds to the environment and what conditions in the environment can be manipulated to maintain or change behavior. As previously indicated, mental retardation is compounded by a lack of appropriate behaviors or responses to the environment. Therefore, the concern is to identify the appropriate behavior(s) and develop the program in such a way as to increase appropriate behaviors and to reduce or eliminate inappropriate behaviors.

Behavior modification involves a deliberate and systematic process of establishing and systematically programming for specific objectives in the training program. The structuring of this process involves several steps in assessment, programming, and reassessment to determine whether the behaviorial criteria have been met.

1. *Definition of goals.* The first step in a program of behavior modification is to observe accurately and assess the behavior(s) that need to be changed. Secondly, we must define the goals for change or desired terminal behaviors. The terminal behavior must be defined in observable, measurable terms and reflect exactly what the student is expected to do. One of the frequent problems in this analysis is that the goals are stated as broad generalizations like, "To toilet train Leonard." This is too global or long-range and does not define the specific conditions under which Leonard will be considered toilet-trained.

2. *Determine the criterion.* Once the goal is defined, the next step is to determine what criterion must be met to complete the terminal behavior. For example, must Leonard go to the toilet spontaneously and demonstrate complete extinction of "accidents" before terminal behavior is met? Or is going to the toilet spontaneously 90% of the time with a 10% "on-demand level" an acceptable criterion?

3. *Select the procedure.* What must now be determined is whether we wish to increase the behavior, shape or maintain it, or reduce or eliminate it. The procedures may change as the process progresses. In the initial stages, we wish to eliminate Leonard's toileting "accidents" and shape, maintain, and extend his toilet training. These procedures will be discussed later in the chapter.

4. *Identify appropriate reinforcers.* Although food is a frequently used reinforcer in behavior modification programs, its use in the classroom may be impractical and expensive. Moreover, Fred might like M & M's, but what if George does not like candy? The teacher will have to determine what reinforcers are appropriate for George.

5. *Communicating the process.* The teacher must make sure that the student understands the desired behavior and the contingencies for reward. The environmental consequences for a given response must be defined. For example, George should understand that when he pulls the button through the button hole, he gets a "Fruit-Loop"; or if George is more advanced than that, he should understand that if he buttons his coat (the contingency), he can go outside (the reward).

6. *Structure the environment.* A favorable environment, where the teacher can control the contingencies, must be defined. In terms of George, the buttoning process is most likely to occur or be meaningful at times immediately prior to going outside. However, the teacher has noticed that George's friend Fred, whose locker is right next to George, frequently assists George by buttoning his coat for him. Therefore, it would be appropriate to rearrange locker assignments, placing Fred away from George.

7. *Initiating the program.* The first step in beginning the program is to determine the frequency that a behavior does or does not occur. This measurement is the *baseline data.* As an example, before initiating toilet training for Leonard, we need to know the frequency of "accidents" at various time intervals during the day. This will tell us how often it occurs and when it occurs, which may have some implications for timing of toilet training (that is, if there is a high frequency rate immediately prior to lunch and prior to going home, the toileting schedule for Leonard would be most appropriate at these times). The baseline or preliminary measure of behavior should be repeated to determine the effectiveness of the procedure (that is, is the behavior increasing or decreasing?) and to determine when the criterion has been met.

8. *Maintenance of behavior.* Once the criterion is met, some sort of reinforcement schedule must be continued. Behavior that has been changed or developed, if ignored, will not continue. Although the reinforcers may be gradually reduced in frequency, the behavior must continue to pay off through some sort of extrinsic or intrinsic reward.

This process for changing behavior is usually accomplished through a systematic process of positive reinforcement or reward for appropriate behavior and the withholding of reinforcement for negative behavior. The basic principle of the reinforcement system is that the child does what pays off and avoids behavior that does not pay off. Thus, a behavior that is reinforced will increase in frequency, and that which is not reinforced will decrease in frequency. The critical issue, then, is close attention to the child's behavior and a systematic manipulation of the environment to insure that appropriate behaviors are reinforced and inappropriate behaviors are not reinforced (Chalfant & Silikovitz, 1972).

Reinforcement Systems

The teacher creates, maintains, and manipulates the learning environment. Teachers are constantly—consciously or unconsciously—creating conditions within the classroom that have a profound effect on the student's learning. In terms of our own educational experiences, preferred participation was often in those subjects or other activities where we were rewarded for our performance with good grades or praise from the teacher. However, conversely, how many of us have experienced the threat of, "Twenty-five more arithmetic problems if you don't sit down" or "If you don't get busy, you will have to write your spelling words twenty-five times." Surely, our teacher was interested in our learning arithmetic or being able to spell, but the inadvertent use of these subjects as threats may have shaped us out of an interest in arithmetic or spelling because they became a vehicle for punishment. How much better mathematicians or spellers we might have been had we been rewarded for performance in these areas!

From these brief examples, we can see that reinforcement systems are already used in the classroom. The problem is to insure that they are consciously applied in a systematic manner in order to increase or maintain appropriate behavior and to reduce or eliminate inappropriate behavior.

Increasing or Maintaining Behavior

The critical issue in increasing or maintaining appropriate behavior is the maintenance of a positive environment where appropriate behavior is identified and systematically reinforced or rewarded. The structuring of the environment through a system of positive rewards can be a powerful tool in the learning process. The use of positive reinforcers will increase the frequency of appropriate behavior and may also be used to eliminate inappropriate behaviors.

Bensberg (1965) identified a positive reward as anything that is pleasant to the child. He defines these in terms of primary reinforcers, such as food, and secondary reinforcers, such as social rewards like "good boy," a pat on the head, or a hug. Other reinforcers may involve a favorite toy, a chance to engage in a favorite activity, or tokens that can be exchanged for tangible items or select activities. These are all effective reinforcers for the development and acceleration of appropriate behaviors.

MacMillan (1970) offers a hierarchy of type and use of positive reinforcers that includes:

1. Food
2. Tangible rewards (toys or trinkets)
3. Tokens or check marks redeemable for tangible rewards
4. Symbolic rewards (letter grades or graphs)
5. Social approval
6. Being correct
7. Sense of mastery

This continuum reflects a progressive system of rewards from the most concrete (food) to the abstract satisfaction of "mastery."

Although food is a primary and powerful reward, its use in an educational setting poses some problems. The environmental and staff contingencies in a classroom may preclude the possibility of a stringently controlled environment where extensive use can be made of primary reinforcers. Also, many educators have a philosophical resistance to their use and relegate the use of candy or other food to the level of "bribery." The problems notwithstanding, the more abstract reinforcers do not work with some TMR pupils, and circumstances may necessitate the use of food or other primary reinforcers in the early stages of training. However, when they are used, it is incumbent upon the teacher to plan the program towards an early acceptance of secondary rewards. This can be accomplished by the introduction of social rewards concurrently with the primary reward. For example, if food is used in the early stages of training, a "good boy" or "good girl" can be expressed at the time the food is given. In the later stages, the primary reward should become intermittent and the social reward constant until such time as the need for primary reward decreases, and the child understands and accepts the social reward in lieu of food.

In the beginning, the reinforcement schedule should be continuous, and each successive approximation should be reinforced accurately and consistently. This technique is referred to as *shaping,* where simple behaviors are rewarded and molded into more complex behaviors. Continuous reinforcement also precludes failure at any level of performance and provides for what Chalfant and Silikovitz (1972) refer to as "error-free learning," which is intrinsically reinforcing to the child and the teacher.

As learning progresses, the frequency of reinforcement can be reduced, and the cues or assistance can be faded. *Fading* is a process where the cues are reduced to encourage independence and spontaneity in the behavior. Also, the reduction of reinforcers is necessary if satiation is to be avoided (that is, to avoid causing the reinforcer to cease to be reinforcing). As an example, how many of us have indulged in a favorite food until we could no longer stand the sight or smell of it?

An additional dimension of external cues and reinforcement is the process of modeling. *Modeling* is simply a "look at me, do it" procedure. Altman and Talkington (1971) suggest that modeling procedures have considerable potential in programs and recommend its use in conjunction with reinforcement for appropriate imitative behavior. Their contention is that modeling has far-reaching implications for "highly imitative lower-level retardates" and that acquisition of additional behaviors through modeling procedures should be explored with the TMR population.

Whatever the technique employed, it must be remembered that we want to work away from external cues or reinforcers to the point that the TMR child performs on command (for example, removes her coat when she is told to), or initiates behavior (spontaneously removes her coat upon entering the building). However, in decreasing the reinforcement schedule, the teacher must be careful to avoid withdrawal too quickly, with subsequent disintegration of the behavior, or complete withdrawal of reinforcers and subsequent extinction. Although higher levels of intrinsic reinforcement are desirable and hoped for, in all probability continued intermittent extrinsic reward will be necessary if the behavior is to be maintained.

There are numerous and complex schedules for teaching and maintaining behavior. The knowledge in this area has grown to the extent that it is neither appropriate nor possible, within the scope of this text, to discuss all the variations on reinforcement schedules. However, Table Five provides an example of the four major schedules of reinforcement.

Table Five

Four major schedules of reinforcement

Schedule	Behavior	Reinforcer
Fixed ratio	Puts on smock before painting	Permitted to paint at easel every time smock is on
Variable ratio	Attempts to join and play with other children	Accepted by group on the average of 1 out of every 3 times
Fixed interval	Works quietly for 15 minutes	1 token
Variable interval	Waits for the teacher's help on seatwork	Teacher comes to child's desk on the average of once every 20 minutes

NOTE: Portion of a table in J. T. Neisworth & R. M. Smith, *Modifying Retarded Behavior.* Copyright © 1973 by Houghton Mifflin Co. Reprinted by permission of the publisher.

In the training sequence, receiving the reinforcer is contingent upon completion of a specific task. The child must understand that he or she must do something to obtain the reinforcement. For example, lunch (the reinforcer) may be contingent upon washing hands, or going outside (the reinforcer) may be contingent upon putting on a coat. A contingency principle postulated by Premack (1959) is that high-frequency or preferred behavior, can be used as a contingency for low-frequency or nonpreferred behavior. Therefore, scheduled access to the high-frequency behavior as a contingency can reinforce low-frequency behavior. However, the critical factor in applying this principle is that the teacher must determine that the seemingly preferred behavior is, *in fact,* preferred, rather than one which just appears to be enjoyed.

There are several additional factors that will influence the success or failure of reinforcement systems in the classroom. The most common among these are problems in timing, continuity, and inadvertent reinforcement. The teacher must remember that the reinforcer acts upon the behavior displayed at the moment of reinforcement. Thus, the reward must be immediate to insure that it is generalized to an appropriate behavior. A time lapse of as little as a few seconds could result in the reward being generalized to an inappropriate behavior. For example, Barbara sits down on command, but in the ensuing time lapse between response and reward, she hits Chuck. Consequently, the behavior that is reinforced is hitting rather than sitting and attending.

Continuity is also a critical factor in reinforcement. One of the common errors in programs is that once the child has mastered a skill, the teacher withdraws reinforcers and extinction occurs. An example of this would be Tim, who has learned to remove his coat and hang it in his locker upon entering the room. For two weeks, he does this without any reinforcement from the teacher because, "He is expected to do it." However, for Tim, this behavior is not paying off and he stops it.

There are other patterns of reinforcement that the teacher must attend to in order to avoid inadvertently reinforcing inappropriate behavior. For example, David's mother reports that he is toilet-trained at home. However, he persists in having numerous "accidents" during the school day. Each time an "accident" occurs, David receives immediate attention from the teacher; she immediately undresses him, gives him a bath, and puts on clean clothing. In this situation the teacher is inadvertently rewarding inappropriate behavior by the extra attention given David. In addition, if the other children pick up on the cues or consequences of David's behavior, the teacher may ultimately spend the whole teaching day bathing and changing children who were all formerly toilet-trained.

A final caution in the reinforcement system and its application to the development of appropriate behavior is that the teacher often inadvertently extinguishes appropriate behavior. For example, imagine that you have been working for six weeks under a continuous reinforcement schedule to get Bonnie to sit and attend. Your efforts are paying off, and

Bonnie will now sit and attend for periods of up to five minutes. One day, Bonnie begins to run around the room in random fashion disrupting the class. Without thinking, you grab Bonnie and forcefully place her in a chair. In so doing, you have taken a step towards extinguishing what you have worked six weeks for, and sitting in a chair is now associated with punishment.

The reinforcement system can be a powerful tool in increasing, shaping, and maintaining behavior. However, inappropriate or disruptive behaviors often interfere with the learning process and must be eliminated. Reward systems are an effective means of increasing behavior but are not as effective in the reduction or elimination of inappropriate behavior.

Reducing and Eliminating Behavior

The teacher is often confronted with behaviorial circumstances that seriously interfere with the child's learning or, in extreme cases, pose a threat to the general welfare of the class. The reduction or elimination of these behaviors will involve (1) determining what behaviors are interfering with learning, (2) establishing target behaviors, and (3) developing a schedule for their reduction.

The TMR child's entering behaviors may present the teacher with a number of problems (for example, the child hits, bites, drools, and runs around the room). The teacher's first inclination is to "shotgun" the behaviors and attempt to reduce them all or to target on the behaviors that are personally most offensive. The teacher cannot reduce or eliminate all the behaviors at once, and the target behaviors should be determined on the basis of what benefits the child rather than the teacher.

In order to reduce behaviors effectively, the teacher must determine what behavior has the highest rate of occurrence and interferes most with the child's learning. Admittedly, some behaviors (such as drooling) may be more personally offensive, but a high frequency rate of running around the room probably interferes more with learning and general classroom management.

Ignoring behavior as a technique. Once the behavior is targeted, there are several techniques that can be used to eliminate the inappropriate or undesirable behavior. Extinction of inappropriate behavior may be obtained by simply ignoring the behavior. The simple process involved is that by ignoring the behavior, it does not pay off, and the child stops it. Although simple in its approach, there are some inherent disadvantages. In the process of ignoring the behavior, the teacher must be prepared to deal with an increase in the behavior as the child tries to force attention or try the teacher's patience by increasing or intensifying the behavior. Also, the effects of extinction are not immediate, and the incidence and intensity decrease slowly. These factors often contribute to the teacher "giving in" before the process has had any appreciable effect. Furthermore, extinction requires cooperation from all those who come in contact with the child. For example, the teacher will have limited success in extinguishing a behavior by ignoring it if it is attended to and subsequently rewarded at home. Finally, there are certain behaviors that are so dangerous that they cannot be ignored. For example, if George is chasing Fred with an axe, with obvious malice in his eye, the teacher obviously cannot ignore George, for he will surely rend Fred asunder. This is, of course, an extreme example, but there are certain behaviors that simply cannot be ignored.

Time-out technique. Another frequently used method for reducing behavior is "time out," or the removal from positive reinforcement. The assumption behind this approach is that the classroom is a positive environment. The use of this technique usually requires that the child be physically removed from the environment and placed in isolation for a specified time. If this particular technique is used, the teacher must intervene on the behavior in such a way as to avoid unwittingly reinforcing the behavior by attending to it. When intervening, the teacher must not pause to chastise the child for a period of time prior to placement in the time-out area. Although the teacher's chastisement is negative, it may be reinforcing to the child, because—no matter the consequences—the child has gained the attention of the teacher for a period of time. Therefore, the child must be placed in the time-out area in a very neutral manner, with nothing more than a cursory explanation of the contingencies for removal.

Although often effective in the management of behavior, the time-out process has some environmental and social limitations. Environmentally, the teacher may simply lack the space or extra room for a time-out area. Socially, parents and some professionals have expressed concerns or reservations about "locking up" a child, and consequently the use of "time out" could produce severe reactions and recriminations from parents or school administrators. Finally, and perhaps most devastating, is that time out may have limited impact and may even be rewarding, because the child may like it.

Satiation or overcorrection. Satiation, or overcorrection, is also an effective means of eliminating inappropriate behaviors. The principle involves overattending to the behavior. An example of behavior susceptible to satiation would be that of a child whose eating habits entail grabbing food with her hands and gulping it down without chewing.

Obviously, this behavior must be eliminated before an effective eating program can be initiated. Often our first inclination is to withdraw the food, which merely reinforces the child's fear of deprivation. Reduction of deprivation would be better achieved by supplying food to the satiation level—even unto vomiting—until the fear of deprivation is reduced. Another example of satiatable behavior would be that of the child that continually runs out of the room and up the stairs. The overcorrection procedure would be to make the child repeat the behavior (that is, running up and down the stairs) for a specified period of time.

Punishment.   In some instances, punishment or other forms of aversive therapy are used to reduce or extinguish behavior. This dimension of management is subject to serious controversy. While some behaviorists support certain forms of punishment as an effective means of controlling behavior, others contend that there is never a sufficient reason for the use of these particular procedures. In addition, there is even some marginal disagreement among the proponents on the means and intensity of the process when it is used.

Bensberg (1965) suggests that when punishment is necessary, it should (1) be as mild as possible, (2) fit the child not the crime, and (3) take place at the beginning of the act. Although agreeing with some dimensions of Bensberg's suggestions, Sulzer and Mayer (1972) suggest that the intensity of the punishment be maximized and applied without warning. It is their contention that when punishing, severe punishment tends to be more enduring in terms of eliminating the behavior.

When punishment is used, there are certain principles that should be observed in the process. It must be remembered that timing is critical. Punishment must occur at the moment the act is committed in order for it to be appropriately generalized to the inappropriate behavior, and to insure that there is not time lapse to allow for inadvertently punishing appropriate behavior. In addition, punishment communicates that something is wrong, but does not always specify what; nor does it define appropriate behaviorial alternatives. Therefore, when punishing, the child needs to be informed of what he is being punished for, and what the alternative appropriate behavior is. Some cautions in the use of punishment are that it may cause withdrawal and a negative self concept. Also, there may be some modeling of the aggression and displacement on their peers, or the peers may model the teacher and repeat the punishment (Sulzer & Mayer, 1972).

Certain severe aversive therapies such as shock have been strongly resisted on moral and ethical grounds by many parents and professionals. Subsequently, these are outside the alternatives available for teacher use. If they are used at all, they should be under controlled clinical conditions, and with the full knowledge of all concerned.

Environmental management. A final means of reducing inappropriate behaviors often involves a simple process of environmental management. This is simply eliminating those factors in the environment that may precipitate inappropriate behavior or programming for them in order to eliminate them. For example, short breaks in the day for a few minutes of exercise may tease off excess energy and reduce hyperactivity. In addition, the teacher should maintain an awareness of circumstances or activities that provoke inappropriate behavior. Examples of this would be poor scheduling, an overstimulating classroom environment, or other environmental events like seating arrangements that may precipitate inappropriate behaviors.

One final mention of inappropriate behavior that intrinsically resists extinction. Masturbation, for example, often creates considerable consternation in training programs. The problem is that the behavior is so self-stimulating that elimination of the behavior is nearly impossible. In the case of behavior such as this, the teacher has few alternatives. Increasing the activity level of the class to reduce idle moments or boredom will possibly reduce opportunities for masturbation. Other than this, the teacher will have to be content with defining appropriate areas for the behavior (for example, the bathroom as opposed to public places).

In summary, good teaching is based upon principles of behavior modification that encompass a number of scheduled events that affect behavior. The procedures involve:

1. presenting reinforcing events;
2. withholding reinforcing events;
3. withdrawing aversive events;
4. presenting aversive events;
5. scheduling stimulus events to occur frequently;
6. scheduling stimulus events to occur intermittently. [Haring & Phillips, 1972, p. 17]

These events occur in every classroom, but they must be administered systematically. The critical difference between a well-defined and purposeful program and a "happening" is in the systematic application of these principles.

The evidence to date of success through the employment of behavior modification techniques in training programs is encouraging. However, there is some cause for concern about its too rapid future growth. Bijou (1973) points to a general misunderstanding of the process, limited strategies for training teachers, parent programs, and modification of the curricula as serious problems in including behavior modification in schools on a large scale. In addition, there has been an emerging concern expressed for basic human rights and legal responsibilities in the use of behavior modification, particularly in the ethical issues of imposed value judgments related to the definition of appropriate behaviors and the use of aversive therapy (Martin, 1974).

The resolution of these issues, if they are ever resolved at all, may have implications for the future use of behavior modification techniques. However, at this point in time the available research indicates considerable success in the systematic teaching of a wide variety of skills that were previously determined as unobtainable for TMR population.

Thus far, we have discussed some general principles of behavior modification that may be employed in the training or extinction of certain specific behaviors. The dimensions of the process have been generalized to a total program process, and the current application of behavior modification principles in the classroom has focused on a total systematic precision-teaching model. This is a goal-referenced instructional model based on each learner's behavior, with the objectives of the program being stated in behavioral terms rather than global content areas.

Precision Teaching

Precision teaching is not a new methodology, but a deceptively simple means of providing consistent, systematic instruction. Lindsley (1971) describes precision teaching as an extension of the procedures of operant conditioning to the classroom setting using materials which are familiar to the teacher. He emphasizes that the process is not the dispensing of "synthetic rewards" to the child for repeating the task he has failed; rather, it involves a precise analysis and sequencing of curricular tasks, and the measurement and recording of behavioral frequency to determine progress. In this same context, Haring (1970) has defined precision teaching as "procedures . . . designed to enable the teacher to discover the abilities of each child and allow him to advance at his own individual rate" (p. 7).

The precision process occurs through the determination of instructional objectives that are consistent with individual ability levels. The process involves:

1. Determining instructional goals
2. Assessing entering behaviors

3. Defining instructional procedures
4. Assessing performance or terminal behaviors (Glaser, 1962)

In this model, instructional goals or behavioral objectives are determined by the expressed desirable behavior. Unlike content-referenced goals, these are stated in terms of behaviors that *each* student should display at the termination of instruction.

The entering behaviors are the repertoire of behaviors that the individual exhibits that may need to be increased or decreased to obtain the behavioral objective. The assessment of these behaviors is necessary to determine deficit behaviors (what the student needs to learn) and surplus behaviors (what needs to be extinguished). Once determined, the instructional manipulation and experiences are designed to guide the individual towards the desired terminal behavior. At the termination of instruction, the teacher will reassess the student's behavior to determine how well the individual has learned the expressed behavioral objective.

Determining Behavioral Objectives

Success of the precision-teaching model is dependent upon *specifically* stated behavioral objectives and criteria that are clearly observable and measurable. Deciding on the appropriate behavioral objectives involves observation of the TMR child's behavior in a number of circumstances. Chalfant and Silikovitz (1972) have enumerated eight criteria that may be helpful in the determination of behavioral objectives:

1. Determine prior knowledge. Concentrate on skills and objectives that the child does not already know.
2. Identify prerequisite skills for learning. Determine whether the child has mastered skills that are prerequisite to learning new ones.
3. Determine the relevancy of the objective. High priority should be given to skills that are related to physical well-being and safety.
4. Identify the physical proximity of the objective. Priorities should be given to activities representing people, objects, and situations present in the child's daily environment.
5. Define the frequency of encounter. Determine how frequently a child will encounter or be expected to respond to situations, and give priority to those that they are likely to use most frequently.
6. Express in concrete terms. Concepts based on actual experience should be used before abstractions.
7. Determine the appeal of the objective. Concepts which the child will most likely enjoy will increase the chances of enthusiastic participation.

8. Define behavioral antecedents. Inappropriate or disruptive behaviors which interfere with learning should be dealt with first.

From criteria such as these, priorities can be established for training, goals can be determined, and objectives can be stated in terms of terminal behaviors, or what the child will be expected to do after training.

Stated behavioral objectives are often too broad and general. Teachers often have difficulty in differentiating between a goal or broad generalization and a specifically stated objective. Figure six illustrates the sequential organization of an area of learning and defines the progressive organization of a behavioral objective from a broad curriculum area.

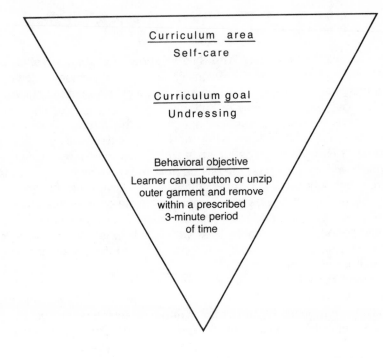

Curriculum area
Self-care

Curriculum goal
Undressing

Behavioral objective
Learner can unbutton or unzip
outer garment and remove
within a prescribed
3-minute period
of time

Figure Six

Progressive sequencing of program

It is important that the objectives be stated specifically and be observable and identifiable through assessment. In addition, the objectives must clearly define the intentions of the instruction process. The proper expression of behavioral objectives is often a simple problem of semantics, where the objective is stated in vague terms, subject to varying interpretations. For example, Mager (1962, p. 11) listed a number of statements that are frequently used in expressing behavioral objectives that are subject to various interpretations:

Words open to many interpretations	Words open to fewer interpretations
to know	to write
to understand	to recite
to really understand	to identify
to appreciate	to differentiate
to fully appreciate	to solve
to grasp the significance of	to construct
to enjoy	to list
to believe	to compare
to have faith in	to contrast

It is not sufficient to say "The child will know how to button a shirt" or "The child will understand the significance of brushing teeth." These statements are not explicit enough and do not define what the children will be doing in the process of buttoning their coats or brushing their teeth. Simply stated, the essential elements of the behavioral objective must describe who, will do what, how well, under what conditions (Payne, 1973). Thus, a better stated objective would be, "Given a garment with buttons, George will be able to button all buttons in the correct buttonholes within three minutes" or "Given toothbrush and toothpaste, Sharon will be able to put toothpaste on a toothbrush and scrub her teeth front and rear, top and bottom, for a prescribed one-minute period." In these objectives we are told what the learner is to work with, how well the task is to be done, and the prescribed time allowed for its completion.

Needless to say, the persistent complaint of teachers is the lack of time for writing these individual objectives. However, once written they can be used repeatedly, and as Isaac and Michael (1971) so succinctly stated, "In helping educators pinpoint their intentions, they will encourage better educational management, more effective classroom procedures, superior feedback to the learner, and a more satisfactory accounting to the public" (p. 164).

Task Analysis

Any behavioral objective has various component parts that lead to successful realization of the objective. A behavioral objective is composed of a hierarchy of tasks that range from the simplest learning to the most complex. The structure for learning any given task is composed of subtasks that must be mastered in an orderly fashion if criterion performance is going to be realized (Gagné, 1967).

Each behavioral objective has various smaller specific tasks that must be ordered sequentially to lead to the terminal behavior. These represent a *chain* of behaviors that are interrelated, with each link of the chain serving as a reinforcer and cue for the next response. The analysis of the objective into a chain of behaviors or responses provides the necessary series of approximations for shaping the behavior through continuous reinforcement and "error-free" learning.

The reduction of the objectives into its constituent parts is a process which begins with the whole (that is, the behavioral objective) and progresses backward to determine the order of tasks or skills that are prerequisite to successful attainment of the objective. This is called "backward chaining," and the last behavior for the completion of the objective is conditioned first. For example, let's continue with George and his buttoning skills. We have determined that George has mastered the prerequisite skills for learning to button his coat. Our behavioral objective is that George will be able to button all buttons in the correct buttonhole within a three-minute period. The objective may be organized like this:

1. Place coat on George with all but the last button in the corresponding buttonholes. The last button is inserted halfway in the buttonhole, and George is instructed to grasp the cloth around the buttonhole and pull the button through, thus completing the buttoning process.

2. The process is repeated, and all buttons but the last button are in their corresponding buttonholes. This time, George must locate the corresponding buttonhole and insert the last button into the buttonhole.

3. The process is repeated, except this time all but the last two buttons are properly inserted. The next to the last button is inserted half way through the buttonhole, and the last button is completely unbuttoned. George is instructed to grasp the cloth around the half-inserted button and pull the button through, and then locate the corresponding buttonhole and button the last button.

This process is continued until George is able to locate and insert every button into its corresponding buttonhole. In shaping George's behavior, we began with the last step or near-completion of the objective. With reinforcement at each level of success, we would proceed with increasingly complex tasks until George has mastered the objective.

The sequencing of this task was appropriate for George, since we previously determined that he had all the prerequisite skills for beginning at the defined task level. However, let us suppose that George is to be joined by three other classmates in this activity. The teacher has defined the task hierarchy for George, but must now determine the different entering behaviors of the three other children. Their prerequisite skills will probably be different from George's, and the teacher must determine whether each child is ready to learn the skill, and at what level in the hierarchy that child is ready to learn. Conceivably, the analysis of the behavioral objective for this group would look something like Table Six.

Table Six

Student performance on task hierarchy for buttoning

Behaviorial objective: Learner will button all buttons in the correct buttonhole within a 3-minute period.

Task level	Student's name
0. No performance	Barbara
8. Buttons with last button half-inserted.	Leonard
7. Buttons last button without assistance	
6. Buttons next-to-last button half-inserted and last button unassisted.	Judy
5. Buttons 3rd button half-inserted and last two buttons unassisted.	
4. Buttons 2nd button half-inserted and last three buttons unassisted.	George
3. Buttons 1st button half-inserted and last four buttons unassisted.	
2. Buttons all five buttons unassisted.	
1. Buttons all five buttons in correct buttonholes within a three-minute period.	

It may be noted that all the children do not begin at the same task level. In fact, Barbara has been found to be unready for even the lowest level of task in the hierarchy (Task 8). Therefore, the teacher will find it necessary to define, through further assessment, the prerequisite skills necessary for Task 8. An example of task analysis of prerequisite skills for buttoning is the following:

1. Barbara can pick up buttons from a flat surface.
2. Barbara can pick up buttons from a flat sufrace and put them in a box.

3. Barbara can pick up buttons from a flat surface and put them in a slot in the lid of a box.
4. Barbara can insert single button in a buttonhole, using a button frame on a flat surface.

Although the children will be expected to progress through the various task levels to the terminal behavior, it must be remembered that Barbara may never reach the task level necessary to learn to button, or that Leonard may never progress beyond Task 8. Therefore, for those children who demonstrate a lack of ability or understanding of the terminal behavior, the teacher will have to develop a compensatory mode of instruction that more realistically reflects the child's ability level. For example, if a child cannot master buttoning skills, the compensatory skill may be instruction in dressing with pullover type shirts, or the use of *Velcro,* a commercially prepared pressure-sensitive tape for closing open garments.

For those children who enjoy successful skill mastery, the teacher must also be careful to continue to reinforce obtained skills. Too frequently the process breaks down because the child will master a subtask and move on to the next level and the teacher assumes well-integrated mastery of the previous task and withdraws reinforcers. It must be remembered that the subtasks are all interrelated, and it is important to increase efficiency in previous skills through a continuing reinforcement system.

In summary, the precision teaching technique is designed to assist the teacher in identifying and structuring learning experiences appropriate to the child's ability and needs which will allow the child to progress at her or his own rate of learning. This technique relies upon a systematic process of identifying instructional goals, evaluation and determination of procedures, and assessment of terminal behaviors.

Precision-teaching Programs

There are a limited number of programs or packages commercially available that use the precision-teaching approach. A few of these prepared programs have gained considerable attention in training programs and have an emerging number of advocates who feel that they have some inherent qualities that may make them a significant force in training programs in the years to come.

The work of Bijou et al. (1966) with a group of mildly and moderately retarded children at the Rainier School in the state of Washington, provided the knowledge and inspiration for the Edmark Reading Program (1972). The Edmark program uses the technology of operant behavior and is designed to teach vocabulary, comprehension, and use of a total of 150 words. The prerequisite skills for students are only that they can repeat words, respond by pointing, and have sufficient receptive language to respond to direction by words or gesture. No special skills or training—other than a positive attitude toward the student—is required of the teacher. The teaching model, illustrated in Figure Seven is a systematic process of stimulus-response-reinforcement. The sequence of presentation is systematic, and reinforcement is intrinsic.

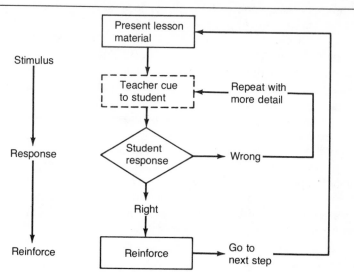

NOTE: Figure from Teacher's Guide, *Edmark Reading Program* (Seattle, Wash.: Edmark Associates, 1972).

Figure Seven

Teacher's model for Edmark program

The program has had seven major revisions since its introduction and currently claims 98% effectiveness in teaching reading to the severely retarded. Although the reported success rate is quite high, there is, at this time, a paucity of research to substantiate these claims. The newness of the material precludes the possibility of longitudinal studies, and there is no reported evidence on the temporal stability of the 98% success rate. However, the publishers believe that the temporal stability of the gains in reading will be a function of where the child goes after leaving the program, and whether the reinforcers are continued.

These limitations notwithstanding, the Edmark program is a research-based program that grew out of extensive clinical research in the application of an operant model to the teaching of academic subjects. The informal reporting of the results in the classroom are promising, but the ultimate relevance of the content for the TMR population and their adult role in society is yet to be determined. The principal value of the Edmark program in the TMR classroom may be the systematic program model that could be applied to other areas of learning.

Another systematic learning package developed for the TMR population is Project MORE (Lent et al., 1974). Project MORE is specifically designed to teach self-help and daily living skills. Although the total program is still under development, there are training packages currently available for teaching eating, nose-blowing, hand-washing, and toothbrushing. Additional programs for teaching other self-help and daily living skills are currently under development.

The MORE programs are designed for use by teachers and aides. The teaching strategy is based on the model illustrated in Figure Eight and is programmed in an easy "how-to" fashion that is result-oriented rather than data-oriented.

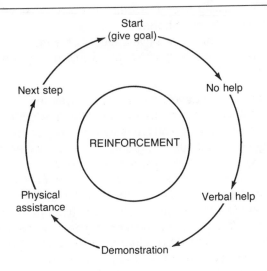

Level 1: *No help*
The trainer waits approximately
10 seconds to see if the student
will perform the step independently.

Level 2: *Verbal help*
The trainer tells the student what
to do.

Level 3: *Demonstration*
The trainer demonstrates
the step while telling
the student what to do.

Level 4: *Physical help*
The trainer physically
helps the student
perform the step.

NOTE: Figure from J. R. Lent, I. Keilitz, C. D. Foster, and B. M. McLean, *Project MORE* (Parsons, Kansas: University of Kansas Bureau of Child Research, Parsons State Hospital and Training Center, 1975).

Figure Eight

Project MORE teaching strategy

At this point in time, the only apparent serious limitation to the use of MORE programs in the classroom is the requirement for a one-to-one teacher-pupil ratio in the instruction process.

The operant technology has also been used in the development of total program training models. Chalfant and Silikovitz (1972) developed an experimental program for the systematic instruction of retarded children in the areas of self-help, language, and motor performance and recreation. This program is based on the contention that the TMR are capable of learning multiple skills through proper instructional procedures when emphasis is placed on behavior modification techniques in the program. In this program, the authors defined four conditions for learning:

1. Systematic instruction based on task analysis
2. Errorless learning based on reinforcing approximations to and leading up to terminal behaviors
3. Reinforcement of the positive aspects of learning
4. Criteria-based teaching which gives information on mastery of each skill level

The authors have developed a precise system for the teacher to use in each of the curriculum areas. The language portion of the program has been field tested, and the results were optimistic in indicating the possibility of a "total push program" where a number of objectives, taught systematically, will complement each other.

The particular limitations of this program are (1) the program was developed on a small number of children (ten children with Down's syndrome), (2) the self-help and motor curriculum have not been field tested, (3) the staff-pupil ratio in the program development (three to one in instructional situations), and (4) there is no determination of the range of population that may profit from the program. These limitations notwithstanding, the information obtained indicates that the *Systematic Instruction Program* merits continued use and exploration in programs for the TMR.

One final total program that merits mention is the program developed by Watson (1972) at the Columbus State Institute, Columbus, Ohio. Watson's program is a behavior modification program that is designed to be used in homes, classrooms, day-care centers, and institutions. The content areas encompass self-help, language, and social-recreational behavior.

The program is very carefully and completely designed to insure success in the shaping of a number of complex behaviors. It is unique in its detail and formation from a conceptual "model child" level. The author contends that human behavior is complex and therefore should be painstakingly written. The "model child" concept, as the antecedent to determining target behaviors, is a model of "normality." The program attempts to make the retarded as normal as possible in the community in which they will be living.

The success of these and other precision-teaching programs using behavior modification techniques has provided a more optimistic outlook for the TMR population. However, these programs are so new that further assessment will be needed to verify their efficacy in terms of persistent life situations and adult prognosis. Our optimism must then be guarded in terms of the ultimate potential of this new technology and its application in teaching increasingly complex skills. Nevertheless, behavior modification and the precision-teaching model have provided a positive step in the remediation and training of certain skills that were previously considered unobtainable for many of the trainable mentally retarded.

There are, of course, other approaches to programs that have been employed with some measure of success. These grew out of an extension of the early processes developed by Itard and Seguin, following closely the physiological method.

Perceptual-Motor Training

Kephart (1971) has defined a neurological framework for developmental organization in terms of integrated motor patterns involving (1) the basic motor skills of movement within the environment, (2) the processing of information at the perceptual-motor level, (3) a perceptual-conceptual organization which ultimately results in (4) a well-integrated conceptual level of functioning. Kephart's contention is that failure to learn any of these basic patterns will interfere with subsequent learning.

According to Kephart (1971), if this developmental hierarchy is disrupted, it is necessary to identify the stage or processing method that is incomplete and train it to an appropriate level to allow for successful achievement and development of subsequent skills. In so doing, he notes, "The crux of the problem is to teach development—to help the child achieve a developmental task, to teach him how to learn rather than presenting him with facts to be learned" (p. 45).

Thus, Kephart advocates a direct attack on the developmental problems of the retarded and training of the processing methods before subject matter is attempted. To do this, a series of activities were designed to observe the child's perceptual-motor behavior (Roach & Kephart, 1966) and to be used as training exercises. These activities are concerned with areas such as (1) sensory-motor training, (2) body concepts, (3) directionality, (4) ocular control, and (5) form perception.

The procedures for training in these areas involve the use of walking beams for training balance and laterality; identification and control of body parts through touch and imitation of movement; sensory-motor activities like "Angels in the Snow," "Stepping Stones," and obstacle courses; chalkboard scribbling to train directionality and smooth movement of motor patterns; visual tracing for the training of ocular pursuit and proper ocular control; and use of puzzles, peg boards, and so on for training form perception.

The Kephart theory of motor learning and development is perhaps more systematic than the "method." The activities are more a series of techniques than a method. Kephart indicates that the techniques should not be considered goals in themselves but merely a means by which the child can be taught generalized skills and abilities.

The importance of neurological organization in the education process has also been identified by Delacato (1959; 1963; 1966). His concern for reading problems led him to study the common characteristics of poor readers. In general, he surmised that the difference between good and poor readers was due to neurological differences or problems. From this early work, the Doman-Delacato Theory of Neuropsychology emerged. This theory is based upon the premise that human development repeats the pattern of man's evolutionary development and that if an individual does not follow a sequential continuum of neurological development, problems in mobility and/or communication will result.

The theories of Kephart and Doman and Delacato are similar in that both programs are developed from the premise that the remediation process should be directed towards factors that interfere with the orderly process of neurological organization and that this development is directly related to psychomotor development. However, Doman and Delacato differ in that their procedures and restorative claims have created considerable controversy, and various professional organizations have seriously questioned their credibility. According to the Doman-Delacato theory, if their measure of "neurological organization" indicates a missing or poorly developed developmental phase, then the individual's performance in that area is below normal. The remediation of this problem is approached by a return to the lowest level of the developmental sequence and a progressive reworking up through the sequence to its highest level of functioning—hence, the frequent reference to the "creeping and crawling curriculum," because the prescribed training sequence for neurological organization often involves returning to the primitive developmental process of early infancy (such as relearning to crawl as a sequential step to walking).

The Doman-Delacato methods have been subjected to very little empirical scrutiny, and various medical organizations, the NARC, and other organizations operating in the interest of the mentally retarded have expressed a concern for the misleading evidence about curative aspects of the program.

Kershner (1967) investigated the application of their theories to TMR children in public schools. The experimental group was provided training consistent with the Doman-Delacato theory, and the control group was trained according to Kephart's procedures. Through pre- and post-testing of the two groups, the investigator did find support for the Doman-Delacato theory by IQ gains obtained in the experimental group. Although this study did provide some validity for the theory, the author indicated a need for a replication of the study on a much larger scale before any conclusion about the efficacy of this approach can be made.

In a more recent study (Neman, Roos, McCann, Menolascino, & Heal, 1975) using sixty-six institutionalized retardates as subjects, the "patterning" program of the Doman-Delacato method was evaluated. The conclusions drawn from this study were that there was no significant improvement in global intelligence or motor performance. However, gains in language development, spatial perception, and in the overall Profile of Development were noted. This led the authors to conclude that the patterning procedures may have a measurable effect on some behavioral domains. However, they cautioned that extensive additional research was necessary to determine the ultimate potency and efficacy of this treatment method over other approaches to program.

The findings of Neman *et al.* (1975) precipitated immediate professional reaction (Zigler & Seitz, 1975). This reaction discounted the positive findings, and it was the contention of Zigler and Seitz that the small, significantly positive findings could well occur by chance. Furthermore, the mechanics of the study were seriously questioned.

Neman (1975), in a counter-reaction to Zigler and Seitz, questioned the validity of their commentary and noted that the study was not intended to mislead. He emphasized again that further studies needed to be done before the efficacy of the Doman-Delacato procedure could be determined.

The relationship between perceptual-motor/psychomotor development and intelligence remains obscure. The evidence to date would serve to indicate that perceptual-motor/psychomotor development may be a viable component in the training process, but would not merit the status of a "total program." The trainable mentally retarded exhibit a universe of behavior that must be acted upon, and current evidence appears to indicate that the operant procedures have been demonstrably more successful than other methods and are the most adaptable to the greater number of program areas and in the maintenance of the general learning environment.

Summary

Early procedures in training programs were usually ineffective and contributed much to the limited impact of programs for the TMR. In recent years, a great deal of interest has been expressed in the use of behavior modification techniques in training programs. The success of these techniques in training skills previously determined unobtainable for the TMR population has resulted in an expanded application of the process into the classroom and the development of a precision-teaching model for training. The precision-teaching model is based upon the identification of specific behavioral objectives for each student's training. These objectives are goal-referenced rather than content-referenced. The implementation of this teaching strategy has been remarkably successful, and there is an emerging body of commercially prepared precision-teaching materials designed to assist the teacher in training academic subjects, self-help, language, social adjustment, and motor skills.

There have been other proposed program models that employ a developmental approach to learning designed to remediate developmental neurological deficits. These programs have not had the credibility or success that the application of behavior modification principles has had; and it appears that the behavior modification-precision teaching strategy holds the greatest promise for significantly increasing the functioning level of the trainable mentally retarded.

References

Altman, R., & Talkington, L. W. Modeling: An alternative behavior modification approach for retardates. *Mental Retardation,* 1971, *9,* 20–23.

Azrin, N. H., Bugle, C., & O'Brien, F. Behaviorial engineering: two apparatuses for toilet training retarded children. *Journal of Applied Behaviorial Analysis,* 1971, *4,* 249–253.

Azrin, N. H., & Foxx, R. M. A rapid method of toilet training the institutionalized retarded. *Journal of Applied Behaviorial Analysis,* 1971, *4,* 89–99.

Bensberg, G. J. *Teaching the mentally retarded: A handbook for ward personnel.* Atlanta, Ga.: Southern Regional Education Board, 1965.

Bensberg, G. J., Colwell, C. N., & Cassel, R. H. Teaching the profoundly retarded self help skill activities by behavior shaping techniques. *American Journal of Mental Deficiency,* 1965, *69,* 674–679.

Birnbrauer, J. S., Bijou, S. W., Wolf, M., & Kidder, J. D. Programmed instruction in the classroom. In L. P. Ullman & L. Krasner (Eds.), *Case studies in behavior modification.* New York: Holt, Rinehart, & Winston, 1965.

Birnbrauer, J. S., & Lawler, J. Token reinforcement for learning. *Mental Retardation,* 1964, *2,* 275–279.

Bijou, S. W. A functional analysis of retarded development. In N. R. Ellis (Ed.), *International review of research in mental retardation.* New York: Academic Press, 1966.

Bijou, S. W. Behavior modification in teaching the retarded child. In C. E. Thoresen (Ed.), *Behavior Modification in Education.* Chicago, Ill.: The National Society for the Study of Education, 1973.

Bijou, S. W., & Baer, D. M. *Child development vol. 1: A systematic and empirical theory.* New York: Appleton-Century-Crofts, 1961.

Bijou, S. W., & Baer, D. M. Operant methods in child behavior and development. In W. Honig (Ed.), *Operant behavior: Areas of research and application.* New York: Appleton-Century-Crofts, 1966.

Bijou, S. W., Birnbrauer, J. S., Kidder, J. D., & Tague, C. Programmed instruction as an approach to the teaching of reading, writing and arithmetic to retarded children. *Psychological Record,* 1966, *16,* 505–522.

Chalfant, J. C., & Silikovitz, R. G. *Systematic instruction for retarded children: The Illinois program.* Springfield, Ill.: Superintendent of Public Instruction, 1972.

Delacato, C. H. *The treatment and prevention of reading problems.* Springfield, Ill.: Charles C. Thomas, 1959.

Delacato, C. H. *The diagnosis and treatment of speech and reading problems.* Springfield, Ill.: Charles C. Thomas, 1963.

Delacato, C. H. *Neurological organization and reading.* Springfield, Ill.: Charles C. Thomas, 1966.

Edmark reading program. Seattle, Wash.: Edmark Associates, 1972.

Forness, S. R. Behavior modification as an educational training tool. In J. M. Gardner (Ed.), *Selected papers from the 94th annual meeting of the American Association on Mental Deficiency, vol. 1.* Orient, Ohio: Department of Research and Development, Orient State Institute, 1970.

Gagne, R. M. *Learning and individual differences.* Columbus, Oh.: Charles C. Merrill, 1967.

Girardeau, F. L., & Spradlin, J. E. Token rewards in a cottage program. *Mental Retardation,* 1964, *2,* 345–351.

Glaser, R. Psychology and instructional technology. In R. Glaser (Ed.), *Training research and education.* Pittsburgh, Pa.: University of Pittsburgh Press, 1962.

Guskin, S. L., & Spicker, H. H. Educational research in mental retardation. In N. R. Ellis (Ed.), *International review of research in mental retardation, vol. 3.* New York: Academic Press, 1968.

Haring, N. G. Preface. In H. P. Kunzelman (Ed.), *Precision teaching: An initial training sequence.* Seattle, Wash.: Special Child Publications, 1970.

Haring, N. G., & Lovitt, T. C. Operant methodology and educational technology in special education. In N. G. Haring & R. L. Schiefelbusch (Eds.), *Methods in special education.* New York: McGraw-Hill, 1967.

Haring, N. G., & Phillips, E. L. *Analysis and modification of classroom behavior.* Englewood Cliffs, N. J.: Prentice-Hall, 1972.

Hunt, J. G., Fitzburgh, L. C., & Fitzburgh, K. B. Teaching 'exit-ward' patients appropriate personal appearance behavior by using reinforcement techniques. *American Journal of Mental Deficiency*, 1968, *73*, 41–45.

Isaac, S., & Michael, W. B. *Handbook in research and evaluation.* San Diego, Ca.: Robert R. Knapp, 1971.

Karen, R. L., & Maxwell, S. S. Strengthening self help behavior in the retardate. *American Journal of Mental Deficiency*, 1967, *71*, 546–550.

Kephart, N. C. *The slow learner in the classroom* (2nd ed.). Columbus, Oh.: Charles E. Merrill, 1971.

Kershner, J. R. *An investigation of the Doman-Delacato theory of neuropsychology as it applies to trainable mentally retarded children in public schools.* Harrisburg, Pa.: Department of Public Instruction, 1967.

Lent, J. R., Keilitz, I., Foster, C. D., & McLean, B. M. *Project MORE*. Parsons, Kansas: University of Kansas Bureau of Child Research, Parsons State Hospital and Training Center, 1974.

Lindsley, O. R. Precision teaching in perspective. *Teaching Exceptional Children*, 1971, *3*, 114–119.

Lovitt, T. Behavior modification: The current scene. *Exceptional Children*, 1970, *37*, 85–91.

MacMillan, D. L. Ground rules for behavior modification. In J. M. Gardner (Ed.), *Selected papers from the 94th annual meeting of the American Association on Mental Deficiency, vol. 1.* Orient, Oh.: Department of Research and Development, Orient State Institute, 1970.

Mager, R. F. *Preparing instructional objectives.* Palo Alto, Ca.: Fearson Publishers, 1962.

Martin, R. *Behavior modification: Human rights and legal responsibilities:* Champaign, Ill.: Research Press, 1974.

McCarthy, J. J., & Scheerenberger, R. C. A decade of research in the education of the mentally retarded. *Mental Retardation Abstracts.* Washington, D.C.: U.S. Government Printing Office, 1966.

Minge, M. R., & Ball, T. S. Teaching self help skills to profoundly retarded patients. *American Journal of Mental Deficiency*, 1967, *71*, 864–868.

Nawas, M. M., & Braun, S. H. The use of operant techniques for modifying the behavior of the severely and profoundly retarded: Part I introduction and initial phase. *Mental Retardation*, 1970, *8*, 2–6. (a)

Nawas, M. M., & Braun, S. H. An overview of behavior modification with the severely and profoundly retarded: Part III maintenance of change and epilogue. *Mental Retardation*, 1970, *4*, 4–11. (b)

Neisworth, J. T., & Smith, R. M. *Modifying retarded behavior.* Boston, Mass.: Houghton Mifflin, 1973.

Neman, R. A reply to Zigler and Seitz. *American Journal of Mental Deficiency*, 1975, *79*, 493–505.

Neman, R., Roos, P., McCann, B. M., Menolascino, F. J., & Heal, L. W. Experimental evaluation of sensorimotor patterning used with mentally retarded children. *American Journal of Mental Deficiency,* 1975, *79,* 372–383.

Pavlov, I. *Conditioned reflexes.* London: Oxford University Press, 1927.

Payne, T., *Behaviorial objectives.* Kettering, Ohio: Behaviorial Products, 1973.

Perline, I. H., & Levinsky, D. Controlling maladaptive classroom behavior in the severely retarded. *American Journal of Mental Deficiency,* 1968, *73,* 74–78.

Premack, D. Toward empirical behavior laws: I positive reinforcement. *Psychological Review,* 1959, *66,* 219–233.

Rentfrow, R. K., & Rentfrow, P. K. Studies related to toilet training of the mentally retarded. *American Journal of Occupational Therapy,* 1969, *23,* 425–430.

Roach, E. G., & Kephart, N. C. *The Purdue perceptual-motor survey.* Columbus, Oh.: Charles E. Merrill, 1966.

Roos, P., & Oliver, M. Evaluation of operant conditioning with institutionalized retarded children. *American Journal of Mental Deficiency,* 1969, *74,* 325–330.

Skinner, B. F. *Science and human behavior.* New York: Free Press, 1953.

Sulzer, B., & Mayer, G. R. *Behavior modification procedures for school personnel.* Hinsdale, Ill.: Dryden Press, 1972.

Watson, L. S. *How to use behavior modification with mentally retarded and autistic children: Programs for administrators, teachers, parents and nurses.* Columbus, Oh.: Behavior Modification Technology, 1972.

Watson, L. S. *Child behavior modification: A manual for teachers, nurses and parents.* New York: Pergamon Press, 1973.

Zigler, E., & Seitz, V. On "An experimental evaluation of sensorimotor patterning": A critique. *American Journal of Mental Deficiency,* 1975, *79,* 483–492.

Chapter 6

General Program Planning

In planning a class for the trainable mentally retarded, there are several factors that must be considered. The program will essentially reflect the teacher, the physical facility, and the type of student enrolled in the class. Although the aegis of administrative responsibility for training has, for all practical purposes, fallen to the public schools, there are frequent problems with the facilities used for classrooms and in the definition of types of student to be enrolled in the program.

Physical facilities for training programs have often, historically, been somewhat less than adequate. As was noted in Chapter Two, the early programs were usually located in the basements of churches or other community facilities that often, at best, barely met minimum fire and safety standards. The early influx of the TMR into the public schools did not significantly alter these circumstances, and space was usually allocated on the basis of what was available, rather than what was appropriate or amenable to the type of program offered and the children to be served.

The Facility

Baumgartner (1955) has noted that the proper choice of building or room is very important in carrying out the curriculum. In recent years, remarkable progress has been made in the quality and organization of classes for the TMR, and there are currently several alternatives employed in the housing and administration of community classes.

Administrative Alternatives

The Special Class

This type of provision for a program usually entails the location of the class within the physical confines of the public school. It is usually limited to a single class serving a heterogeneous group of TMR children. Although inclusion of the TMR in the mainstream of public education has been advocated, their best interests have not usually been met through this arrangement; and this is, perhaps, the least desirable alternative for a program. The type of class provided is often restricted by available classroom space, which was designed for a traditional educational program. These rooms are usually not self-contained, and often have

171

numerous physical barriers (such as stairways and traditional toileting facilities), which limits the program and the type of children that can be served. In addition, location within the public school usually means numerous interruptions during the day (such as bells signaling changes in class) and restrictions in the scheduling of important program areas (such as having to eat in the lunchroom rather than the classroom, on the usual public school schedule of twenty minutes—"eat, burp and go").

The Special Center

This type of facility is usually a separate building located on the school grounds or in an abandoned school building made available by the public school. There is usually sufficient space in the special center to provide for all age levels in homogeneous classes ranging from six years of age to adolescence. This arrangement is much preferred over the special class but may still have certain limitations. Abandoned school buildings or other traditional school facilities are just that— traditional school facilities. These were not built with a handicapped population in mind, and unless extensively renovated, may have numerous physical barriers and safety hazards. In addition, although designed to serve a wider range of the TMR, this alternative still often represents single-agency responsibility. The school provides for and administers the total program, with limited to no service from other disciplines (for example, Mental Health, Public Health, Vocational Rehabilitation) that are often necessary to meet unique training needs.

The Comprehensive Community Center

This alternative for program is often much like the special center. The physical facility is usually a building that has been renovated or constructed to serve a wide range of the TMR in homogeneous classes. It differs only in that it is operated and financed by a cooperative group (such as the public school, Department of Human Resources, public health, child welfare) and designed to provide total comprehensive services to the TMR and their families at all ages from preschool through adulthood. If appropriate services are to be provided, this alternative appears to be the most viable of the three in providing total community programs for the TMR and their families.

Space Requirements

The appropriate type and size of the training facility must, almost by historical axiom, be large and spacious. In 1866, Seguin (1971) noted that:

> The buildings of the institution must have a special character, unlike those of any other educational establishment, to correspond with

certain idiosyncrasies of the children and with numerous exigencies of their treatment. Idiots vitiate the air very rapidly; hence the necessity of supplying them with more than an ordinary share of it, by making their rooms very high and large, very airy and easily ventilated, accessible equally to natural and artificial heat. Their training, unlike that of ordinary children, requiring movement, noise and show, demands a special distribution of the building. [p. 252]

A review of various program guides indicates that large space is still a current consideration in providing the TMR an opportunity for freedom of movement. Single-floor plans and areas of 900 square feet are recommended for rooms or sixty square feet per child, exclusive of storage space and equipment (Baumgartner, 1955; Molloy, 1972; Williams, 1963).

Equipment and Materials

Other classroom standards, such as equipment, furniture, and supplies, are usually dictated by the type and age level of TMR in the program. It is the general opinion of most educators that the classroom should be self-contained to allow the teacher to structure the total learning environment. This means that there should be appropriate equipment and furniture within the classroom to allow for training in toileting and other health habits. In addition, other pieces of equipment, such as stove, refrigerator, sink and cabinets, workbenches, and tables, should be provided for training. Additional supplies will be dependent upon the individual teacher, the age of the students, and the focus of the program. Baumgartner (1955) and Johnson and Lavely (1966) have provided representative lists of items and smaller equipment that may be useful in specific areas of training. These include items such as those listed in Table Seven.

Table Seven

Items for Various Activities

Grooming Aids

mirror
soap
towels
washcloths
toothbrushes
toothpaste
combs
nail file
nail clippers
nail brush
deodorant

water cups
shoe polish & brush
facial tissues

Table & eating equipment

dishes
silverware
glasses
napkins
placemats
straws

(continued next page)

Table Seven
Table and eating equipment, cont.

trays
cooking utensils
dish towels
dish clothes

Cleaning equipment

broom
dust mop
dust pan
dust cloth
sponges
small mop
pan
bucket
soap & detergent
cleanser
aprons

Communication skills

play telephones
picture books
picture file
puppets

Toys & games

balls
blocks
puzzles
dolls
dollhouse
doll stroller
jumping ropes
rubber animals
train

trucks
cars
bean bag & ring toss
tricycles

Resting

aluminum cots for young
children

Music

records
record player
autoharp

Arts & crafts

paper—newsprint & construction
paint
brushes
crayons
chalk
scissors
paste or other adhesive
wood scraps
felt
sandpaper
clay
hammer
saw
wood file
nails
yarn
plaster
string
finger paint

In addition, items such as the following may be useful for training activities in the classroom:

Self-care training

buttons
buckles
zippers
ribbon for tying

Economic usefulness

lawn & garden tools
lawn mower
furniture for home living area
iron

Self-care training	Economic usefulness
old shoes	ironing board
old adult clothing	washing machine & dryer

Safety

safety signs
survival vocabulary cards
play traffic apparatus

There are numerous other materials and equipment that are commercially available and may be useful in the classroom. These have become so numerous in recent years that the teacher must choose wisely the merits of the various materials available.

Bleil (1975) has offered some guidelines that may assist the teacher in the decision-making process about "What to buy?" He cautions teachers to watch out for:

1. The use of superlative adjectives, indicating magic solutions without publisher guarantees
2. Diagnostic labels ("Specifically designed for the trainable classroom") applied to materials without substantiation that the material is, in fact, appropriate for the population so labeled
3. Fad words or phrases like, "high interest-low vocabulary" used in the material without defining the circumstances of this claim or whether the concept is measurable
4. Grade-level designation for material without specific information on how this particular level was arrived at

In selecting materials, he indicated that the teacher should:

1. Apply common sense or instinctive values in the determination of the appropriateness of the material
2. Look for honest, realistic statements about the projected outcomes from the use of the material
3. Determine whether the materials are realistic in terms of the fundamental management problems in the classroom
4. Identify editorial quality control
5. Evaluate the expertise of the author or authors
6. Obtain information on the success rate of previous users of the material under circumstances similar to your own

Unfortunately, the material is often unavailable for teacher evaluation, and money is wasted or poorly spent on materials that prove to be of limited value in the classroom. In recognition of this problem, the U.S. Office of Education, Bureau of Handicapped Children and Youth, was provided funds in 1963, under Title III, Section 302 of PL 88–164, to begin to establish a regional network of Special Education Instructional

Materials Centers (SEIMC) to assist in the development and evaluation of materials. Table Eight is a list of the currently existing centers and the areas that they serve.

The centers are designed to serve teachers and other professionals working with handicapped children. The SEIMC's provide many material-related services. They can make material available for teacher evaluation and provide additional evaluation and consultation on the efficacy of materials to be used in the classroom.

In the development of a training program, the materials, curriculum, and general procedures should also reflect the children who are enrolled. Circumstances such as age, handicapping condition, and criteria used for selection will largely determine the major thrust of the program. The criteria used for admission will vary, depending upon the type of agency supporting the program. Public school program eligibility may differ significantly from the admission criteria of a state agency-supported program (such as child welfare).

Selection of Students

The criteria for admission of TMR children into the public school program vary from state to state. However, there has been some commonality in specific criteria for placement of TMR children in special classes. These have been and will continue to be altered by court action. Court decisions like those of Pennsylvania *(Pennsylvania Association for Retarded Children* v. *Commonwealth of Pennsylvania)* and the District of Columbia *(Mills* v. *Board of Education of the District of Columbia)* have had a profound impact on the selective criteria usually employed in the admission of TMR children into the public schools. The courts, in these decisions, ordered that *every* child must be provided a free public education according to ability level.

Criteria for Eligibility

Various authors (Baumgartner, 1955; Gardner & Nisonger, 1962; Johnson & Lavely, 1966; Rothstein, 1971) have listed a number of general criteria that have frequently been used in placing a TMR child in special classes in the public school. They involved consideration of circumstances such as the following.

1. Must comply with state required minimum chronological age standards (most states use a minimum CA of 6)
2. Must have been determined ineligible for a class for educable mentally retarded
3. Must have a measured IQ at least three standard deviations below the mean of the test used

Table Eight

Learning resource centers for handicapped children and youth

Resource center	Area served
Clinical Services Building University of Oregon Eugene, Oregon	Alaska, Hawaii, Samoa, Guam, Trust Territory, Washington, Oregon, Idaho, Montana, Wyoming
Area Learning Resource Center 600 South Commonwealth Suite 1304 Los Angeles, California 90005	California
New Mexico State University P.O. Box 3AW Las Cruces, New Mexico 88003	Nevada, Utah, Colorado, Arizona, New Mexico, & BIA Schools
Midwest ALRC Drake University 1336 26th Street Des Moines, Iowa 50311	North Dakota, South Dakota, Kansas, Nebraska, Oklahoma, Iowa, Missouri, Arkansas
Texas ALRC University of Texas at Austin 2613 Wichita Austin, Texas 78712	Texas

(Table Eight continued next page)

177

Table Eight continued

Resource center	Area served
Great Lakes ALRC P.O. Box 420 Michigan Department of Education Lansing, Michigan 48902	Minnesota, Wisconsin, Michigan, Indiana
Educational Media and Information Service Department for Exceptional Children Illinois Office of Education 100 North First Street Springfield, Illinois 62777	Illinois
Ohio Division of Special Education 933 High Street Worthington, Ohio 43085	Ohio
Northeast ALRC 168 Bank Street Hightstown, New Jersey 08520	Maine, Vermont, New Hampshire, Massachusetts, Rhode Island, Connecticut, New Jersey
New York State LARC New York State Education Department Division for Handicapped Children 55 Elk Street Albany, New York	New York

National Learning Resource Center of Pennsylvania
443 South Gulph Road
King of Prussia, Pennsylvania 19406

Pennsylvania

Mid-East ALRC
University of Kentucky
123 Porter Building
Lexington, Kentucky 40506

Delaware, D.C., Maryland, Virginia,
West Virginia, Kentucky, Tennessee,
North Carolina, Puerto Rico,
Virgin Islands

Southeast LRC
Auburn University at Montgomery
Montgomery, Alabama 36109

Louisiana, Mississippi, Alabama,
Georgia, South Carolina, Florida

Serving all ALRCs:
NCEMMH Coordination Services for ALRCs
National Center on Educational Media and Materials for the
    Handicapped
The Ohio State University
220 West 12th Avenue
Columbus, Ohio 43210

179

4. Must be ambulatory
5. Must be able to see and hear well enough to participate in class activities
6. Must be toilet-trained
7. Must have sufficient communication skills to make their wants known
8. Must not have serious personality problems that would preclude adjustment to the classroom situation
9. Must be physically able to attend class on a full-day basis
10. Must pose no physical danger to themselves or others
11. Must be able to profit from the training program

The interpretation and application of criteria such as these is usually at the discretion of the local school system. However, exclusion from the program on the basis of these or any similar criteria is going to become increasingly difficult and is inconsistent with current court-ordered standards. Also, interpretation of individual criteria should be made in consideration of circumstances such as classroom facilities, staff-pupil ratio, and the teacher's ability to handle the situation. For example, a child in a wheelchair may be "ambulatory" and eligible for placement in the classroom if there are no physical barriers and sufficient provisions for wheelchairs have been made. Other criteria, such as a measure of intelligence, are also insufficient cause for exclusion, since by current definition (Grossman, 1973), we would have to consider the broader dimensions of adaptive behavior.

Once a child is determined eligible for placement in the classroom, it is often recommended that admission be on a trial basis (Baumgartner, 1955; Williams, 1963) to determine whether the child is appropriately placed, how well the child can adjust to the training situation, and whether the child can profit from the training program. In order to assess these factors, the trial period should be approximately four to six weeks in duration, with teacher options for extension in those cases where a final determination of continued participation cannot be made.

Other provisions for community programs through the Department of Human Resources, child welfare, or a similar agency must be provided for those children who are determined ineligible for public school special class or who, because of age or handicapping condition, cannot meet criteria for public-school, special-class placement.

Staff-Pupil Ratio

The number of children who can be accepted in a special class is usually contingent upon facility, staff, and the homogeneity-heterogeneity of the group. As previously discussed, the facility or classroom space should be sufficient to provide ample square footage per child to prevent overcrowding and other safety or health hazards.

It is usually recommended that programs for the TMR have a minimum staff ratio of one aide per two teachers, but it would be most desirable if each classroom had a teacher and a full-time aide. Staff-pupil ratio is usually determined by state standards, but a recommended staff-pupil ratio for TMR classes is approximately six children per adult, or a classroom of twelve children with a teacher and an aide (National Association for Retarded Citizens, 1971).

Staff-pupil ratio may be affected by circumstances such as the homogeneity-heterogeneity of the class and the children's previous program experience. The maintenance of a reasonable training environment will depend upon the heterogeneity of the handicapping conditions. For example, if the class has a number of nonambulatory children or a number of hyperactive children, six children per adult may be excessive. Also, the age range of the group will affect what may be considered a manageable number of children; classes of very young children, or classes comprising a wide age range may need to be reduced in number for safety as well as training reasons. Finally, if the class is newly organized and none of the children has participated in program previously, the initial enrollment may need to be somewhat less than would be necessary for a class of children with previous experience in training programs.

An additional consideration that may affect program and planning would be the teachers—their training and qualifications. Historically, the lack of teacher training programs for working with trainable children and adults resulted in the employment of teachers with little or no training, other than, perhaps, having children of their own and being identified as warm, responsive people. This practice is rapidly changing. Colleges and universities are beginning to respond to the need for trained personnel in training programs in the public schools, and degree requirements and certification are being imposed on persons aspiring to work with the trainable mentally retarded.

Teacher Qualifications

The various states usually require a valid teaching certificate for teachers in public school classes for the trainable mentally retarded. College preparation for this certification usually involves a four-year baccalaureate, with program emphasis in areas deemed appropriate for teaching the trainable mentally retarded. The focus of this training varies according to state requirements but usually has emphasis on course work in:

1. Child development and early childhood education
2. Introduction to the general area of mental retardation

3. Curriculum and methods for the TMR
4. Behavior management
5. Speech and language development
6. Family counseling
7. Practicum in teaching the TMR

In addition to the formal training, certain personal characteristics such as (1) an understanding and sensitivity for children, (2) patience and durability, (3) confidentiality, (4) a sense of humor, and (5) a willingness to accept and understand small gains over extended periods of time, are recommended as being helpful (Johnson & Lavely, 1966; Molloy, 1972).

Although there are certain assumptions relative to teacher training programs, there is, currently, no general agreement concerning the type of training that is necessary to develop an effective teacher of the trainable mentally retarded. The various states require certification for teachers to work in public schools, and it is a stated policy of the National Association for Retarded Citizens (1971) that teachers of the retarded should meet the same technical and personal qualifications as those teachers working with nonretarded pupils. However, there has been some expressed concern over the need or efficacy of a baccalaureate-trained teacher in programs for the TMR. Much of this concern is the result of several factors:

1. Trained teachers were historically unavailable, and those who directed the programs without formal training felt that they had done an adequate job.
2. Some parents resent the "Johnny-come-lately" intervention of trained professionals in a program that was, for so long, ignored by them.
3. Limited evidence of what specific type of training makes a good teacher of the TMR has resulted in many "trained" teachers to be ill equipped to cope with the realities of the TMR classroom.
4. There has been and still is a question among many workers in training programs as to the efficacy of taking fours years (the usual time for a baccalaureate degree) to do what they are convinced can be better accomplished at the Associate Arts level (i.e., two years of junior college training) with immediate and intensive emphasis on training and practicum in training programs and elimination of the "superfluous" course work in the arts and sciences.

Blackwell (1972) attempted to provide some insight into the problem of determining what made an effective or ineffective teacher of the TMR. The results of his study, involving seventy teachers of the TMR, indicated that there were certain characteristics that were considered to be significant and insignificant in determining teacher effectiveness. These characteristics were identified as:

1. Women teachers were rated higher than men teachers.
2. Those teachers teaching at the preschool level are more often rated as effective teachers. The teachers at the vocational level are rated more often as ineffective teachers.
3. The number of years that these teachers attended school did not contribute to teacher effectiveness.
4. The years of teaching experience that these teachers had did not contribute to teacher effectiveness.
5. The teachers' previous teaching experience in different areas of education did not contribute to teacher effectiveness.
6. Previous contact with exceptional children before becoming teachers did not add to teacher effectiveness.
7. Knowledge of teacher occupation before employment has little to do with teacher effectiveness.
8. Knowledge of teachers' previous training at the preschool, lower primary, and upper primary levels is related to the predictability of teacher effectiveness.
9. Knowledge of a teacher's previous training with secondary-level students, special education mentally retarded, or other teaching areas did not add to predictability of teacher effectiveness.
10. The type of degree that these teachers have does not increase the predictability of their being effective teachers.
11. A teacher's interest in a number of hobbies does not add to his effectiveness. [p. 142]*

It may be of particular significance to note that years of school, degrees obtained, and previous training in special education were not considered contributors to teacher effectiveness. The author suggested that his findings may have certain implications for training, certifying, and employing teachers of the TMR, but indicated that the issue needs to be investigated further. As Williams (1963) noted some time ago, there is a "great amount of pathfinding that still needs to be done" (p. 61).

The final consideration in general classroom planning involves the process of scheduling. Although this is essentially an area of individual teacher responsibility and a reflection of the individual classroom, there are several general factors in timing and content that may be common to the various levels of training.

---

*Reprinted from "Study of effective and ineffective teachers of the trainable mentally retarded," *Exceptional Children,* 1972, 39. Copyright 1972 by The Council for Exceptional Children, 1920 Association Dr., Reston, Virginia 22091.

Program Scheduling

Scheduling and choice of activities are largely dependent upon the age and the sophistication of the group being trained. Since we are principally concerned with a school-age population, the youngest group to be served will, in all probability, encompass a chronological age of five or six to ten years of age; the intermediate group will be expected to range in age from eleven to approximately thirteen or fourteen; and the secondary or adolescent class will reflect an age range of approximately fourteen to eighteen or twenty-one. The upper age range of the adolescent class will usually be determined by local or state school policy concerning the maximum age for participation in public school programs.

Although the groups are usually defined by chronological age, the factor of mental age must also be considered in scheduling the program content. For example, a class or group may all be chronologically adolescents, but because of handicapping conditions, a primary program with emphasis on self-care may be deemed more appropriate than the anticipated prevocational experiences usually considered for this group.

General Scheduling for a Primary Class

Because of age, handicapping conditions, and limited exposure to program, the school day for this group may vary. Although we would anticipate a full five-hour day, conditions may dictate a half-day program for the primary class. See Table Nine for a sample schedule.

Table Nine

Sample schedule for a primary class

9:00 – 9:15	Pupil arrival. Removal and storage of outer garments.
9:15 – 9:30	Opening exercises. Although the routines may vary, the teacher uses this time to stage or structure the day.
9:30 – 10:00	Toileting or other washroom routines in self-care such as washing face and hands, toothbrushing, etc.
10:00 – 10:30	Self-care instruction in specific areas such as safety, dressing skills, nose blowing, or other areas of personal hygiene.
10:30 – 10:45	Break for light snack. If snacks are inappropriate or unavailable, the break time may be used as an activity break for a teacher-directed group game.
10:45 – 11:15	Communication skills with activities such as picture interpretation or games involving listening and responding.

Table Nine continued

11:15—11:45	Recreation period (outside if possible) with teacher-directed activities or games.
11:45—12:00	Clean up and preparation for lunch.
12:00— 1:00	Lunch. The training cycle continues with instruction in eating skills, table manners, etc., where appropriate.
1:00— 1:30	Rest period if necessary. The need for a rest period will be dictated by the class. If it is obvious to the teacher that the children do not need or want a rest period, it can be eliminated.
1:30— 1:45	Music or art activity. When additional time is needed for a planned activity in this area, the rest period can be reduced or eliminated.
1:45— 2:00	Clean up and preparation for going home. Putting on coats, etc.

General Scheduling for an Intermediate Class

Although the age range of this group would cause us to anticipate a reduction in the need for instruction in self-care skills, the teacher may need to continue specific training in this and other primary-level skills. Also, it must be remembered that continuous practice and reinforcement must be provided for skills previously learned. Table Ten is a sample schedule for this age range.

Table Ten

Sample schedule for an intermediate class

9:00— 9:15	Pupil arrival. Removal and storage of outer garments.
9:15— 9:30	Opening exercises. Although the routines may vary, the teacher uses this time to stage or structure the day.
9:30— 9:45	Toileting and other washroom routines with continued instruction in self-care where appropriate.
9:45—10:30	Functional academics to include recognition of survival vocabulary, number concepts, prewriting skills, etc.
10:30—10:45	Break for game or activity. This should involve an active rather than passive type of activity designed to tease off excess energy.
10:45—11:30	Independent living skills to include communication, safety concepts, or continued self-care where appropriate.
11:30—11:50	Recreation (outside when possible) with teacher-directed activity or game.
11:50—12:00	Clean up and preparation for lunch.

Table Ten continued

12:00– 1:00	Lunch with continued instruction in eating skills, use of utensils, and table manners.
1:00– 1:30	Economic usefulness with instruction or practice in clearing tables, washing dishes, and other home living skills.
1:30– 2:00	Unit instruction in environmental awareness, social participation, etc.

General Scheduling for an Adolescent Class

A continued caution in scheduling is that chronological age does not ensure mastery of certain skills. Therefore, the schedule may need to be adjusted to include skills more reflective of an earlier age group. Also, remember that practice and continuous reinforcement must be provided for skills previously learned. A schedule for this age group is shown in Table Eleven.

Table Eleven

Sample schedule for an adolescent class

9:00– 9:15	Pupils' arrival and storage of garments.
9:15– 9:30	Opening exercises. Although the routines may vary, the teacher uses this time to stage or structure the day.
9:30–10:30	Functional academics to include recognition of survival vocabulary, number concepts, developing writing skills, etc.
10:30–10:45	Break for game or activity. This should involve an active rather than passive type of activity designed to tease off excess energy.
10:45–11:30	Independent living skills to include communication skills, social or adaptive behavior skills, or continuing self-care skills where appropriate.
11:30–12:00	General cleanup and preparation for lunch. This instructional period should have focus on training in food service or other kitchen and dining room activities involved in preparation for meals.
12:00– 1:00	Lunch with continued instruction in eating skills, use of utensils, and table manners.
1:00– 2:00	Instruction in economic usefulness, and prevocational work skills.

The schedules offered here are sample plans to be improvised upon according to facility, staff, and the functioning level of the group. Whatever the circumstances, it is important that routines be established, and specific procedures be designed to reflect the needs and ability levels of the class.

Summary

General classroom planning and scheduling will be influenced by the type of facility, administrative provisions for the program, level of student to be trained, and staff training.

There are various options for organizing a training program; however, optimally the training facility should reflect a multi-agency approach to training. It should be organized to serve a wide range of abilities and provide for homogenous grouping according to age and ability levels.

Eligibility criteria for admission to public school special classes are usually specified by local school regulations or by state statute. However, the interpretation and implementation of the selective criteria are being questioned by the courts, and there is an emerging concern for their elimination and provisions for training being extended to all children, regardless of their handicaps. These factors notwithstanding, certain eligiblity criteria for various types of programs are often in the best interest of the child and assist in ensuring that they are placed in a program appropriate to their needs.

A determination of what makes an effective teacher of the TMR appears to be elusive. Although state departments of education usually require certification to teach in the public schools, the level of training necessary for this level of certification is subject to some controversy. Evidence to date indicates that extensive training may not contribute as much to teacher effectiveness as does the teacher's personality and skill in pupil-teacher relationships.

Whatever the circumstances of space, admission criteria, and teacher training, it is important that schedules for programs be defined, and routines established as antecedents to effective programming.

References

Baumgartner, B. *A curriculum guide for teachers of the mentally retarded.* Springfield, Ill.: Superintendent of Public Instruction, 1955.

Blackwell, R. B. Study of effective and ineffective teachers of the trainable mentally retarded. *Exceptional Children,* 1972, *39,* 139–143.

Bliel, G. Evaluating educational materials. *Journal of Learning Disabilities,* 1975, *8,* 12–19.

Gardner, W. I., & Nisonger, H. W. A manual on program development in mental retardation (monograph supplement). *American Journal of Mental Deficiency,* 1962.

Grossman, H. J. *Manual on terminology and classification in mental retardation* (Special publication no. 2). Washington, D.C.: American Association on Mental Deficiency, 1973.

Johnson, G. O., & Lavely, C. D. *Guidelines for the establishment of training programs for severely mentally retarded children.* Albany, N.Y.: New York State Interdepartmental Health and Hospital Council Committee on Mental Retardation, 1966.

Molloy, J. S. *Trainable children curriculum and procedures.* New York: John Day Co., 1972.

Rothstein, J. H. *Mental retardation readings and resources* (2nd ed.). New York: Holt, Rinehart, & Winston, 1971.

Seguin, E. *Idiocy and its treatment by the physiological method.* New York: Augustus M. Kelley, 1971.

Williams, H. M. *Education of the severely retarded child.* Washington, D.C.: U.S. Government Printing Office, 1963.

Reference Note

1. National Association for Retarded Citizens. *Policy statements on the education of mentally retarded persons.* Unpublished manuscript approved by the Board of Directors April 24, 1971.

Chapter 7

The Trainable
Mentally Retarded Adult

The emergent interest in programs for the TMR and the expansion of programs to include all levels of handicapping conditions have resulted a marked expansion of facilities for training. However, many programs have only looked at the "tip of the iceberg" and have done little in planning for the TMR beyond the school years. In view of this lack of planning, Stanfield (1973) commented that:

> If the school district is willing to commit up to twelve years of programming and specialized personnel to develop within the students the potential for functioning in a post-school sheltered setting, then it should be equally committed to insuring graduates placement in such a setting or providing services until such facilities become available. [p. 552]

The public schools have done little to provide for the TMR beyond maximum age for school attendance. They have often been insensitive to the fact that TMR children grow up to be TMR adults and that, unlike the educable adult, they are not readily assimilated into society. In addition, various other agencies have been penurious in their efforts and have been content to abrogate their responsibility for the TMR adult. Therefore, alternatives for post-school programs are frequently limited, and the TMR adult languishes in the home or is institutionalized.

These attitudes toward adult programs have some historical precedent in the assumptions that many TMR people die at an early age and that the remainder could be adequately served in an institution. These attitudes are no longer viable. Advances in medical science have contributed significantly to the increased life span of the TMR population, and the institution is no longer considered a "total program" for the adult. In general, though, we frequently continue to wish the adults out of existence by simply ignoring them.

These complacent attitudes toward the TMR adult have had severe limitations on life planning for the TMR adult, with the resultant fact being that we currently have less knowledge of what constitutes an appropriate program for this population than any other level of retardation currently being served. New programs are being developed for the TMR adult and we are learning from our successes and mistakes, but history continues to dictate many attitudes toward the position or role of the TMR adult in society.

Historical Role of the TMR Adult in Society

The early treatment of children and adults who were mentally retarded was discussed previously in Chapter Two. From the early beginnings to the scientific approach of the 1800s, child and adult were usually treated or mistreated alike. However, Seguin (1971) advocated that:

> The superintendent should consider the important questions relating to the propagation of schools for idiots where they may be needed; to the creation of *asylums* proper, in which adult idiots, left friendless or imperfectly improved, might find a happy home. [p. 290]

Those children who grew up "unimproved" or abandoned were to be provided lifetime care in an institution. Seguin (1971) conceived of this "asylum" as a "happy home for those who could have no other" (p. 74), rather than just containment, as they soon became.

In a further discussion of his successes and failures in the development of programs for the retarded, Seguin (1971) enumerated what he considered to be important objectives necessary to advance progress in the treatment of idiocy. Among these he expressed a concern for the total life of this population and determined that:

> Among these various *raisons d'etre* of idiocy, the most urgent, the most neglected arises from the light to be thrown on . . . observations of idiots from the cradle to the slab. [p. 75]

While not exactly representing the genesis of adult programming, Seguin did recognize that there are differences in training for the child and adult, and that additional information on all age ranges was needed. These concerns of Seguin did not reach fruition. It became clear that the existing programs, in general, were having no appreciable effect on improving the severely retarded, and after 1848, the institutions for cure or respite care rapidly evolved into lifetime asylums for the incurable.

The status of the adult retarded was again, at this point in time, not significantly different from the young TMR. Both were either institutionalized or placed in jails or almshouses. Those that remained in the care of the family were often locked away or fulfilled the dubious role of the harmless village idiot. However, this was soon to change.

By the 1900s, the eugenics movement began to receive some attention in this country. The eugenics movement, as an expressed concern for the improvement of the human race, was organized by Sir Francis Galton around 1865. The impact of this movement was a determination that heredity was a principal etiological factor in mental retardation, and that the mentally retarded represented a menace to society. Not only was "feeblemindedness" considered hereditary, but the greater ills of society were accounted for by the presence of this population. Certainly, the young retarded were not feared as much as the adults who were considered to be prolific breeders, with a potential birth rate that could overwhelm civilization (Davies & Ecob, 1962).

Although the entire TMR population carried a collective guilt for this menace, it was frequently the TMR adult rather than the TMR child that was indicted, and social remedies ranging from segregation and sterilization to euthanasia were proposed to control this population. Society "mercifully" decided upon the alternatives of segregation in the institutions—at least for the reproductive years—and/or sterilization as the proper means of control.

The alternative of total segregation was doomed to an early failure. It was simply found to be impossible to incarcerate all the retarded adults that existed in society, and even so this would not necessarily reduce their fecundity and subsequent multiplication. Therefore, sterilization was viewed as a proper alternative to the problem. Subsequently, various states enacted statutes permitting involuntary sterilization for any retardate possessing cacogenic potential. The process usually employed was vasectomy for the males and salpingectomy (cutting or tying the fallopian tubes) for the females. Although castration was occasionally used for medical reasons, it was considered entirely too radical for eugenic purposes. As early as 1894, the practice of cutting the vas deferens (vasectomy) was introduced; and since 1899, vasectomy became the preferred form of sterilization of male retardates for eugenic purposes. In the same context, the performance of a hysterectomy was also considered to be too radical a procedure; and as early as 1823, the practice of cutting or tying the fallopian tubes was advocated for the sterilization of females (Gosney & Popenoe, 1929). While both practices were legal in many states, sterilization was not as widespread as it may seem and made no greater contribution to the control of mental retardation than did segregation (Davies & Ecob, 1962).

The two means of social control—institutionalization and sterilization—continued to be employed wherever possible or appropriate, and institutionalization represented, essentially, the only program for the TMR adult. Community programs, where available, usually served only children. However, the common belief was that they too, would sooner or later have to go to the institution.

The program options of home or institution for the TMR adult persisted. The prevailing opinion in society was that the TMR adult could not and should not live in the community and therefore must be institutionalized. It was not until the 1950s that professionals began to refute this assumption.

Saenger (1957) determined from a population of adults, all of whom were former pupils in community classes for the TMR, that many of them were capable of adjusting to the home and community to the extent of entering into activities in the home and moving about in the community. Also, Tisdall (1960) noted in a study of 126 trainables that, after five years of enrollment in community classes, 80% were still in the community. His major conclusion from this study was that the growing size of the TMR population remaining in the community posed a serious need for community-based, post-school programs. Thus, contrary to prevailing opinion, evidence began to indicate that the greater number of TMR adults were remaining in the community and in instances functioning quite adequately.

The fallacy of institutionalization as total program for the TMR adult was further substantiated by Gardner and Nisonger (1962) who determined that, in actuality, the institutions were only serving 5% of the total retarded population; the other 95% were residing in the community. Needless to say, the 95% figure had a representative adult population that was, for all practical purposes, being ignored by society. Although by this time there was a reemerging interest in provisions for community programs for the TMR, the adult was still being routinely institutionalized or maintained in the home with limited alternatives for program or development other than that which the family could provide.

In recognition of the limited alternatives for the adult retardate and other extant problems in services to the retarded, the President's Panel on Mental Retardation (1962) recommended a decentralization of institutional facilities and a movement of services into the community to provide for the total age range of the TMR population from preschool through adult life. The panel proposed to provide for post-school work opportunities in sheltered environments, adult activity centers, and community-based group homes as the appropriate alternatives to institutionalization. These recommendations encompassed a concern for improved institutional programs for those who needed them. They defined a continuum of care for all ages and levels of retardation, and society was now confronted with a population, so long ignored, in need of community services without the knowledge base to define what type of services were appropriate.

The Present Problem

Adult TMR present a contradiction in terms. Because of chronological age, they are physically adults; but, because of their intellectual and social deficits, they are often treated as children. This poses a serious paradox in the development of community services. In instances, their "adult" status creates aspirations or demands from society that they be adults in the sense of taking a self-directed role and participating in the "work ethic" as productive, responsible humans. Conversely, their psycho-social development, which is consistent with their mental age, often leads us to regard the TMR adult as what Dybwad (1964) calls "eternal children" and to program accordingly. Parenthetically, it is interesting to note that the National Association for Retarded Children, organized to promote the welfare of all retardates regardless of age, did not change their title to National Association for Retarded Citizens until 1973—twenty-three years after its organization in 1950.

This dysjunction between what we see (that is, a physical adult) and the reality (that is, behavior that is consistent with the mental age of the TMR) has created within society some persistent assumptions about the role of the TMR adult and his ability to live in the community. In addition, the spectre of the adult TMR "loose" in the community and the age-old fears surrounding his "moral imbecility" have contributed to considerable reluctance on the part of many to accept any alternative other than institutionalization for the TMR adult. As Mamula and Newman (1973) remarked, "No more formidable obstacle exists to the development of a meaningful community placement program than community fears and ignorance" (p. 58).

These fears are, perhaps, substantiated by existing evidence that indicates that there were previously several problem areas in placing or maintaining retardates in the community. Mamula and Newman (1973) reviewed literature concerning community placement of over 13,000 retardates and identified the following problem areas:

I. Patient factors:

Antisocial actions—Sex offenses, problems of undue attachment to the opposite sex, indecent exposure, promiscuity, pregnancy, illegitimate children, repeated theft, assault, public mischief, serious community problems, consistent contact with various social and legal agencies, courts, associated with problems.

Undesirable social/personal conduct—Untidy, destructive, unruly, hyperactive, sleeping problems, refusal to take medication, eating habits, toileting, etc.

Inadequate interpersonal relations—Uncooperative, moody, jealous, insolent, quarrelsome, quick-tempered, etc.

Unsatisfactory work habits—Unreliable, too much time off, frequent lateness, low work output, too old, inefficient, lazy, etc.

Escape or voluntary return to the institution—Running away from community placement facilities or returning to the institution without permission.

II. Health problems:

Physical ill health, physical disability, seizures, superimposed mental illness, ambulation, etc.

III. Adverse environmental factors:

Includes indifference or lack of natural parents, relatives, economic dependence, community objections, illness of family caretakers, closing of placement facility, etc. |pp. 51−52|

The authors indicated that the data used in the literature they reviewed are only suggestive and that the majority of research on problems of community placement of the adult retardate has not met empirical scrutiny. However, the aforementioned factors or problems they identified are not surprising. They would probably be consistent with a census of educated guesses on what problems could be anticipated when placing the retarded in or back in the community.

The reduction of many of the problems in community placement is possible if all the referral and receiving agencies that are in contact with the TMR adult plan appropriately. These agencies taking the responsibility for placement can and should be effective in the reduction of problems in the community by adhering to a few simple guidelines:

1. Insure that community placement is the appropriate alternative for the individual. It must be remembered that some TMR adults cannot or should not be placed in a community program.

2. Train the adult for community living. This is especially important for those adults being moved out of an institution or those with no previous training. It is also important not to move these people too

fast; there must be ample evidence that their level of training has reached a level of functioning sufficient for reasonable success in the community program.

3. Insure that placement is appropriate to the TMR adult's needs, training, and ability level. This guideline would include considerations of appropriate type of residential care (for example, residing with the natural family vs. other residential arrangements in the community) and type of program (for example, sheltered workshop placement vs. other adult activities). In addition, the placement should be open-ended to allow for movement from residence or program as circumstances change.

4. Provide proper supervision and follow-up in the placement. The TMR adult's circumstances, like our own, are subject to change. Proper follow-up and supervision must be provided to accommodate change and to insure the continued appropriateness of the placement in the community.

5. Initial and continuing community education will be necessary to alleviate or prevent resistance and fear over the TMR adult being in the community. In addition, many community-based programs for TMR adults can rarely, if ever, become self-supporting, and active solicitation of community support is important for program survival.

All the problems notwithstanding, there is sufficient evidence to indicate that it is most beneficial to the TMR and their families if they remain in the community. In addition, society has a commitment and/or mandate to decentralize the large institutions and, wherever possible, to provide appropriate programs for all ages and levels of the retarded in the community. Thus, the presence of the TMR adult is being increasingly encountered in the community, and it is incumbent upon the community to develop appropriate habilitation and rehabilitation services and programs.

Community Placement

The early impetus given community programs for the retarded by the President's Panel on Mental Retardation (1962) has resulted in the beginnings of the development of a number of alternatives in services for the TMR adult. The current focus of these programs is to maintain as many retardates as possible in the community, and the President's Committee on Mental Retardation (1972) has defined the return of one third of the retarded in institutions to the community as a national goal. In order to accomplish this, the committee identified four areas of action needed:

1. Reduce intake into institutions by offering alternative types of placement
2. Increase capabilities and independence of current residents through highly skilled care and training
3. Increase community placement by developing qualified community facilities and homes
4. Promote the public acceptance of the retarded as neighbors and employees

Figure Nine illustrates the committee's design for residential alternatives to accomplish the goal of deinstitutionalization.

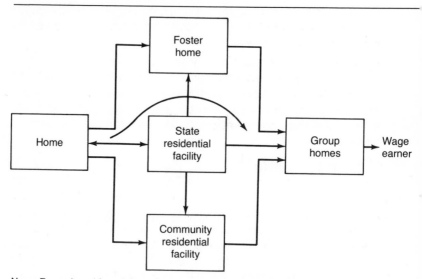

NOTE: Reproduced from President's Committee on Mental Retardation, *MR 72 Islands of Excellence* (Washington, D.C.: U.S. Government Printing Office, 1972).

Figure Nine

Alternatives for returning residents to the community

The focus on increased community alternatives has been developed to return as many institutional residents as possible to the home or community residential facility. Another goal is to provide alternative programs, to decrease the necessity for or desirability of institutionalization. Some of the more salient features or advantages to this alternative are:

1. It is consistent with the normalization principle—providing oppor-

tunities for as normal a life as possible and for development in the community.

2. It provides for an increase in the quality of care through smaller community residential units closer to the home or within the natural family unit.
3. The shared responsibility of various community agencies provides a broader spectrum of services in habilitation and rehabilitation programs for the TMR population.
4. Maintenance of the TMR child or adult in the community eliminates the "retarding" process of institutionalization.
5. The maintenance of the TMR in the community eliminates the potential guilt factor in the family who may feel forced to abandon a retarded child or adult to some faraway institution.
6. The provision of community services will hopefully reduce the institutional population, allowing for a higher quality of service for those needing institutional care.

Although some limitation was necessary, the alternatives for program at the community level have principally focused on the TMR population from birth to eighteen years of age. The literature is burgeoning with reports on alternatives for the school-age TMR, but there remains a remarkable paucity of information on the availability or success of community-based adult programs. When available, the literature continues to indicate that a significant number of TMR adults are still not being provided post-school habilitative and rehabilitative programs in the community, other than life-long, family-bound care (Stanfield, 1973).

If we are to be consistent with the concept of "continuum of care," it is apparent that we must equalize our focus on the TMR population, and expand the community programs to include *all* the TMR—children and adults. Over a decade ago, Dybwad (1964), at the White House Conference on Children and Youth reflected on this problem when he said, "It remains to be seen whether education of the public will create as favorable a climate for the young adult and the adult retardate as now exists for the retarded child" (p. 207). Regrettably, we can observe that although significant in their beginnings, programs for the TMR adult are still inadequate.

Community Programming

The principal objective, often stated in the development of community programs for the retarded adult, is rehabilitation. The early thrust of the President's Panel on Mental Retardation (1962) was directed towards increasing the retardate's self-sufficiency and rehabilitating him into society. While some TMR adults may have to be rehabilitated from the institution, the hoped for results of community programming is that it will prevent or at least postpone institutionalization. Therefore, as increased numbers of the retarded are retained in the community, the principal focus will be habilitation rather than rehabilitation.

Habilitation for the TMR represents a lifetime program designed to develop their capacities, reduce dependency, and make them as capable and independent as possible through whatever program is appropriate to their needs and ability levels. Rusalem (1966) defined several dimensions of habilitation training as involving:

1. Reshaping the environment by providing sheltered industry and developing special living arrangements
2. Reducing the distorted social perceptions by integrating as many retarded as possible into the community
3. Reducing the history of failure through acceptance and reinforcement for positive achievements
4. Providing meaningful goals and appropriate reinforcers which advance the retardate towards ultimate employment and independent living
5. Developing, in addition to specific skills, adaptive behaviors which permit them to cope with change and new conditions

Programs that are designed to habilitate or rehabilitate the adult retardate usually focus on vocational development and/or vocational rehabilitation. The objectives of this type of program were defined by the Vocational Rehabilitation Administration (1963) as:

1. Rendering the client capable of productive work which is beneficial to the community
2. Assisting the retardate to develop, through work, a satisfaction in one's ability to work and the self-esteem derived from such satisfaction
3. Appreciating the worth of work and achievement at the level they are capable of performing without overemphasis on material possessions and objectives out of their grasp
4. Preparing the retardate to live in a community and to cope with the demands of everyday life

Although vocational development programs for the TMR adult are defended on the basis of being consistent with the normalization principle, the "work ethic," and adult expectancy, there have been a number of problems in developing the work potential of the TMR. Several problems or lags in the vocational development of the TMR were identifed by Blue (1964). He noted that preparation for sheltered employment requires early and extensive training in gross and fine motor skills, persistence, performance over extended periods of time, and the development of a response to motivation and rewards. His conclusion was that failure to initiate programs at an early age to accomplish this training often leads to subsequent failure of the adult in a workshop setting.

Further guidelines for overcoming lags in vocational development of the retarded were identifed by the Vocational Rehabilitation Administration (1963). They recommend that:

1. The retardate should develop a work role.
2. The TMR should be trained in skills relative to job performance as determined through assessment of sensory-motor status, be provided task analysis to assist in assignments consistent with their sensory-motor status, and be trained in task performance providing reinforcement to promote a sense of competence.
3. They should be trained to operate effectively in the work-related community, including training in such concepts as getting to and from work, interpersonal relationships at work, and recognizing hazardous situations in the work environment.
4. The retardate's vocational potential should be increased through continuous assessment, increasing goals for performance, and assisting in transferring existing achievements to new areas of work.
5. A self-concept of a worker should be developed through an "I can do it" feeling, in order to help them perceive themselves as competent adults.

Vocational preparation and work activities for the TMR adult have been subjected to various questions and interpretations. Ultimately, what is at issue are the actual benefits of work that is often little productive and does not contribute significantly to the individual's financial independence. Regardless of the level of productivity or financial benefits, Wolfensberger (1967) countered this concern by proposing a vocational creed for the retarded that he felt was consistent with the cultural values of the American society and contributed to the habilitation of the retarded:

1. A working retardate is generally a happier person. Work gives self-esteem and a feeling of accomplishment and worth.
2. Work lends adult status to a retardate, and thus adds to his dignity in the sight of others.
3. In our work-oriented society, positive attitudes will generally be expressed towards the worker, and negative ones toward the drone. Thus, the retardate's adjustment will be enhanced by the community attitudes he encounters.
4. The family of the working retardate is, generally, a better adjusted

family. Since work tends to make the retardate more acceptable, it engenders positive attitudes in the family benefiting the retardate indirectly.

5. A retardate capable of working will be less likely to become an economic burden to his family or society.
6. A working retardate contributes to the economic welfare of society.
7. He earns an income that is likely to give him more of the material benefits enjoyed by the majority of our citizens.
8. Idleness can lead to nonadaptive or maladaptive behavior. [p. 233]

Wolfensberger extended this "right to work" creed to all retardates whether gainfully employed in the competitive labor market or in sheltered workshops. Whatever the level of retardation, it is his contention that the retarded have a right to work and can profit from some sort of work that is consistent with their ability level.

In summary, the current emphasis in community programs for the TMR adult has a strong work orientation. Community programs for TMR adults, where they exist, have focused on some sort of work evaluation, training, and placement in locally organized workshops or adult activities. However, the existence of actual programs is often inadequate and limited in service capacity.

Post-school programs are frequently only available to the TMR adult living in a community where sheltered workshop or other program arrangements have been organized. The TMR adult who lives fifty miles from an existing program is usually home-bound and dependent upon his or her family because transportation to the program is usually not feasible.

In addition to availability and/or accessibility of program, there are other problem areas to be considered in developing community programs for the adult. The parents of the TMR are not immune to illness, nor are they immortal. What if severe illness or death occurs in the natural family? Also, what about the TMR adult who is moved from an institution into a community program away from his natural parents or other family members? These adults should have some alternative other than the home for residential care.

Contingencies such as those mentioned make it obvious that there are at best two critical components to consider in the development of a community program for the TMR adult: (1) we must develop appropriate work or other adult activities that are as accessible as possible and (2) we must develop alternatives for residential services that provide for emergency contingencies in the home and make the work or activity program accessible to a broader geographic area and population. In order to accomplish this, there are various alternatives that a community may develop to extend the continuum of care to the adult population.

Alternatives in Community Programming

The concern for community-based habilitative and rehabilitative programs has identified a right to work and a desire for the TMR to live as independently as possible. However, evidence to date indicates that few TMR adults can participate in competitive labor or manage their affairs independently of some supervision or support. As a result, the most common work placement for the TMR adult usually involves some form of sheltered employment, most often in a sheltered workshop.

Sheltered workshops have been established for the handicapped in this country since the mid-1800s. They were first developed for the blind and over the years have been expanded to include many handicapping conditions. The inclusion of the TMR population into sheltered workshops is only as recent as the 1950s. This was a direct result of the efforts of the newly organized National Association for Retarded Children. These early ventures in the placement of the TMR in sheltered workshops were considered successful and indicated that some of the TMR had vocational potential.

The Sheltered Workshop

The development of sheltered workshops for the TMR is a relatively new concept but follows essentially the same patterns as those previously developed for other handicapping conditions. The type of work done in these workshops can usually be divided into three categories:

1. *Production of new products:* This usually involves the manufacturing of items of an arts and crafts nature that are sold at a small profit.
2. *Repair or salvage:* This type of work usually entails soliciting items from the community, like old furniture, to be repaired or refinished on a contract basis or for resale.
3. *Subcontract with business or industry:* This is usually the most lucrative of the options. It involves specific contracts with industry for packaging, sorting, assembling, or performing other types of production on a piecework basis.

Even within these options for work, the major problem in establishing workshops for the TMR is that they usually cannot become self-supporting. In reality, the workshop is a paradox of labor. The true mission of the sheltered workshop for the TMR adult is employment for a population that would otherwise be unemployed. Therefore, the real "product" of a sheltered workshop is an employed TMR, rather than the production of a product for profit. Farber (1968) took note of this when he cautioned that the sheltered workshop, while having value, may only provide retardates and their families with the opportunity to pretend that they are part of the labor force.

Nevertheless, the sheltered workshop is a viable component of the post-school program for the TMR adult, and Wolfensberger (1967) proposed that:

1. A retardate that is capable of self-care is almost certainly capable of at least sheltered work.
2. A retardate who can profit from arts and crafts or who is capable of purposeful play is very likely to be capable of at least sheltered work.
3. Inability to walk, lack of speech or language and even incontinence are not necessary indicators that the retardate is incapable of at least sheltered work. [p. 233]

The provision of sheltered work for such a broad range of handicapping conditions as are extant in the TMR population will make it necessary to develop different types of sheltered employment and different goals for these alternatives. To meet this need in program, there are usually three alternatives or types of workshops (Gold, 1973; Katz, 1968):

1. *Transitional sheltered employment:* In this type of workshop, the focus is on rehabilitation-habilitation, and the client is trained for ultimate competitive employment.
2. *Long-term sheltered employment:* This program provides for terminal placement in a sheltered work environment for those retardates who will be unable to function in competitive labor.
3. *Multidisability sheltered employment:* A workshop of this type is usually comprehensive enough to serve numerous handicapping conditions and to include all levels of retardation. It is designed to provide for transitional as well as terminal placement.

The TMR adult is usually considered a client for long-term or terminal placement. However, in rare instances, he may be able to obtain and maintain gainful employment in the community.

Whatever the option for placement, the objective of sheltered employment has been to provide, where appropriate, a work-oriented, post-school program and, when possible, to provide a small remuneration to contribute to the TMR client's economic self-sufficiency. The efficacy or success of this type of post-school program for the TMR, while supported intuitively, has had little in the way of determination through empirical research.

Huddle (1967a) reviewed the existing literature and indicated that there were fewer than ten studies on work behavior and performance of

TMR adults enrolled in sheltered workshops. From this review, he was able to draw the following implications:

1. The TMR can perform industrial tasks, and the sheltered workshop should shed its traditional role of handicrafts, minor manufacturing, and salvage and repair and seek more involvement with industry.
2. Small work teams rather than individual work stimulates greater productivity.
3. Reinforcement in the form of money and social reward contributes to higher production.
4. Challenging tasks and proper incentives should be provided to reduce supervision.
5. Training should be standardized, and the use of clients to train clients can be expanded.
6. The school curriculum needs to be revised for early identification of pupils who have the potential for sheltered workshop work, and socialization and self-help skills should be introduced earlier in the curriculum for those pupils with workshop potential.

From these implications, it would appear that traditional attitudes towards the TMR's concept of work (that they are incapable of performing complex tasks) and remuneration (that they neither need nor understand money) are unfounded. It would further appear that improvements in sheltered workshops are needed to upgrade the work potential of the TMR and that the sheltered workshop *should* contribute to some economic self-sufficiency. Parenthetically, we might add that Huddle (1967b), citing his own research, indicated that intrinsic motivation is not enough to sustain interest and/or performance and that money or monetary reward was the best incentive.

In a later study, Gold (1969) determined that there was a discrepancy between the abilities of the moderately and severely retarded and that which has been traditionally expected of them. He demonstrated that the retarded were able to perform at a much higher level than what has been traditionally expected. He noted that a low level expectation was, perhaps, a function of the training and experience of workshop staff who frequently ignore cognitive and skill development and direct their efforts toward the social experiences in the work environment. He concluded that:

> The level of functioning of workshop clients, then, remains essentially unchanged, apart from improvement gained through the alleviation of maladaptive social behavior. Workshops presently accept subcontracts that require little in terms of ability. As a result it is a low level of habilitative training and a low level of remuneration. This restriction

in selecting contracts is a major cause of the unprofitable operation of most sheltered workshops. Increasing sheltered workshop income, both for the clients and the workshop would allow for improved services and programs, and a better life for those served. [p. 30]

It is apparent that the growing body of literature relative to sheltered workshop programs is rather iconoclastic. It is becoming obvious that previous expectancies for the TMR adult's performance were somewhat less than he is capable of. However, we must keep the current optimism in proper perspective and remember that this higher level performance is relative to *sheltered workshop performance* and should not be considered as tantamount to the ability to engage in competitive employment outside the sheltered environment.

While appropriate training for optimum productivity is a critical issue in workshop programs, other problems and possible solutions have been identified by Garner, Lacy, and Creasy (1972) that could also have a significant impact on the success of the workshop:

1. Location is often a problem when the workshop is established in areas of limited economic growth. The solution to this problem is obvious—workshops should be located in areas of economic growth providing industrial, government, and service support.
2. Staffing and labor resources are often poor because there are few skilled workshop personnel. The answer to this problem is to avoid generic objectives that demand large staffing; rather, the workshop should develop a clear definition of objectives that define the need for specific personnel to accomplish specific goals in the program.
3. Isolation of services or single-disability services, focusing interest on the retarded alone, should be avoided. Services programs should be developed to meet the needs of all the disabled.
4. The job performance potential of the retarded should be defined, and the number of terminal placements should be reduced by placing the retarded worker into business wherever possible.

Whatever the future holds for the sheltered employment of the TMR adult, Huddle (1967a) pointed out that the sheltered workshop is not appropriate for all TMR adults. Intellectual and/or physical limitations will preclude the possibility of successful performance for some people in a workshop setting. The specific reasons for exclusion may vary, depending upon the individual or the facility, but one study (Tobias & Gorelick, 1963) suggested that mental ages of three years and less and IQ's less than 20 represent a reasonable cutoff point for sheltered workshop placement.

Admissions criteria for placement in a workshop will vary. There is a representative population of the TMR whose circumstances are such that they will not be eligible for sheltered employment but are still in need of some sort of post-school program involving appropriate adult activities.

Adult Activities

An alternative to sheltered workshops is a continuation of training and prevocational experiences in an activities program for those adults who do not have or may never possess sufficient skills to be placed in a workshop.

The adult activity center is essentially an extension of the day-care training program provided for the younger TMR. The National Association for Retarded Children (Cortazzo, 1967) defined this aspect of adult programming as:

> an organized rehabilitation service for moderately and severely retarded individuals beyond school age which enables them to live with less dependence upon others. It offers them training in basic daily living activities and adjustment based upon the individual's needs in society and geared to the functioning level of the individual in accord with his potential. [p. 244]

This level of training reflects a continuation of programs in self-care, socialization, recreation, and other programs or activities deemed appropriate for the functioning level of the adults participating. Although differing from sheltered workshops, training in prevocational experiences may also be provided as an ongoing assessment and reevaluation of the individual's progress to determine whether continuation of the adult activities program is appropriate, or whether the individuals are ready for workshop placement.

Although the program may vary in content, Cortazzo (1967) has defined five major objectives for the adult activities program:

1. To provide the mentally retarded with a socially acceptable pattern for daily living . . . The appropriate behavior for most adults is to leave home some time during the day, engage in some purposeful and acceptable activity, and then return home later.
2. To help the mentally retarded make the important transition into adult living through training in the adult living skills and adjustments such as proper and appropriate grooming, homemaking, traveling, work habits and skills, etc.
3. To work closely with parents and help them understand, accept, and develop the new role of the severely retarded adult in the family. By the very nature of this condition the parents must be involved in the program.

4. To provide an alternative to institutional living. Parents who had to place their retarded sons or daughters in an institution due to lack of community services would be given an opportunity to withdraw them and place them in an activity program.

5. To prepare the mentally retarded who have the potential in the necessary skills and adjustment for advanced programs, such as workshops and other vocational centers. [p. 248]

An additional objective in the provision of adult activities would be the continuation of reinforcement systems for skills previously learned. Oftentimes the desirability of institutionalization increases as the TMR adult's management problems increase. Management may not have been a serious issue during childhood, when training programs were available; however, the lack of program alternatives during the post-school years not only places the TMR back in the home without training, but also contributes to the extinction of behaviors previously learned. Consequently, management problems and dependency will increase.

A final factor to consider in determining the efficacy of such a program is the delay or prevention of physical and/or mental deterioration of the TMR adult. Early senescence is often an accepted fact in the adult life cycle of many TMR. The onset of adolescence or adulthood often creates a deterioriation usually attributed to multiple factors such as poor health and general handicapping conditions—all with a physiological base. However, it may be postulated that this is also a sociological/psychological phenomenon. The removal of reinforcers, social interaction, and removal from society in general would prompt many of us to "give up" on life. TMR adults are not significantly different. Regardless of their functioning level, removing them from a program and isolating them within the home may contribute significantly to their "giving up," regressing in their behavior, and filling out their remaining years as "senile" adults.

The maintenance of community programs for the TMR adult, such as those previously discussed, are often confronted with several critical realities. Although community programs for the adult TMR are rapidly becoming a viable alternative to institutionalization, the problem of guardianship for this population poses some serious problems. The three principal concerns are:

1. A natural family unit may not be available for caretaking. The parents may be dead or unable physically to maintain the adult in the home; or, the parents and/or other family members may be unwilling to provide the necessary maintenance and support outside the institution.

2. Because of the relatively small size of the adult TMR population, necessary financial support, facilities, staff, and so on, it is only

feasible to operate adult programs on a regional basis. The location of these programs is usually in an area of population density, but designed to serve adults in outlying areas. The distance to be travelled from home to program may pose problems, if not preclude the possibility of participation.

3. Because of the TMR adult's level of competence, he cannot be expected to function completely independently in the community.

Therefore, the management of the retarded adult at the community level will demand that some sort of living arrangement, close to the program, be made for his supervision and care. This should, whenever possible, be a family-type facility that provides for as normal as possible experiences and participation in community living.

Community Residential Programs

The office of the Special Assistant to the President for Mental Retardation (Department of Health Education and Welfare, 1967) proposed a plan for the supervision and care of the TMR adult in community cooperative boarding houses. The operational plan and protections were defined as:

1. *The mission:* To permit the young trainable retarded person to integrate as fully as possible in the community, so that he or she may participate to the extent possible in the community's industrial, religious, social, and recreational life and programs. To provide some degree of management of their financial affairs, which takes under consideration the fact that they should be contributing to their own support and building up an estate for their future care.

2. *The operation:* The facility of ten to twelve young adults would have a parent-team, preferably a middle-aged couple without children of their own, to act as stand-ins for their parents. They would provide the home atmosphere and home supervision that parents would normally exercise and act as their day-to-day advisors on matters with which teenagers, for example, would normally come to their parents for assistance. This couple may be hard to find. They should have completed a short-term training course before assuming responsibility and should have the services of a social worker or trained counselor readily available. The retarded accepted into the facility would have to have had proper vocational training and special education, be in good physical condition, and have demonstrated an ability to maintain social and emotional stability. From their earnings the residents would be expected to pay a sum to be determined to help pay the parent team, to pay costs normally associated with the operation of a residence (rent or mortgage payments, maintenance, depreciation, utilities, insurance etc.); to pay for their food, clothing, medical care, transportation, recreation, and towards individual retirement and disability benefits.

3. *Protection for the retarded:* It must be assured that the structure selected meets all building code requirements; that medical, surgical, dental, psychological care be insured for every resident; that constant vigilance be given by the Board, reinforced by the aid of trained workers, to assure that employment is maintained . . . and that the facility's parent team is conducting the facility in the best interest of its residents and fully stays "up to the challenges." [pp. 369–370]

Although a beginning, the criteria for admission to such a facility was obviously selective and concerned with residential care for only the higher functioning adults who have had special class training and who could be gainfully employed. The criteria as stated would eliminate the major portion of TMR adults from consideration for community living.

Current thinking relative to community residential facilities reflects a more liberal approach and a concern for serving a larger and more diverse adult population. Thomas (1972) has described a recent structuring of community facilities that more realistically reflects a continuum of care through group home living. He defines the group home as:

A group home is a residential facility capable of serving, among others, a small number of mentally and/or physically handicapped individuals—up to a maximum of twenty—who are able to participate in a variety of jobs, sheltered workshops, day-care centers, activity centers, educational facilities, and/or other community-based programs that are meaningful for their training, rehabilitation, and/or general well-being. [p. 2]

He defined the major objective of these homes as the provision of residential care in a community, home-like atmosphere. The homes should be located where maximum community resources for training, education, and rehabilitation are available. The physical structures could be homes or other suitably remodeled buildings that meet safety and health standards. They are operated on a nonprofit basis but answerable to a citizens advisory board. The specific objectives of the program are to avoid the mass living conditions of the institutions and to afford each individual as much privacy as possible. The in-house program was designed to encourage variety rather than uniformity in programming.

The community group home described by Thomas is a relatively new, but rapidly growing, program of community placement for those adults who can profit and participate in this type of experience. Wolfensberger (1972) indicated that this type of alternative, when implemented, precipitated a remarkable decline in the retarded population in the institution, and Thomas noted that this arrangement, while not quite the epitome of normalization, places us closer to the principle than the present institutional model.

Although impressive in its potential for reduction of institutional populations and implementation of broader based community programs, resistance to this type of community facility is a very real consideration. Consider the neighborhood that is informed that a "home for retarded adults" is to be established in their neighborhood. The range of reaction—the fears and the outright resistance—can be potentially damaging. In addition, zoning restrictions and other state regulations may force the location of the group home in a less-than-desirable area of the community. Therefore, rather than wait for these reactions after the fact, community education and demonstration of the effectiveness of this program will have to be implemented in order to prevent problems and develop support for the program before it is implemented.

The advent of community alternatives for training and residential programs reflects a growing antipathy towards the maintenance of large isolated institutions. The abuses of the past 150 years have resulted in the rejection of the institutional concept as "total program," and the institution is rapidly becoming an anathema. Nevertheless, within the continuum of care, the institution must remain as an alternative for that population of retardates who are in need of twenty-four-hour residential care, or whose handicapping conditions are so severe as to preclude successful participation in other alternatives in the community.

Although the institution is not exclusively an adult alternative, the increase in community-based programs has frequently been more child than adult-oriented. Therefore, the lack of adult community services and potential management problems in the home is most critical for this population and often makes institutionalization of the adult a more viable alternative for services.

Butterfield (1969) reported that 82% of the approximately 200,000 retardates in institutions have IQ's below 50, and that 70% of the total population of institutionalized retardates are fifteen years of age or older. These figures would imply that more trainables are being institutionalized and that the majority (although not overwhelming) are maturing adolescents and adults. The clear implication is that the institution is still being used as a primary locus for care and/or program for a large number of adults. However, the large institution currently represents an anachronism of sorts, and it is the general consensus of opinion that when institutionalization is necessary, it should be accomplished in smaller residential units closer to community resources and services.

The Alternative of Institutionalization

The current antipathy towards the quality of care provided the residents of large institutions was previously discussed in Chapter Two, and the continuing deleterious effects of this alternative for care are readily apparent in publications such as *Willowbrook* (Rivera, 1972) and *Christmas in Purgatory* (Blatt & Kaplan, 1966). However, the institution will always be necessary to serve that segment of the population who, because of handicapping conditions, management problems, or lack of other community alternatives, must be institutionalized.

The need to reorganize the old institutional program model of isolation and dehumanization has been recognized for some time, but the question of the survival of the institution, as we have known it, remains. Over a decade ago, the President's Panel on Mental Retardation (1962) urged the elimination of the large isolated institutions. In their proposed program, the institution was to be only one of several alternatives for care and closely linked to the community program. The custodial aspects of the institution were to be eliminated, and residential care was to be provided only when necessary, and only for as long as necessary.

The American Association on Mental Deficiency (1964) concurred with the need for smaller residential units whose programs represented an extension of the community. Under their minimum standards, they directed that the new multipurpose facilities should not exceed a residence population of 1,000, and that special-purpose short- and long-term care facilities should not exceed a resident population of 500. They further directed that the existing residential facilities should regroup the residents according to their specialized needs into homogeneous groups of about 500 for service as smaller residential groups.

Scheerenberger (1965) noted that new institutions developed after 1960 had a rated capacity of less than half those previously constructed, but the large institutions are still with us. Wolfensberger (1971) has proposed that the large institutions can and should disappear and other alternatives for institutionalization be developed. This proposal is by no means an accomplished fact, but Budde (1972) indicated that what may be done is to eliminate institutionalization without eliminating the institution through a systems technology to provide a broader, more meaningful program model. Thurman & Thiele (1973) have also proposed that the existing institution can take on a viable role by "self-destructing" into a community-based program that provides a community model for education and training for community-based personnel, while preparing the residents for community living.

It is quite clear that a trend developed over a decade ago to deinstitutionalize the institution and bring the retarded closer to their homes and communities for short- and long-term service in a residential setting. Different systems, programs and techniques have been tried to reduce the large institutional population—some have succeeded and some have failed (Scheerenberger, 1974).

The Changing Role of the Institution

The changing concepts in residential services are well reflected in a series of papers edited by Kugel and Wolfensberger (1969). They defined the extant problems of residential care as a national disgrace involving overcrowding, understaffing, and underfinancing, and proposed a number of alternatives for care. The various contributors to this monograph made recommendations for new service models involving administrative changes, new rationales and program models, and the application of the normalization principle to the institutional care of the retarded.

Dunn (1969) noted that the current concerns for institutional programs provided the propitious moment for changing the structure of institutional services from large multipurpose facilities to smaller special-purpose facilities. His proposal entailed the establishment of facilities to serve populations not to exceed 100, that would provide short- and long-term treatment appropriate to the retardates' needs.

In summary, the evolutionary process or trend in institutional programs has taken on four distinct features: (1) the development of a new rationale for program, (2) the reduction in size of facilities for services, (3) the movement of all residential programs closer to the community, and (4) the designation of the institution as only one of several alternatives for care, treatment, and education of the retarded.

The concerns for changing patterns in residential care are further reflected in the current set of standards developed by the Joint Commission on Accreditation of Hospitals (1971). These standards are consistent with current knowledge and concerns for the improvement of residential care and delivery of services for the mentally retarded. The basic philosophy of these standards is the principle of normalization and increasing the resident's ability to cope with the environment. The standards for facilities are described as small living units that are community-oriented, and they direct that the resident should, as much as possible, participate in community life for schools, recreation, shopping, and so on.

The standards are quite comprehensive and define guidelines for resident welfare in admissions, resident living, and programs and services. These are all consistent with current focus on the institution as an alternative program. However at this point in time, accreditation of residential facilities by these standards is only voluntary (that is, the existing institutions are not under any general mandate to be reviewed by the Joint Commission or to meet the commission's standards). Needless to say, few institutions have voluntarily requested review by the Joint Commission. Sadly enough, the current proposals for changing residential services is only a vague reality involving precious few institutions, and White and Wolfensberger (1969) have noted that the attitudes that contribute to the dehumanizing of the institutional population still exists.

The potential mandate for change is currently in the courts. The outcome of the litigation discussed in Chapter Two (*Wyatt* v. *Aderholt* and *Burnam* v. *Georgia*) may create a court-ordered mandate for the improvement of residential services. Accreditation by the Joint Commission, or at least the meeting of court-ordered standards, may become mandatory. But if this occurs, the question may still remain whether these imposed standards will precipitate a genuine change in residential services or merely provide for new, clean, and efficient warehouses.

The concern for the rights of the retarded to live as normal a life as possible is a philosophy that is nowhere near fruition. The institutional experience is an issue yet to be dealt with. In addition, other rights to "normal" adult experiences have been posed but are as yet unanswered. Society will be slow to respond to these questions for various reasons; however, there are a number of persistent issues that are seeking resolution on the road to normalization for the TMR adult.

Some Questions to Be Answered

The transition into adulthood carries with it certain rights and expectations for life. The period of dependency upon parents has ended, and as adults, we are expected to become gainfully employed, get married, and perhaps have children of our own. These are considered to be normal adult experiences. The issue at point is how "normal" are these experiences for the TMR adult?

We have already discussed work potential and alternatives for employment, but what about marriage and procreation, and what about the right to normal heterosexual experiences with or without marriage? These are issues that in some instances have been resolved by statute, or in our minds by assumed physiological incapacity. States have enacted laws prohibiting marriage for the "incompetent" and sterilization of the "incompetent" where appropriate. There has also been a historical assumption that many of the lower levels of retardation were sterile and/or sexually impotent. The restrictive statutes in some states are being repealed, and we know that we can no longer look upon the TMR adult as asexual and impotent. The rights of marriage, procreation, and expressions of sexuality for the TMR adult are being explored by many parents and professionals. The right to these rights is yet to be accepted by many.

The Right to Marriage

The current concerns for normalization and habilitation of the TMR have created the question of the right to marry as a normal adult experience. The sentiments on this issue vary, and arguments are proposed, pro and con. There are those who contend that, with proper supervision, a union between two TMR adults could be a successful and gratifying experience. Others contend that the TMR do not have sufficient sense of responsibility to maintain a successful marriage.

In some states, the issue is a moot point. These states, by statute, prohibit marriage of persons determined "incompetent." Krishef (1972) reviewed the various state laws on marriage, and his findings are reflected in Table Twelve. In summary, he reported that 37% of the states had no law, 29% provided no information, 24% prohibited marriage, 6% permitted marriage, and 4% gave no reply.

The existing restrictive laws on marriage are being challenged in some states. The categorical denial of the right to marry, based upon the criteria of mental retardation, is subject to serious question. Various authors (Andron & Sturm, 1973; Edgerton, 1967; Mattinson, 1973) have discussed the efficacy and/or success rate of marriage among the mentally retarded. Their findings reflect the desire among many retarded to be married and reveal that among the marriages reviewed, the greater number were considered to be successful and mutually satisfying. However, there is a note of caution in the interpretation of these findings. The sample in each of the studies was relatively small and encompassed ranges of intelligence from 38 to 93, with the majority scoring in the 50s and 60s (Mattinson), mean IQ's in the 60s (Edgerton), and known IQ's from 40 to 84 (Andron & Sturm). Although some TMR were measured, it appears that the majority of the sample in all three studies were within the educable range of intelligence.

Hall (1974), in an excellent review of the literature concerning marriage and the mentally retarded, concluded that the number of mentally retarded who marry is actually small, and that the advisability of marriage for those retardates with IQ's below 50 is questionable. Saenger (1967) also noted that marriage in the TMR population is rare, and Bass (1964) questioned the efficacy of marriage of severely retarded persons except under unusual circumstances and where supervision was available.

Table Twelve

*State Statutes Regarding Marriage of
the Mentally Retarded*

No law	Law prohibits	Law permits	No information	No reply
Alabama	Indiana	Hawaii[4]	Arizona	Alaska
Arkansas	Kentucky	New Mexico	Delaware	New
California	Massachusetts	South	Florida	Hampshire
Colorado	Michigan	Dakota[5]	Iowa	
Connecticut	Minnesota[1]	Washington[6]	Louisiana	
District of	Mississippi		Maine	
Columbia	Missouri		Montana	
Georgia	New Jersey		Nebraska	
Idaho	North		North	
Illinois	Dakota[2]		Carolina	
Kansas	Ohio		Oregon	
Maryland	Rhode		Pennsylvania	
Nevada	Island[3]		Texas	
New York	Virginia		Utah	
Oklahoma			West Virginia	
South			Wisconsin	
Carolina				
Tennessee				
Vermont				
Wyoming				

[1]Law prohibits unless permission is obtained from legal guardian.
[2]Law prohibits unless woman is over 45 or man is going to marry a woman over 45 years of age.
[3]Law prohibits unless the person has not been adjudicated incompetent.
[4]Law permits marriage if superintendent of hospital gives permission. Superintendent's authorization is based on a board decision. Board assesses ability to be self-supporting and lack of behavior and social problems.
[5]Law permits marriage if individual granted license is sterile.
[6]Law permits marriage after counseling and approval of superintendent of hospital.

NOTE: C. H. Krishef, State laws on marriage and sterilization of the mentally retarded, *Mental Retardation*, 1972, *10*, 36–38.

At present, there appears to be little support for marriage among TMR adults, but as Andron & Sturm (1973) have noted:

> As more and more of the state institutions return their retarded citizens to the community and the "normalization" principle gains wider acceptance, the question of whether or not the retarded should marry and how we can help them will become more pressing. A great deal of research is necessary to provide the knowledge needed in the field. [p. 34]

Another expressed concern, in conjunction with the right of the TMR adult to marry, is the frequent product of marriage—children. The question is not whether these people can but whether they should be allowed to have children. Krishef (1972) noted that in instances where legislation was enacted concerning the TMR's right to marry, there was an expressed concern for the production of offspring.

Sterilization has been the historical means that society has used to cope with the problem of procreation of the retarded. However, Carnahan (1973) indicated that the United States Supreme Court has reaffirmed the individual's right to conceive and raise children as a basic civil right that the state cannot hinder.

Sterilization and the Right to Have Children

The history of involuntary sterilization as a eugenics measure was discussed previously. Although not frequently employed or permitted in many states, there has been a reemerging interest expressed towards its use as a protective means of birth control for retarded adults. As in the case of marriage, it is a moot point in some states. Krishef (1972) reviewed the state laws on sterilization, and the results of his findings are illustrated in Table Thirteen. He reported that 47% of the states permit sterilization, 43% had no law for sterilization, 4% prohibited it, 4% gave no reply, and 2% gave no information. In addition, Krishef noted that most states, where sterilization was admissible, could not make indiscriminate or arbitrary use of the sterilization law. The final authority, by state, is defined in Table Fourteen.

The propaganda for and against sterilization of the mentally retarded is emotionally charged and/or laden with fear. The historical fear factor was that retardation was hereditary, and that the indiscriminate propagation of mentally retarded offspring posed a threat to the social and economic welfare of society. Conversely, others plead that sterilization is religiously and morally wrong, as well as being a violation of the retardate's civil rights. Further, the sterilization excesses of National Socialist Germany are frequently brought into the controversy as an example of wholesale sterilization as being the action of a police state.

Whitcraft and Jones (1974) made a survey of attitudes relative to the sterilization of retardates. Their findings indicated that out of a sample of parents, professionals, and others, 85.8% favored voluntary sterilization, and 95.5% viewed voluntary sterilization as a "morally right" means of controlling the incidence of mental retardation.

Although such actions may find support in the abstract, there is evidence (Edgerton, 1967; Sabagh & Edgerton, 1962) to indicate that the mentally retarded person, after sterilization, does not approve of the process. Among the retarded surveyed, it was determined that their

Table Thirteen

*State Statutes Regarding Sterilization of
the Mentally Retarded*

No law	Law prohibits	Law permits	No reply
Alabama	New Jersey	Arkansas	Arizona
Alaska	Texas[1]	California	New Hampshire
Colorado		Connecticut	
District of		Delaware	
Columbia		Georgia	
Florida		Indiana	
Hawaii		Iowa	
Idaho		Maine	
Illinois		Michigan	
Kansas		Minnesota	
Kentucky		Mississippi	
Louisiana		Montana	
Maryland		New Mexico	
Massachusetts		North Carolina	
Missouri		North Dakota	
Nebraska		Oklahoma	
Nevada		Oregon	
New York		South Carolina	
Ohio		South Dakota	
Pennsylvania		Utah	
Rhode Island		Vermont	
Tennessee		Virginia	
Washington		West Virginia	
Wyoming		Wisconsin	

[1]Law prohibits for those who are wards of the state, however, does not apply to those who are not state wards.

NOTE: C. H. Krishef, State laws on marriage and sterilization of the mentally retarded, *Mental Retardation,* 1972, *10,* 36–38.

inability to have children was a source of great distress, and those surveyed often used their sterility as a reason for marital problems.

In answer to the recent concerns surrounding sterilization of the mentally retarded, the American Association on Mental Deficiency (1974) has proposed an official policy statement on sterilization. In these guidelines, involuntary sterilization was strongly opposed, and conditions for voluntary sterilization were clearly defined to guard against unwanted or unnecessary sterilization. For the purposes of considering sterilization, the policy divides the general population into three classes:

1. *Competent persons:* It was determined that this population should

---

Table Fourteen

Final Authority for Sterilization in States with Laws

1. Parent/ guardian/ retardate	2. Court/agency board/ institution	3. Required consent of both 1 & 2	4. Other[2]
Georgia	Arkansas	Connecticut	Maine
Montana	California	Minnesota	Oklahoma
New Mexico	Delaware[1]	North Dakota	South Dakota
Oregon	Indiana	Vermont	
	Iowa		
	Michigan		
	Mississippi		
	North Carolina		
	South Carolina		
	Utah		
	Virginia		
	West Virginia		
	Wisconsin[1]		

[1]Does not provide a formal appeal procedure.
[2]Maine and South Dakota have separate sterilization requirements for institutionalized and noninstitutionalized retardates. Oklahoma has a law which provides for "adequate protection" for proposed sterilization of retarded men under 65 and women under 47.

NOTE: C. H. Krishef, State laws on marriage and sterilization of the mentally retarded, *Mental Retardation,* 1972, *10,* 36–38.

---

have the right to free and informed choice. They should be free from involuntary constraints; they should be informed of less restrictive alternatives; and they should be fully notified and understand the consequences of sterilization.

2. *Legally incompetent persons:* The guidelines directed that no legally incompetent person should be involuntarily sterilized except where the case was reviewed and approved by the courts. In the court proceedings, legal, social, and ethical safeguards should be rigorously applied to insure that the action taken is in the best interest of the retarded person.

3. *Persons of impaired capacity:* It was noted that these persons should not be sterilized except with the approval of the court, under the same conditions as outlined for legally incompetent persons, the one exception being that the approval of next of kin can be substituted for the legal guardian if there is no legal guardian other than a public official.

Informed consent is the central issue of sterilization. It is always a problem, and sterilization—voluntary and involuntary—will probably remain a controversial issue. However, the benefits of sterilization merit its continuing consideration. This policy frequently relieves the parents of fears about the TMR adult's potential for heterosexual relationships and potential pregnancy. It also, in instances, relieves society of the potential burden of care for retarded offspring. Therefore, it appears that sterilization should be made available to those who desire it, and for those parents who, through informed consent, desire it for their TMR child as a protective and/or preventive measure.

Concurrent with the moral and legal issues surrounding sterilization is the frequent concern for promiscuity among the retarded once the fear of pregnancy is removed. The potential for promiscuous sexual behavior—or for that matter any sexual behavior—in the TMR adult population is a source of considerable consternation to society. The TMR adult is frequently regarded as a neuter sexually and is expected to behave in like fashion. Violation of this expectancy through any type of heterosexual or homosexual activity creates considerable anxiety in parents, professionals, and others who are in contact with the TMR adult. The right to be a human sexually has been tacitly denied TMR adults because "they are not supposed to be interested in such things."

The Expression of Human Sexuality

In addition to the rights to marry and bear children, the TMR's right to expressions of human sexuality is receiving an increasing amount of attention in programs. Although parents and professionals are beginning to look at appropriate sexual expression as an important dimension of training in programs, sex education and human sexuality for the TMR has not reached a level of general acceptance. There are those who contend that exposure to information on sexuality increases interest and potential experimentation in sexual relationships, and that without the safeguards of sterilization or other forms of contraception we will have to deal with increased incidence of pregnancy in the TMR population. In addition, the fear of sexual assaults by the TMR adult is omnipresent. These fears notwithstanding, there is a growing counter-contingent that contends that sex education will reduce, rather than increase, the potential for maladaptive sexual behavior and develop in the TMR adult a means of expressing his sexuality appropriately. This expression is often regarded as a right and is consistent with normalization.

Sex education, or instruction in sex-related behavior for the TMR, is a different dimension of what is usually regarded as sex education. Although the TMR have in the past been regarded as immoral, they are actually amoral. Their sometimes overt sexual behavior is committed without a sense of propriety or responsibility, acting merely in response to natural impulses. Therefore, socially appropriate behaviors in expressions of sexuality, as in other forms of adaptive behavior, will have to be learned. Even though their sex drive may not, in certain instances, be as intense as that of a normal adult, and their ability to sustain a meaningful relationship may be questionable, the TMR need to be instructed in the means of expressing sexuality in a socially acceptable manner.

The manual *Sex Education and the Mentally Retarded: A Community Approach* (1974) noted that the retarded have not been instructed in appropriate ways of expressing sexuality and are therefore unaware of the inappropriateness of "indecent exposure," masturbation in public places, and other displays of sexuality that are inappropriate. They simply have never been taught differently.

Although the TMR often display poor internal controls in expressions of sexuality, most can learn appropriate forms of sexual expression. In determining the desired outcomes for this instruction, the American Association for Health, Physical Education and Recreation (1971) defined three areas for consideration:

1. How does one help the retarded establish realistic and sound attitudes about sex relationships?
2. How does one help the retarded channel natural drives into socially acceptable behavior?
3. How does one provide the retarded, where necessary, with some form of lifetime supervision over relationships of a sexual nature? [p. 6]

Attempts at resolving these issues are beginning to be incorporated into training programs, and resources and curriculum guides for instruction are beginning to become commercially available. Most of the available programs advocate a visual approach to instruction, using a vocabulary familiar to the pupil. The guide developed by Fischer, Krajicek, and Borthick (1974) is representative of this approach. The guide has a number of "relatively unsensational" pictures to be used for discussion in the areas of:

1. Sexual identification of male and female adults and children
2. Identification of male and female sexual body parts
3. Emotional functions of embracing, kissing, and intercourse
4. Body functions of urination, bowel movement, menstruation, and male and female masturbation
5. Identification of pregnancy and discussion of the birth process

Although society is approaching a more realistic attitude towards sexuality and the TMR adult, we are still in need of additional information on the TMR's attitudes and knowledge of sex and improved methods for teaching appropriate sexual behavior. In addition, the critical issue of teacher attitudes and the teacher's willingness to deal with such information will have to be determined and perhaps trained for, in order to provide an appropriately informative program for the TMR.

Commentary

The foregoing discussion on the questions of marriage, sterilization, and sex education poses a number of issues without solutions. At present, the information concerning these issues is often more emotional than empirical. The sum total of these questions is "How normal is normal?" Are we overreacting to a set of issues that are, for the most part, unnecessary and unobtainable for the TMR adult population? The TMR adult is an adult who has severe deficits in intelligence and adaptive behavior. He is, by definition, not normal. Therefore, we have yet to understand and respond to his needs or abilities to (1) sustain or understand the responsibility of marriage, (2) procreate at the risk of society by producing a number of additional retardates, and (3) understand his sexuality and appropriate means of expressing it.

Summary

The TMR adult, throughout history, has been an often ignored, or much maligned individual. The interest in programs for the TMR in general is just beginning to catch up with the TMR adult, and program alternatives for this population are beginning to be implemented. The development of these programs is, for the most part, the result of a concern for decentralizing the institutions and the retention of the TMR in the community for program and services.

The program alternatives that have been developed for the TMR adult have a strong emphasis on work and work-related activities. These programs are usually concerned with the placement of the TMR adult in some sort of sheltered employment. For those unable to participate in this type of program, it has been suggested that other appropriate adult activities be provided.

The establishment of community programs and the movement away from the institution as the sole residential alternative has also precipitated the development of group homes or other small residential facilities for those TMR adults who cannot be maintained in the home with their natural family.

Although there has been a concern for reducing the size of the institutions, the institution remains as an alternative for those TMR adults who cannot participate in community programs or other residential facilities. However, there is an emerging trend towards reducing the size of these institutions and making them more community-oriented, in an attempt to extend the normalization principle as much as possible to the institutionalized adult.

The retention of a greater number of TMR adults in community programs and the concern for providing as normal a life as possible has also raised additional issues—those concerning the experience of marriage, sterilization, and expressions of human sexuality in the TMR adult population. To date, it appears that marriage is not as critical an issue as are sterilization and appropriate expressions of human sexuality. Although sterilization is allowed or required in many states, there has been a concern expressed for safeguarding the mentally retarded against its indiscriminate use. Appropriate expressions of human sexuality in the TMR population have been recognized as learned behavior, and there is an increasing concern for the inclusion of sex education in training programs to reduce maladaptive behaviors in the expression of sexuality.

Many questions remain to be answered about the "normalization" of the TMR adult. Since this is a population that has been long ignored, it will take time and research to determine what is appropriate in programs for this population. However, current efforts are promising, and the TMR adult is beginning to be reintegrated into society.

References

American Association for Health, Physical Education, and Recreation. *A resources guide in sex education for the mentally retarded.* Washington, D.C.: AAHPER Press, 1971.

American Association on Mental Deficiency. *Standards for state residential institutions for the mentally retarded* (monograph supplement). *American Journal of Mental Deficiency,* 1964.

American Association on Mental Deficiency. Sterilization of persons who are mentally retarded. *Mental Retardation,* 1974, *12,* 59–61.

Andron, L., & Sturm, M. L. Is "I do" in the repertoire of the retarded? A study of the functioning of mentally retarded couples. *Mental Retardation,* 1973, *11,* 31–34.

Bass, M. S. Marriage for the mentally deficient. *Mental Retardation,* 1964, *2,* 198–202.

Blatt, B., & Kaplan, F. *Christmas in Purgatory.* Boston, Mass.: Allyn & Bacon, 1966.

Blue, C. M. Trainable mentally retarded in sheltered workshops. *Mental Retardation,* 1964, *2,* 97–104.

Budde, J. F. Will institutionalization survive? *Mental Retardation,* 1972, *10,* 24–28.

Butterfield, E. C. Basic facts about public residential facilities for the mentally retarded. In R. B. Kugel & W. Wolfensberger (Eds.), *Changing patterns in residential services for the mentally retarded.* Washington, D.C.: U.S. Government Printing Office, 1969.

Carnahan, W. A. Rights to love, marry and bear children, to vote, hold property, have a job and go to court. In B. J. Ennis & P. R. Friedman (Eds.), *Legal rights of the mentally handicapped, vol. 2.* Practising Law Institute, 1973.

Cortazzo, A. D. A guide to establishing an activity program for mentally retarded adults. In E. L. Meyen (Ed.), *Planning community services for the mentally retarded.* Scranton, Penn.: International Textbook Co., 1967.

Davies, S. P., & Ecob, K. G. *The mentally retarded in society.* New York: Columbia University Press, 1962.

Department of Health, Education, and Welfare. Boarding facility for the trainable adult retarded. In E. L. Meyen (Ed.), *Planning community services for the mentally retarded.* Scranton, Penn.: International Textbook Co., 1967.

Dunn, L. M. Small, special-purpose residential facilities for the retarded. In R. B. Kugel & W. Wolfensberger (Eds.), *Changing patterns in residential services for the mentally retarded.* Washington, D.C.: U.S. Government Printing Office, 1969.

Dybwad, G. *Challenges in mental retardation.* New York: Columbia University Press, 1964.

Edgerton, R. B. *The cloak of competence.* Berkeley, Ca.: University of California Press, 1967.

Farber, B. *Mental retardation: Its social context and social consequences.* Boston, Mass.: Houghton Mifflin, 1968.

Fischer, H. L., Krajicek, M. J., & Borthick, W. A. *Sex education for the developmentally disabled; a guide for parents, teachers, and professionals.* Baltimore, Md.: University Park Press, 1974.

Garner, R. E., Lacy, G. H. & Creasy, R. F. Workshops—why, what, whither? *Mental Retardation,* 1972, *10,* 25–27.

Gardner, W. I., & Nisonger, H. W. *A manual on program development in mental retardation.* Washington, D.C.: American Association on Mental Deficiency, 1962.

Gold, M. W. *The acquisition of a complex assembly task by retarded adolescents* [Final report. Project no. 8–8060, grant no. OEG–0–9–232021–0769 (032)]. Washington, D.C.: Department of Health, Education and Welfare, U.S. Office of Education, Bureau of Education for the Handicapped, 1969.

Gold, M. W. Research on the vocational habilitation of the retarded: The present and future. In N. R. Ellis (Ed.), *International review of research in mental retardation.* New York: Academic Press, 1973.

Gosney, E. S., & Popenoe, P. *Sterilization for human betterment.* New York: Macmillan, 1929.

Hall, J. E. Sexual behavior. In J. Wortis (Ed.), *Mental retardation and developmental disabilities, vol. 1.* New York: Brunner/Mazel, 1974.

Huddle, D. D. Sheltered workshops for the trainable mentally retarded. *Education and Training of the Mentally Retarded,* 1967, *2,* 65–69. (a)

Huddle, D. D. Work performance of trainable adults as influenced by competition, cooperation, and monetary reward. *American Journal of Mental Deficiency,* 1967, *72,* 198–211. (b)

Joint Commission on Accreditation of Hospitals. *Standards for residential facilities for the mentally retarded.* Chicago, Ill.: Accreditation Council for Facilities for the Mentally Retarded, 1971.

Katz, E. *The retarded adult in the community.* Springfield, Ill.: Charles C. Thomas, 1968.

Krishef, C. H. State laws on marriage and sterilization of the mentally retarded. *Mental Retardation,* 1972, *10,* 36–38.

Kugel, R. B., & Wolfensberger, W. *Changing patterns in residential services for the mentally retarded.* Washington, D.C.: U.S. Government Printing Office, 1969.

Mamula, R. A., & Newman, N. *Community placement of the mentally retarded.* Springfield, Ill.: Charles C. Thomas, 1973.

Mattinson, J. Marriage and mental handicap. In F. F. de la Cruz & G. D. LaVeck (Eds.), *Human sexuality and the mentally retarded.* New York: Brunner/Mazel, 1973.

President's Committee on Mental Retardation. *MR 72 Islands of excellence.* Washington, D.C.: U.S. Government Printing Office, 1972.

President's Panel on Mental Retardation. *A proposed program for national action to combat mental retardation.* Washington, D.C.: U.S. Government Printing Office, 1962.

Rivera, G. *Willowbrook.* New York: Vantage Books, 1972.

Rusalem, H. Rehabilitation problems of the mentally retarded. In E. M. Kelly (Ed.), *The new and more open outlook for the mentally retarded.* Washington, D.C.: The Catholic University Press, 1966.

Sabagh, G., & Edgerton, R. B. Sterilized mental defectives look at sterilization. *Eugenics Quarterly,* 1962, *9,* 372–385.

Saenger, G. *The adjustment of severely retarded adults in the community.* Albany, New York: New York State Interdepartmental Health Resources Board, 1957.

Saenger, G. Social and occupational adjustment of the mentally retarded. In J. Zubin & G. A. Jervis (Eds.), *Psychopathology of mental development.* New York: Grune & Stratton, 1967.

Scheerenberger, R. C. A current census of state institutions for the mentally retarded. *Mental Retardation,* 1965, *3,* 4–6.

Scheerenberger, R. C. A model for deinstitutionalization. *Mental Retardation,* 1974, *12,* 3–7.

Seguin, E. *Idiocy and its treatment by the physiological method.* New York: Augustus M. Kelley, 1971.

Sex Education and the Mentally Retarded: A community approach. Atlanta, Ga.: Roger Blue, 1974.

Stanfield, J. S. Graduation: What happens to the retarded child when he grows up? *Exceptional Children,* 1973, *39,* 548–552.

Thurman, S. K., & Thiele, R. L. A viable role for retardation institutions: The road to self-destruction. *Mental Retardation,* 1973, *11,* 21–22.

Tisdall, W. J. A follow-up study of trainable mentally handicapped children in Illinois. *American Journal on Mental Deficiency,* 1960, *64,* 11–16.

Tobias, J., & Gorelick, J. Work characteristics of retarded adults at trainable levels. *Mental Retardation,* 1963, *1,* 338–344.

Vocational Rehabilitation Administration. *Proceedings of a conference on special problems in vocational rehabilitation of the mentally retarded.* Washington, D.C.: U.S. Government Printing Office, 1963.

Whitcraft, C. J., & Jones, J. P. A survey of attitudes about sterilization of retardates. *Mental Retardation,* 1974, *12,* 30–33.

White, W. D., & Wolfensberger, W. The evolution of dehumanizing our institutions. *Mental Retardation,* 1969, *7,* 5–9.

Wolfensberger, W. Vocational preparation and occupation. In A. A. Baumeister (Ed.), *Mental retardation appraisal education rehabilitation.* Chicago, Ill.: Aldine, 1967.

Wolfensberger, W. Will there always be an institution II. *Mental Retardation,* 1971, *9,* 31–37.

Wolfensberger, W. *Normalization.* Toronto: National Institute on Mental Retardation, 1972.

Reference Note

1. Thomas, J. K. *An overview of Washington State's group homes for developmentally disabled persons.* Unpublished manuscript. Presented at the seminar sponsored by Research and Training Center in Mental Retardation, Texas Tech, Lubbock, Texas 1972.

Chapter 8

The Family of the Trainable Mentally Retarded

Research on the family of the TMR is rapidly reaching immense proportions. The acceptance-rejection factor, coping strategies, and family crisis reaction to the TMR child or adult will all have a decisive impact on the training process. The literature is full of discussions on the dimensions of the various crisis factors, and I recommend, for the student wishing additional supplementary information in this area, Wolfensberger's (1967) excellent review of the literature or texts such as Tizard and Grad (1961), Wolfensberger and Kurtz (1969), or the Farber monographs (1959; 1960).

The family of the trainable mentally retarded is often confronted with a variety of problems beyond the usual ones of child rearing and family living. Not the least of these is an acceptance of the fact that the child is retarded. The problems are principally involved with the parents' efforts to develop and maintain desirable foundations for their child's early and prolonged training, as well as making positive and necessary adjustments in their own personalities. Often, without training or assistance, the parents must be specialists in the developmental problems of retarded children, while lacking an understanding of the problems inherent in the nurture and rearing of a TMR child. Characteristically, this lack of knowledge often precludes the possibility of the family formulating meaningful or appropriate coping strategies.

The presence of a TMR child usually has a disrupting influence on the family. The emotional reactions and coping strategies of the family will, in turn, have a decided impact on the development of the TMR child and her or his future. While reactions and intensity of reactions will vary, the family of the TMR child will almost always have some negative or undesirable attitudes toward the child's presence in the family group.

The impact of the TMR child is borne most heavily by the parents. The mental health of the parents is frequently threatened when they try to cope, and they often become desperate in their pleas for knowledge of the condition and for help in coping with the circumstances.

The disruptive influence of the TMR child has been described in terms of a number of crisis situations which often have a deleterious effect on the ability of the parents to accept the retardation. Some examples of parent reactions to the retarded child have been defined by Wolfensberger and Menolascino (1970):

1. *The novelty shock:* This crisis arises out of the identification of

229

the retardation and the determination that the child is less than the perfect or normal child that was expected. The major contribution to this crisis is a discrepancy in the parents' expectancy for the anticipated normal child and the diagnosis of retardation. The parents frequently become disorganized as a result of this discrepancy, and the lack of information on the meaning of the diagnosis and realistic expectancies for their mentally retarded child.

2. *The value crisis:* The salient feature of this crisis is emotional and/or physical rejection of the retarded child. The parents, in this crisis, may respond to the retardate and his or her lack of potential as a normal child by ambivalence and overprotection or by denial of the retardate's existence and possible early institutionalization.

3. *The reality crisis:* This may occur as a reaction to genuine management problems which make it difficult, if not impossible, to maintain the retardate in the home unless community support and help is available. In addition, other factors, such as social pressures or unexpected events like death of one of the parents, would constitute a reality crisis in the continuing maintenance of the retardate in the home.

The disruptive influence of the TMR child or adult is not a discrete effect. The TMR's presence will have a profound effect upon the total family unit. The parents may react collectively or individually, and the siblings will certainly share in the crisis. In addition, factors such as the socioeconomic status of the family and the sex of the retarded child will all contribute to the intensity and variability of the reaction.

The Family Crisis

There is a rapidly growing body of literature that is witness to the feelings of the parents of retarded children. These various emotions have been described as:

> Alarm, ambivalence, anger, anguish, anxiety, avoidance, bewilderment, bitterness, catastrophic reaction, confusion, death wishes, denial, depression, despair, disappointment, disbelief, disassociation, embarrassment, envy, fear, financial worries, grief, guilt, helplessness, identification, immobility, impulses to destroy the child, lethargy, mourning, over-identification, pain, projection, puzzlement, regret, rejection, remorse, self-blame, self-pity, shame, shock, sorrow, suicidal impulses, trauma, etc. [Wolfensberger, 1967, p. 330]*

---

*Reprinted by permission from Alfred A. Baumeister, editor, *Mental Retardation* (Chicago: Aldine Publishing Company) copyright © 1967 by Alfred A. Baumeister.

Emotional reactions such as those indicated are often sufficient to provoke a crisis of monumental proportions in the family of the retarded child. The parents, through introspection about the "why" of the re-tardation, often begin to engage in recriminations directed towards themselves and others; or they develop a very strong pattern of ego-defensive behaviors that become debilitating and mutually self-destructive. Subsequently, the family unit may begin to disintegrate as a result of the presence of the retarded child.

The disruptive effects of the TMR child have been well docu-mented. Farber (1960) has defined the family crisis as:

> The breakdown of patterns and conduct which have been developed to guide the activities of the family members through the family's life cycle. The crisis can be limited or general in its severity. For example, having a first child in any family disrupts previous family routines and modifies the value of the parents. The parents, however, can usually maintain most of their occupational, friendship, and kinship commit-ments. In contrast, having a severely retarded child frequently creates a situation of utter chaos. [p. 5]

The effects of the presence of a TMR child on the family was determined by Schonell and Watts (1956) to be restrictive and disruptive in nature and to effect the family economically, socially, and emotionally. Furthermore, they concluded that the mental health of the parents (more often the mother) frequently deteriorated.

Other factors involved in the family crisis have been identified as poor marital integration (Farber, 1960), fear of additional pregnancies (Holt, 1958), physical and mental health problems (Tizard & Grad, 1961), emotional problems among the siblings (Farber, 1959; 1960), frequent attempts at early institutionalization (Jolly, 1953), and general frustration (Grebler, 1952). Although these are all generalizable to the total family life cycle, crisis reactions to the TMR frequently vary in type and intensity, depending upon the age of the retardate.

The Crisis at Birth

Burton (1974) has noted that:

> The birth of a child is usually an occasion of joy and relief. The question, "Is he normal or retarded?" is not so much the concern of parents as is "Is it a boy or a girl?" Parents view their children as extensions of themselves and, therefore anticipate only that the child will be as "normal" as they are. [p. 432]

The identification of retardation at birth, then, occurs when the parents are most vulnerable (Jordan, 1972). Their reactions, although variable, often create havoc in the family. The birth crisis is frequently compounded by a lack of information, or misinformation. Parents are often informed of the retardation without a discussion of its implications for care or are informed in such terms as, "Your child is a vegetable, he will never walk, talk, etc., and immediate institutionalization is recommended." Fortunately, this attitude and approach are changing, but unfortunately not rapidly enough.

The crisis may be no less severe in instances where the information at birth is honest and instructive. The parents will still react to the crisis of retardation. Whatever the level and quality of the initial diagnosis and information, Kanner (1953) defined the reaction according to three levels of acceptance:

1. Acknowledgement and acceptance of the child as he or she is
2. Disguising the reality and attempts at correction
3. Complete denial of the problem

In addition, consistent with the level of reaction, Wolfensberger (1967) concluded that guilt was the most prevalent emotion in parents when the retardation was diagnosed at birth.

The initial reaction and guilt are usually generalized to a number of other fears and problems. Kanner (1953) enumerated several questions that are frequently asked by the parents. These involved concerns such as:

1. The cause of the retardation
2. Whether the parents did something to contribute to the condition
3. Why it had to happen to them
4. Whether the condition was hereditary
5. Whether it was safe to have another child

In addition to being plagued by these concerns, the parents often leave the hospital with minimal, if any, knowledge of the developmental lag and face extended problems of infant care for their retarded child in areas such as feeding, toilet training, ambulation, and speech. All of these factors can produce parental exhaustion (more often in the mother than the father), bitterness and jealousy in the siblings for being ignored, and a restriction on the family's social contacts.

The inability to cope with the circumstances and the continuing reaction and growth of the crisis frequently leads the parents to seek an early resolution to the problem through institutionalization; or they engage in "doctor or agency shopping," in an effort to reverse the diagnosis or displace the responsibility for cause or care.

The current overcrowded conditions of institutions and a reluctance to admit young infants frequently precludes the possibility of institutionalization as an early alternative. If the infant is placed in an institution, parents may suffer additional problems of guilt for having "abandoned" the child to an isolated institution. Remarkably enough, Fotheringham, Skelton, and Hoddinott (1971) reported that institutionalization did not improve the family's functioning. The actuality of institutionalization of the retarded infant is simply usually not available, and TMR children are, for the most part, retained in the home.

"Doctor and agency shopping" is the more common reaction to the crisis of the retarded child and is a further manifestation of the parents' unwillingness to accept the initial diagnosis of retardation. "Shopping behavior" involves repeated visits to physicians and other professionals and agencies, in attempts to get an acceptable diagnosis and/or restorative educational and treatment programs. This behavior is usually costly, exhaustive, disruptive, counterproductive, and needless to say, usually futile (Anderson, 1971).

An example of this behavior would be the family who consults with every available physician in the community, several specialists, and ultimately a major diagnostic clinic before the diagnosis of Down's syndrome is "accepted." The presence of Down's syndrome may be acknowledged or "accepted" by the parents, but they then begin a series of agency consultations seeking a means of correcting or "fixing up" their retarded child. The process can be economically and psychologically devastating to the family.

Although many TMR children are readily diagnosed at birth because of the extant syndrome or other physical stigmata, many escape the early diagnosis through omission or commission and are not identified until sometime during the preschool years or upon entering school.

The Crisis of Delayed Diagnosis

Delayed diagnosis frequently occurs as a result of two factors: (1) the problem of retardation is not medically identifiable at birth, or (2) the physician(s) withholds the information from the parents.

Although retardation may go undetected for a few years, it is usually the mother who begins to suspect that something is wrong. Delayed development or failure to achieve anticipated developmental milestones is usually the first indicator of problems. Parental recognition of this "slowness" usually occurs much earlier when there are older normal siblings which provide a basis of comparison for normal development. Although discovery during this period is not as abrupt and overwhelming as the diagnosis of retardation at birth, it is no less severe in its impact (Jordan, 1972).

The crisis is similar to that of the discovery at birth. The patterns of parental and family reaction are essentially the same. However, in instances it can be magnified by professionals' refusing to confirm the parents' suspicions at an early date or to confront the parents with the realities of retardation. The parents are often fended off with explanations such as, "The child will outgrow it." In so doing, professionals contribute substantially to the "shopping behavior." For want of information, the parents will frantically seek to find out what is wrong with their child. This approach may also contribute to post-diagnostic denial of retardation as the primary cause of the child's problem. After all, why should the parents believe the professional that finally confronts them with the harsh reality, when others have given a much more palatable "The child will outgrow it." Additional problems in delayed diagnosis, even as late as school age, may contribute to a lack of planning or limited resources for services for the child.

An example of delayed diagnosis would be the child that was finally diagnosed as having Down's syndrome at four years of age. Prior to the diagnosis, the parents knew that the child looked different but did not know why. Diagnosis came, inadvertently, when the parents overheard the family physician make reference to their child over the telephone to another physician as a "mongoloid." The parents consulted their home edition of a popular baby book for the first descriptive diagnosis. Even after initial "diagnosis," and the physician's subsequent confirmation of the child's problem, the parents report that they continued to deny and fantasize about the child's condition until the first day of school of his sixth year. Their attempt to enroll the child in the first grade was denied, and they were informed that he was ineligible for any of the existing public school programs. The delayed diagnosis and later denial of the circumstances not only resulted in a severe emotional crisis in the family, but delayed for two years the child's admission to an available and appropriate training program in the community.

It has often been remarked that TMR children, like kittens and puppies, have a bad habit of growing up. The implication is that as long as they are small in size, the management problems are not as severe, and they do not pose any real physical threat to the family or the community. Nevertheless, the TMR do grow up and, in so doing, pose additional concerns and potential crisis in the family.

The Crisis of Growing Older

Although factors such as developmental lag in the TMR are often crises in themselves, this problem reaches greater proportions as the lag persists into later childhood, adolescence, and adulthood. The nonambulatory infant, by nature of size and weight, poses little in the way of management problems; but, as he or she grows older and heavier, lack of ambulation can pose a crisis by the sheer physical problem of moving the retardate about. Other problems in feeding and toilet training also become increasingly severe as the child grows older. In addition, the community often begins to see the growing TMR as a threat to their safety and welfare. Fears about the onset of puberty, and parental anxieties concerning potential overt and/or public expressions of sexuality or sexual experimentation become ominous. Also, it may be recalled, from our discussion in Chapter Seven, that programs for the older TMR may not be available. The parental crisis is then frequently one of home maintenance of the TMR adult; and the crisis of institutionalization, for lack of other alternatives, begins again.

It is at this point in time that other concerns may develop into crisis situations. As the child grows older, so will the parents. The parents' increasing age could pose additional physical problems in management. In addition, the probable reality that the TMR adult will outlive the parents creates a crisis over after-care, deciding who or what agency will be responsible for this care.

In summary, there has been, over the last few decades, an expressed concern for the effects of the TMR on the family. It is well recognized that the problem is not isolated in terms of providing programs and services for the TMR only but that it is a total family problem that has implications for the maintenance of the family unit and the mental health of its members.

There has been some reference in the literature on retardation to parental awareness and acceptance as an "overstated case" and to parent management problems as "sacred cows" that may be unwarranted (Wolfensberger, 1967). The genuine evidence of this issue, as in many other issues involving the TMR, is unresolved. However, from the extant literature, it is apparent that the existence of a retarded child in the family poses certain problems that will have to be confronted if we are to provide programs for the TMR and assist the parents in coping with the TMR child or adult in the home and community.

Coping and the Acceptance-Rejection Factor

There are a myriad of circumstances that influence our means of coping with crisis. These circumstances may be supportive or nonsupportive in their influence. The parent, confronted with the crisis of a retarded child, will be influenced by many factors. Factors or circumstances such as religion, socioeconomic status, and the sex of the retarded child will all have an impact on the family's adjustment.

The acceptance of a retarded child is often thought to be facilitated by a strong religious conviction. In instances, religion can serve a supportive role, but may also contribute to the crisis by facilitating denial. The cliché, "The retarded are God's children," is often used by parents as a badge of honor ("this is my cross to bear") or by parents who are in reality saying, "It's God's responsibility, let him take care of it." Further guilt may also be precipitated in religious parents by the feeling that God has visited past sins upon the parents by punishing them with a retarded child.

The literature on the supportive role of religion and acceptance of the retarded child, although insufficient, indicates that Catholics usually have a higher rate of acceptance of the retarded than do Protestant or Jewish families. This is assumed to be the result of certain elements of Catholicism which absolve the parents of the guilt of having a retarded child (Zuk, 1959).

Socioeconomic status has long been recognized as contributing significantly to the impact of a retarded child and the family's ability to cope with the circumstances. The extensive research conducted by Farber (1959; 1960) and later commentary (Farber, 1968; Michaels & Schulman, 1962) have resulted in a general conclusion that the presence of a TMR child in families of middle to high socioeconomic status poses the greater crisis. However, Wolfensberger (1967) noted several shortcomings in the work of Farber and others. He commented, relative to the topic of socioeconomic status, that much of the data collection and discussion on parent adjustment has been with middle- to upper-middle-class families and that the data have not been representative. The limitation, then, is that the existing information does not reflect the attitudes and feeling of other socioeconomic groups (that is, the lower classes).

These limitations notwithstanding, the achievement orientation of the middle and upper class for their children would tend to give credibility to the "middle-class crisis" and support Farber's (1968) contention that the diagnosis of mental retardation in families of low socioeconomic status is not significantly different from other low-status labels and therefore not particularly damaging or crisis evoking in families of low socioeconomic status.

The sex of the retarded child, as a contributor to crisis, has also been investigated. Farber (1959; 1960) noted that a severely retarded boy has a greater effect on the family and that as he grows older he has an increasingly disruptive effect. Farber also indicated that the retarded child's sex has a greater impact on the parents than on the siblings. This difference was presumed to be the result of parental aspirations for the life careers of a boy and the transcending of death through the anticipated role of the boy as a physical extension of the family and its traditions (Ryckman & Henderson, 1965).

Up to this point, we have principally focused on the factors of parental reaction to the TMR family member. But what of the normal siblings and their adjustment and/or reaction to the crisis? The siblings are no less interested or affected by the TMR child's presence in the family.

Farber (1959) identified several factors that were disruptive to the normal siblings. Principal among these were:

1. The siblings were affected by the dependence of the retarded child. This finding suggests that the mother's added responsibility for the care of the retarded child resulted in the normal siblings' getting less attention and influenced their adjustment in relation to their mother.

2. Institutionalization of the retardate appeared to be of greater benefit to the female siblings, while the male siblings' adjustment was slightly higher if the retardate was at home. When the male and female siblings were compared, the maladjustment of the male siblings appeared to be greater when the retardate was institutionalized. Further implications were that the retention of the retardate in the home contributed to role diffusion, and the female siblings were expected to take on an increased mother role in terms of the retardate and house work. Whereas, if the retardate was institutionalized, the male sibling's role in the home was expanded and additional points of stress and conflict were created between the male sibling and his mother.

While noting a surprising number of siblings who appeared to have benefited from growing up with a retarded child, Grossman (1972) reported that, in general, brothers and sisters of retarded children were frequently:

> bitterly resentful of the family's situation, guilty about their rage at their parents and at the retarded sibling, fearful that they themselves might be defective or tainted; sometimes truly deprived of the time and resources they needed to develop because every support the family had to give was used in the care of the handicapped child. [p. 176]

Additional research (Fowle, 1968) has also indicated that the marital integration factor and the retention of the retardate in the home was not as much a problem as was role tension of the siblings. Therefore, he concluded that the siblings should be given consideration in the process of counseling families of the severely retarded.

We have, thus far, discussed various factors that affect coping and/or acceptance-rejection without defining patterns for adjusting to the crisis of the TMR child or adult. There are a multitude of strategies that we use to cope with various circumstances. Some of these strategies are realistic and appropriate, others are inappropriate and deny the reality of the circumstances. The family of the TMR, in seeking a resolution to the crisis, will develop various means of coping. These strategies can compound the crisis or assist in a realistic adjustment to the acceptance and management of the TMR in the home.

The frequently assumed coping strategy is simple rejection; that is, the retarded child as an extension of the parent represents a narcissistic shock, and the child is deemed unacceptable and therefore rejected. Gallagher (1969) commented on the various dimensions of the parents' expression of rejection in terms of:

1. *Strong underexpectation of achievement:* In this instance, the parent views the child as completely useless and incapable of even the most elementary skills. In instances, this frequently results in the child fulfilling the prophecy by reducing their motivation or subsequent attempts at achievement.

2. *Setting unrealistic goals:* The establishment of high goals or aspirations is often used by the parents as a means for justifying their negative attitudes toward the child. When the child fails to realize these parental expectations, the parents feel justified in their expression of rejection because the child has failed them.

3. *Escape:* This particular strategy involves the physical removal of the child from the home to a distant school or institution or the actual desertion from the home of the mother or father (most frequently the father).

4. *Reaction formation:* Many times parents find their psychological rejection of the child so unacceptable to their own vision of themselves that they adopt the psychological reaction of denying their negative attitudes and overtly presenting the opposite attitude of loving and accepting parents, while actually wishing to be rid of the child.

While rejection is a very real factor in coping with the TMR, Gallagher (1969) contends that it may be relatively appropriate, or at least an expected reaction to the presence of a retarded child, and that we should anticipate a certain degree of resentment from the parents.

Jordan (1972) has defined other elaborate strategies that parents may use to ignore the reality of retardation. He identifies these as understandable ego-defensive behaviors and as a defense against the anxieties experienced by the parents:

1. *The argument in child development:* In this strategy, the parent is not reluctant to accept the diagnosis of retardation, but will reject the ultimate expectancy for adult performance. Parents employing this strategy would argue that the early slow development does not imply continuing and/or eventual retarded performance (that is, the developmental process will "catch up" and the child will be normal).

2. *The argument in ballistics:* The growth pattern of the child in this defense is considered to be analogous to the path of a bullet aimed at a target. The argument is that the child's development is on an inaccurate trajectory and that the path of the bullet needs only to be corrected, or to correct itself, to reduce the error on the target. In essence, the parents are saying that changes can be made in the child's growth pattern, and that the early patterns of development can be changed or altered to achieve a closer-to-normal child or adult.

3. *The key to unlock the powers of the mind:* This strategy essentially evokes the time-worn ubiquitous "mental block." The parents in this case are searching for a means to remove this "block" and to restore the child to normal life and learning.

4. *The uncertainties of differential diagnosis:* Because many conditions have manifestations similar to retardation, the parent will frequently opt for some clinical explanation other than retardation. These parents are frequently more willing to accept a diagnosis of blindness, deafness, or mental illness because of its potential for remediation, rather than the finality of a diagnosis of mental retardation.

Jordan (1972) commented that all four of these reactions were avoidance techniques to protect the parents from the reality of retardation by seeking a more acceptable reason for their child's progress and behavior.

Farber (1960; Note 1) referred to the family reaction to a retarded child as a game of strategy and described several strategies in the following terms:

1. The integrative *child-oriented* family was one in which both husband and wife were both favorably inclined toward high social mobility; the husband emphasized traditional rather than companionate values in family life; the wife identified highly with at least one of her normal children; under certain conditions, interaction between normal and retarded siblings was limited; and emotional support was provided by the wife's mother or the community.

2. The integrative *home-oriented* family was one in which either the husband or wife cared little about social mobility; the husband stressed companionate values in family life; under certain conditions, interaction between normal and retarded siblings was limited; and either the parents were highly integrated in the neighborhood or the husband identified highly with the wife.

3. The integrative *parent-oriented* family was one in which the parents were favorably inclined toward a high degree of social mobility; the husband stressed companionate rather than traditional values in family life, and the husband identified highly with his wife [Note 1, p. 2]

In essence, the *child-oriented* strategy placed emphasis on a family life structured around the needs of the normal children; the *home-oriented* strategy was concerned with good interpersonal relations in the home and the mental health of the siblings; and the *parent-oriented* strategy subordinated the demands of the children and stressed achievement in the middle-class system (Farber, 1960). Table Fifteen is a summary of the characteristics of these three strategies.

Table Fifteen

Characteristics of child-oriented, home-oriented, and parent-oriented families

Characteristics	Child-oriented family	Home-oriented family	Parent-oriented family
Source of emotional support			
Within family		X	X
Outside family	X		
Valuation of children			
High	X	X	
Low or indifferent			X
Division of labor between husband & wife			
Sharply defined	X		
Hazy		X	X
Status-oriented community participation			
Very important	X		
Somewhat important			X
Of little importance		X	

NOTE: From B. Farber, *Family organization and crisis: Maintenance of integration in families with a severely mentally retarded child*. Monographs of the Society for Research in Child Development, 1960, *25* (Series no. 75), p. 40. Copyright 1960 by the Society for Research in Child Development, Inc.

The families not meeting criteria for one of these strategies were classified as "residual." The conclusions drawn from the study (Farber, 1960) were that adjustment and marital integration were significantly higher in the families employing an orientation towards family life which placed emphasis on the welfare of the normal siblings (child-oriented), the home (home-oriented), or the parents themselves (parent-oriented).

In summary, the coping and/or acceptance-rejection strategies appear to point to the presence of a TMR person in the family as a crisis-producing element which precipitates a number of adjustments in "normal" family living. The potentially deleterious effect of the TMR in the family is well documented but frequently ignored or mismanaged. Parents often, as a result of lack of information or misinformation, become hostile and/or reticent in coping with their TMR child. The parents frequently feel isolated in their problems of guilt, rejection, disappointment, and the social stigma of having a retarded child. Therefore, it is not remarkable that they frequently develop a number of maladaptive behaviors so frequently maligned by professionals. As Gallagher (1969) commented, "We should expect that these parents will . . . become downcast and discouraged over the special problems that have sometimes seemed to set them apart from other parents. In short, they will act like human beings" (p. 126).

While ignored only a few years ago, there is an emerging concern for the parents and the impact of the family crisis. As previously noted, professionals are beginning to realize that the concerns accompanying the TMR population are not limited to the child, but extend—perhaps more importantly—to the total family unit. As Burton (1974b) commented in a plea for a reevaluation of program priorities for the TMR:

> The second, and perhaps most important emphasis in program would be family- rather than child-oriented. There is adequate evidence to indicate that the TMR poses a serious crisis to the family. Therefore, in a reevaluation of program it appears logical to provide supportive services to the family while maintaining the TMR in the home and community, and to assist the family in accepting the child for what he is rather than what the family wishes him to be. [p. 46]

It is becoming increasingly apparent that we must focus on the family members with counseling and guidance services. Parents and siblings are usually unable to cope with the circumstances of the TMR in the home. Therefore, services must be available to the family to assist them in adapting to the TMR and to prevent the development of severe maladaptive behaviors.

Counseling the Family

Counseling families of the TMR will vary in time and technique. It frequently begins as an unsolicited statement from the physician at the time the child is born and varies from a simple direct statement about the child's retardation with recommendations for immediate institutionalization to a sensitive, well-structured session with the parents, involving the physician(s) and perhaps other professionals and a parent of another retarded child, informing the parents of the newborn infant about retardation and its implications for care and the availability of services for the family and the child. As discussed previously, the diagnosis may be delayed, but the initial counseling or information session will represent the same continuum of quality as that which occurs at birth.

Regardless of the quality of the initial diagnosis and information about the implications of retardation, the parents will usually need continuing counseling on problems such as (1) accepting the retardation, (2) adjusting to the prolonged dependency, and (3) planning for their child's future. How this counseling is provided is a serious consideration, and as Sarason (1959) commented:

> The failure adequately to communicate to the parents the nature and implications of a diagnosis of mental deficiency probably causes more unnecessary problems and suffering than any other factor, with the obvious exception of those factors which originally produce the mental deficiency. [p. 331]

Who Should Counsel?

It is often the physician who fulfills the initial role of counselor. This level of counseling is frequently inadequate and often contributes to the crisis through the physician's failure to handle the circumstances appropriately (Wolfensberger, 1967; Wolfensberger & Menolascino, 1970). Ehlers (1964) concluded that physicians have difficulty communicating the circumstances of retardation to families and that they frequently frighten and confuse the parents.

The American Medical Association (1965) in recognition of the physician's responsibility to retardates and their families, published a handbook for physicians to increase their information and competence in the area of mental retardation. However, over a decade later, Connaughton (1974) reported that physicians were still in need of information about mental retardation and the counseling of parents.

It is apparent that possessing a medical degree does not insure the ability to be an effective counselor. Furthermore, Wolfensberger (1967) contends that one's professional training is unimportant and that no one degree qualifies or disqualifies a person for counseling parents of retarded children. He further proposes ten criteria for determining an appropriate counselor for parents of retarded children:

1. Knowledge of the broader medical, social, educational, habilitational, behavioral, etc., aspects of retardation;
2. knowledge of resources in the broadest sense (i.e., agencies, services, long-range local prospects, reading materials, "gadgets" useful in home management, etc.);

3. competency, acquired through training, in counseling principles and techniques in general;
4. experience in the applied clinical area of retardation;
5. freedom from stereotypes about retardation;
6. possession of genuinely positive attitudes toward retardation, the handicapped, and their parents;
7. an orientation to the current community-centered management approach;
8. a sensitivity to the reality needs of the family;
9. willingness to go beyond traditional approaches to help parents, even at the cost of personal convenience; and
10. great patience. [p. 355]*

In addition, Stewart (1974) noted that the attitudes and characteristics of (1) an interest in helping people, (2) an adequate personal adjustment, (3) acceptance, (4) understanding and empathy, (5) rapport, (6) genuineness, (7) attentiveness and a willingness to listen, and (8) a general knowledge of human behavior are all related to the effective counseling of parents. Parenthetically, it may be noted that select parents of retarded children frequently meet many of the criteria listed and often serve as excellent counselors for other parents, especially in the early stages of doubt and concern.

While there is no research to indicate the ideal counselor (Stewart, 1974), parents of the TMR are usually confronted with a number of problems in need of resolution and understanding. Ultimately, they will need some sort of professional or nonprofessional counseling and guidance in order to resolve these problems effectively.

The Dynamics of Counseling

We have noted, in the previous discussion of the crisis that the TMR child poses to the family, that the parents are often confused and painfully unaware of the problems and realities of retardation. Therefore, it is often important, if not necessary, for the counselor to determine the actual level of parental awareness of their child's retardation. Stone (1948) has defined three levels of parental awareness that may be useful to the counselor in determining the initial awareness and as criteria for progress throughout the counseling sessions:

Considerable awareness
The parent states that the child is retarded.
The parent recognizes the limitations of any treatment.

---

*Reprinted by permission from Alfred A. Baumeister, editor, *Mental Retardation* (Chicago: Aldine Publishing Company) copyright © 1967 by Alfred A. Baumeister.

The parent requests information about suitable care and training, usually placement in an institution.

Partial awareness

The parent describes the symptoms of retardation with questions about the causes.

The parent hopes for improvement but fears that treatment will not be successful.

The parent questions his own ability to cope with the problems.

Minimal awareness

The parent refuses to recognize that certain characteristic behavior is abnormal.

The parent blames causes other than retardation for the symptoms.

The parent believes that treatment will produce a "normal" child. [p. 363–364]

An additional dimension to these levels of awareness should be noted—the "over-reacting" or "overly accepting" parent. This parent is usually very verbal in acceptance of the retardation, frequently offering the counselor an indifferent but almost hostile reaction to the retardation with statements such as, "I know he is retarded; I expect nothing from him or from you or any other person. The condition is final and I know it, and I just want to be left alone." This type of parental resignation to the retardation is, perhaps, the most difficult level of awareness to counsel, and such a parent is usually very defensive and difficult to deal with.

In determining the level of awareness, it is important that the counselor see both parents. We cannot assume that they both have the same level of acceptance and understanding of the problem. On the contrary, the mother and father frequently react to the retarded child in substantially different ways. Also, it is important to work with the parents together as a natural unit. If they are counseled individually, the result could be confusion and a "playing off" of the counselor against each other (that is, individual counseling affords an opportunity for displacement of responsibility, blame, etc., with statements such as, "I don't know or care what he/she (the counselor) told you, but he/she told me that . . ."). The results of this kind of parental conflict are obvious and frequently compound the problem by making the counselor the third person in a crisis rather than a mediator.

The literature is rapidly becoming replete with general issues and suggestions for counseling parents of retarded children. Beck (1959) contends that counseling services are not necessary for every parent, but Tretakoff (1969) concluded from a review of the literature that most parents need assistance and that counseling should take place at an early date to reduce anxiety and parental rejection.

Ishtiaq (1972) identified methods of effective counseling to assist parents in facing problems objectively and to reduce such factors as anxiety, emotional stress and worry. Her commentary included suggestions for the counselor to go beyond conveying factual information and assist the parents in working with the child. These involved interpreting the problem in a realistic manner and counseling the parents towards emotional reconciliation of the problem of retardation.

Roos (1963) also defined some important ingredients for the reduction of the "tragedy" of retardation. The basic components of this process were identified as (1) acceptance and respect of the parents, (2) resistance on the part of the counselor to take on an authoritarian role, (3) allowing for a free emotional expression of parental concern and reaction, (4) allowing parents to reach decisions about their retardate, (5) making the interview parent-centered rather than counselor-centered, and (6) honesty in dealing with the parents. He concluded that this type of interview will not only reduce the parental reaction to the retarded but will help them to think constructively about future planning.

Parents have also offered suggestions for professionals conducting the interview. Patterson (1956) has recommended that the counselor should:

1. Tell us the nature of the problem as soon as possible.
2. Always see both parents.
3. Watch your language.
4. Help us to see this is OUR problem.
5. Help us to understand our problem.
6. Know your resources.
7. Never put us on the defensive.
8. Remember that parents of retarded children are just people.
9. Remember that we are parents and that you are professionals.
10. Remember the importance of your attitude towards us. [p. 15]

Skelton (1972) reported some additional concerns of parents that have implications for counseling. She identified seven prime areas, in order of frequency of mention, that parents of retarded children were concerned about:

1. Training and education were needed for the retarded.
2. The retarded child interfered with family life.
3. Other family problems interfered with the ability to care for the retarded child.
4. Physical care and protection were sought for the retarded child.
5. A living situation was sought for the retarded child.
6. Recreation and companionship were sought for the retarded child.
7. The retarded child caused problems in the community. [pp. 38–41]

The pervasive nature of the problem of a retarded child has also been defined by Attwell and Clabby (1971). The authors (Attwell is a parent of a retarded child) identified and commented on 231 specific questions that parents frequently ask concerning problems of (1) definitions, (2) etiology, (3) diagnosis and referral, (4) adjustment, (5) home training, (6) speech, (7) school programs, (8) parent organizations, (9) sex education, (10) institutionalization, (11) vocational planning, and (12) legal provisions and planning.

It is apparent from this discussion of parent problems and concerns that they are in need of counseling directed towards an understanding of their child's condition, appropriate planning, and the development of an adequate means of coping with the retardation. These recommendations clearly indicate that the parents have expectancies beyond the simple communication of the diagnosis, and it is apparent that the diagnosis of retardation is only the beginning, rather than the end of the professional relationship. However, it is remarkable that many workers still assume that the simple communication of diagnosis to the parents constitutes treatment (Beck, 1959; Wolfensberger, 1967).

A good counseling relationship must be developed as a prerequisite to the resolution of concerns where they exist. In addition, specific objectives should be defined for the counseling process. While there are various patterns in counseling, Ehlers, Krishef, and Prothero (1973) have defined some general objectives that may be applied to the counseling process:

1. Helping them to be more objective about their child.
2. Helping them to learn about behavior their child will outgrow and behavior they can expect to continue.
3. Helping them to assimilate ideas about handling various problem situations common to families of a retarded child.
4. Advising them about the help books and pamphlets can provide and making these materials available for their study and use.
5. Assisting them in learning how to handle their retarded child more successfully and with greater acceptance, understanding, and knowledge.
6. Aiding them in helping the child engage in leisure time pursuits and other constructive activities which may result in a happier child and, therefore, a happier family.
7. Advising them regarding the community resources which are available (e.g., clinics, evaluation centers, parents' groups, sheltered workshops, and educational institutions for the retarded. [pp. 185–186]

It is obvious that each family will be unique and different methods will have to be determined after the initial period of diagnosis, the determination of the circumstances and needs of the family, and a definition of goals in counseling (Beck, 1959). Although individual (that is, single-family) counseling may be necessary, the frequently preferred technique for counseling parents of the retarded is through the group process, where parents work together to learn more about their problems.

Group Counseling

The organization of a parent group (that is, an association for retarded children) is often tantamount to group counseling, albeit without professional direction. In this type of group counseling, parents, through routine meetings and contact, have opportunities to discuss common problems and solutions. In addition, the parent group is a therapeutic force, producing the realization that they are not alone and that many of their problems are not unique.

The results of structured group counseling have usually been equally successful in developing positive attitudes in parents of retarded children. Bitter (1963) reported that positive parent attitudes toward the TMR child and family problems were enhanced through scheduled group discussions. Furthermore, Appel, Williams, and Fishell (1964) concluded from their experience with group counseling with parents that:

1. The counseling served as a catharsis for parents.
2. The parents were much more able to accept the medical diagnosis of retardation.
3. Counseling increased discussion of retardation between parents and siblings, increasing the siblings' understanding of retardation.
4. The group counseling helped the parents to understand that others were genuinely sympathetic rather than just curious or pitying.
5. Goal orientation of parents changed from short-range, immediate concerns to long-range planning.
6. Group counseling contributed to greater optimism about the retarded child's future.

Although group counseling appears to hold considerable promise as a technique or method for the resolution of many of the family problems, Sternlicht and Sullivan (1974) noted that group structure with well-defined goals and expert guidance will be necessary for optimum outcomes. Furthermore, Beck (1959) cautioned that group counseling may only be helpful to the mature parents who are only temporarily impaired by the problem and whose needs may be met through group support. She declared that parents with "clearly psychotic tendencies" tend to be poor risks for group counseling. Wolfensberger (1967) further cautioned that the change in attitude noted in various studies of the group process provided no evidence to support the assumption that this attitude was extended to the actual management of the retarded in the home.

Up to this point, we have concerned ourselves with counseling and the maintenance of the TMR in the home environment. Workers are frequently confronted with a different dimension in counseling involving the omnipresent crisis of institutionalization. Frequently the greatest crisis in counseling is the initial reaction of the parents to the diagnosis. The initial diagnosis is often followed by directives from some professionals towards immediate or early institutionalization. In addition, the continuing personal reaction and/or other family and community pressures frequently lead to the decision to institutionalize as "the only alternative."

The Decision to Institutionalize

Although it has been recommended that no child should be institutionalized at an early age (Jolly, 1953), parents frequently see this alternative as an easy and early solution to the family crisis. However, early institutionalization may have disastrous consequences for the parent and the child and create more problems than it resolves (Jordan, 1972; Slobody & Scanlon, 1959).

Various reasons for seeking institutionalization have been reported. Obvious physical stigmata (such as Down's syndrome) have been noted to be major contributing factors (Giannini & Goodman, 1963; Stone, 1967), but the rather consistent reasons for seeking institutionalization appear to be the result of a general reaction to the severity of the retardation, the sex of the retardate (boys are more often institutionalized), poor marital integration, lack of community facilities, and assistance in adapting to the retarded in the home (Farber, Jenne, & Toigo, 1960; Graliker, Koch, & Henderson, 1965; Saenger, 1960; Stone, 1967).

The implications for counseling are quite clear, but the problems not so easily resolved. While institutionalization may be appropriate in instances, other alternatives will need to be explored. Parents will need assistance in finding other solutions and means of coping with the circumstances in the home. In addition, institutionalization, rather than resolving the problem, may create new problems.

Wolfensberger (1967) has proposed a number of principles and considerations in the decision to institutionalize. He recommends that four dimensions be explored:

1. Is the crisis that precipitates the separation question a novelty shock, value, or reality crisis?
2. Do considerations indicate removal of the retardate from the home or placement in the institution? As the range of services increases, the answer to this question will imply different courses of action.
3. Whose welfare is more immediately at stake? Is it the retardate's, the family's, or society's? Is the retardate to be protected from the family, from society, or from himself? Is the family or society to be protected from the retardate?
4. Do the circumstances of the case call for a judgment on whether separation is justified, indicated, or strongly indicated? [p. 373]*

He further elaborated on these by providing fourteen comprehensive guidelines to be used by the counselor, the family, and society in the decision to institutionalize:

1. A diagnostic label (such as mongolism, hydrocephaly, etc.), by itself, is entirely insufficient in evaluating separation need.

2. Separation at birth is unjustified unless there are other reasons than the mere fact diagnosis occurred then. Separation would only be justified if factors are operant that would have justified separation at another time as well.

3. Multiple handicaps, *per se,* should not be sufficient cause for separation unless they are demonstrated to lead to conditions constituting sufficient grounds otherwise.

4. Aesthetic handicaps should not be sufficient reason for separation unless they are irreparable and have been shown to cause unallayable and severe anguish in the family.

5. Embarrassment to a sibling in a courtship phase should not, by itself, be sufficient cause for separation, especially not if sibling counseling has not been attempted.

6. Removal is not justified because a marriage is threatened, unless the chances are good that removal will, in fact, reduce threat of dissolution and unless the family has other children.

7. Placement away from home for educational purposes is only justified if the education will likely result in appreciable, rather than slight, improvement and the detrimental effects upon the removal of the retardate do not cancel or even outweight the beneficial ones derived from placement.

8. Removal is justified if a very high likelihood exists that in the near future the home cannot or will no longer provide minimal physical

and emotional care, as in cases of parental terminal illness or death, mental illness, etc.

9. Removal is justified if the family does not suffer therefrom and the retardate benefits while losing nothing. For example, relatively young grandparents may be willing to raise the retardate so that no one loses and everyone gains.

10. Removal from the home is indicated if the retardate is exposed to unmitigably subminimal physical or emotional care and if the alternate placement is likely to be an improvement.

11. Appropriate placement is indicated to prevent the retardate's certain death or appreciable injury.

12. Removal may be indicated where the emotional welfare of other family members is threatened, if removal does result in improvement of the other member(s), and if such improvement is substantial enough to clearly outweigh disadvantages to the retardate.

13. Removal is strongly indicated where the physical welfare of other family members is clearly threatened and where other measures are ineffective or unavailable.

14. Placement is strongly indicated if the retardate is a demonstrated—not merely suspected—menace to society and if other feasible measures have failed. [pp. 373–374]†

Throughout this chapter, we have discussed the various reactions of the family to the birth and maintenance of the TMR child. Various professional roles have been defined to assist the parents in coping with the circumstances. However, little, specifically, has been mentioned about the role of the teacher. The teacher, as a "front-line" professional, will often be called upon to serve in a number of professional roles, even the role of surrogate parent. While the total dimension of counseling may not be within the responsibility of the teacher, he or she must be prepared to work with the parents in concert with other individuals and agencies to maximize the acceptance and maintenance of the TMR person in the home.

Teacher Responsibility

The typical parent-teacher relationship is frequently limited to progress reports or discussions of parent or teacher complaints about the child's behavior and/or progress. Clearly, the relationship between the parent and teacher of the TMR must be substantially more than this if a meaningful program between home and school is to be accomplished.

---

†Reprinted by permission from Alfred A. Baumeister, editor, *Mental Retardation* (Chicago: Aldine Publishing Company) copyright © 1967 by Alfred A. Baumeister.

Communication between the home and school should be multipurpose. It should be information-seeking and information-giving. Parents usually have more experience with their TMR child in a number of dimensions exclusive of the school program which can prove useful in the formulation of appropriate objectives in the training program. The teacher, in turn, has a responsibility to communicate to the parents the school program's goals and objectives for the TMR. An understanding of these goals and objectives will promote home-school cooperation and reduce problems in parental expectancy for their child in the training program.

The teacher has a responsibility to extend the training program into the home and to train the parents for continuation of the goals and objectives of the classroom. This will provide carry-over of the classroom program into the home and assist in the transfer of classroom training to persistent life situations. It will also enhance the parent's ability to manage the child through instruction in techniques and reinforcement schedules that are consistent with the school program.

Parents must frequently cope with their TMR child on the basis of very limited knowledge. The home management techniques are frequently random, counter-productive, and often destructive in terms of the goals and objectives of the classroom. Therefore, it is advantageous to the child, the parents, and the teacher to develop a home-training program.

The parent program should be designed to establish a cooperative relationship between the home and the school that assists in interpreting the purposes and procedures of the program and in providing periodic reports of progress (Zudick, 1955). Cansler and Martin (1973) suggested that the benefits of such a program will:

1. Foster more continuity and coordination of the child's training.
2. Permit greater individualization for the child and parents.
3. Give parents knowledge and specific skills for child training.
4. Form a supportive community for the families of handicapped children.
5. Keep the center program relevant to the needs of the families and the community.
6. Provide a base of community knowledge and support for the center program. [pp. 1−2]

One of the persistent resistances to parent programs is that the assumed subjectivity of the parent precludes the possibility of the parent's being an effective teacher. This myth is being dispelled by recent literature that has noted that parents can assist in teaching basic self-help skills (Lance & Koch, 1973) and utilize behavior modification techniques in the instruction of language development, motor coordination, and self-help skills in the home (Fredricks, Baldwin, McDonnell, Hofman, & Harter, 1971). Furthermore, the New York Association for Brain-Injured Children (1974) reported that parent programs provided the parents with confidence and consistency in the management of their child and reduced the possibility of damaging the work that was done at school. The parents also reported a sense of accomplishment in contributing to the training of their child.

Cansler & Martin (1973) have provided some guidelines for home programs to supplement the training the child receives at school:

1. If the parent can read, provide simple written instructions for the parent to keep.
2. Demonstrate techniques for working with the child, such as ways to achieve and maintain eye contact, how to prompt and give cues, and use of rewards.
3. After demonstrating the procedures, let the parents practice either with the child or with you role playing the child.
4. Demonstrate how to adapt materials for the individual child (such as making a soft newspaper ball for the child to catch if he shows fear of the harder rubber ball).
5. Involve the parent in suggesting adaptations of materials or procedures for his or her own child.
6. Analyze the tasks the parents must learn, and program for success by training the parent one step at a time. (For example, make sure that he or she can demonstrate ability to get the child's attention before trying to teach the parent to give instructions to the child.)
7. When there is a behavior problem, take an experimental approach. Recognize with the parent that while there are some behavior principles that work, there are no pat procedures for automatic use or success in every case. Let the parent know that if a particular plan for behavior management does not work, you will assist in finding another more workable one.
8. Seek supervision or suggestions from resource persons knowledgable in behavior modification procedures if you have questions.
9. Maintain regular contact with parents implementing home programs. Each time you meet for discussions, let the parent report how the program is working. Is the parent comfortable with the procedures? Is the child responding the way you and the parent expected?
10. Provide support. It is hard to be consistent when the home program recommends procedures such as ignoring tantrum be-

havior. Recognize with the parents that the process of change can be long and hard. Small groups of parents who are simultaneously working on home programs can provide suggestions and mutual support for one another.

11. Reinforce parent's efforts. When the child shows realistic gains, commend the parents on their fine work.

12. Watch for signs that the program is becoming burdensome to the family. Is the parent spending so much time with the handicapped child that other children's or parents' own needs go unmet? Is the parent too anxious about carrying out the home program? [pp. 25–26]

In addition to training parents to work with their retarded child at home, the teacher has a responsibility for individual conferences to report and coordinate the school's progress in the training program. These should be held on a regular basis and provide an analysis and interpretation of the child's progress. It must be remembered that the progress of the TMR is often difficult to recognize, or the parents may be inclined to overreact to progress and begin to develop unrealistic expectations for their child's growth. Therefore, these individual conferences should be as frequent as possible (that is, a minimum of four a year). The individual conference should be mutually beneficial and not just a reporting session. The teacher should also listen to the parents and engage with them in any decisions about appropriate steps that may need to be taken to enhance the child's progress at home and school.

The teacher should take the responsibility for arranging and structuring these conferences. The conferences should be friendly and informal, and not have overtones of authoritative advice-giving. The teacher should be prepared with relevant information that is well documented and, where problems exist, have alternative solutions and/or suggestions for remediation. The conference should always close on a friendly forward-looking note.

In summary, the teacher has a responsibility to share the parents' frustrations and exhilarations and to develop a greater cohesiveness between the home and school program. This will be necessary if we are to maintain the trust and cooperation of the families that have so long been ignored by the school. As Feldman, Byalick, and Rosedale (1975) commented:

Parents have begun to have a greater trust in and satisfaction with special education facilities, professionals, and educators. They have begun to view themselves as being capable to deal with their children's education. Efforts toward including parents on an equal status basis should be pursued vigorously. [pp. 553–554]

Summary

Professional responsibility for the family of the trainable mentally retarded has long been ignored in the development of training programs. However, an emerging concern and appreciation for the family crisis has precipitated an increased willingness on the part of many professionals to assist the parents in coping with the circumstances of retardation.

The effects of the trainable mentally retarded on the family are pervasive and sometimes devastating to the TMR child and the family members. The presence of the TMR child in the family unit has a disruptive influence on the parents and the siblings and often threatens the economic and social status of the family and the mental health of its members.

Although the intensity of the crisis may vary with time, families often develop unique—sometimes maladaptive—coping strategies. Counseling is usually necessary to reduce the continuing crisis and to reduce or prevent the development of maladaptive coping behaviors. While there is no consensus of opinion on who, specifically, should counsel, it is recognized as a multidisciplinary function designed to assist the parents in accepting the retarded child, adjusting to the long-term dependency, and planning realistically for their child's future.

Since the major purpose in counseling the parents of TMR children is to assist in the maintenance of the child in the home, the teacher as a "front-line" professional will share in this and other responsibilities. In addition to counseling and/or consultation on progress in the program, the teacher has an important role in the training of parents. This training should be directed towards the facilitation of home management and coordination of the objectives of the classroom with persistent life situations in the home and community.

References

American Medical Association. *Mental retardation: A handbook for the primary physician,* 1965, *191,* no. 3.

Anderson, K. A. The "shopping" behavior of parents of mentally retarded children: The professional person's role. *Mental Retardation,* 1971, *9,* 3–5.

Appell, M. J., Williams, C. M., & Fishell, K. N. Changing attitudes of parents of retarded children effected through group counseling. *American Journal of Mental Deficiency,* 1964, *68,* 807–812.

Attwell, A. A., & Clabby, D. A. *The retarded child: Answers to questions parents ask.* Los Angeles, Ca.: Western Psychological Services, 1971.

Beck, H. L. Counseling parents of retarded children. *Children,* 1959, *6,* 225–230.

Bitter, J. A. Attitude change by parents of trainable mentally retarded children as a result of group discussion. *Exceptional Children,* 1963, *30,* 173–177.

Burton, T. A. The trainable mentally retarded. In N. Haring (Ed.), *Behavior of exceptional children an introduction to special education.* Columbus, Oh.: Charles E. Merrill, 1974. (a)

Burton, T. A. Education for trainables: An impossible dream? *Mental Retardation,* 1974, *12,* 45–46. (b)

Cansler, D. P., & Martin, G. H. *Working with families.* Chapel Hill, N.C.: Chapel Hill Training-Outreach Project, 1973.

Connaughton, M. C. Physicians' understanding of mental retardation and their advice to parents of mentally retarded children. Unpublished doctoral dissertation, Indiana University, 1974.

Ehlers, W. H. The moderately and severely retarded child: Maternal perceptions of retardation and subsequent seeking and using services rendered by a community agency. *American Journal of Mental Deficiency,* 1964, *68,* 660–667.

Ehlers, W. H., Krishef, C. H., & Prothero, J. C. *An introduction to mental retardation.* Columbus, Oh.: Charles E. Merrill, 1973.

Farber, B. Effects of a severely mentally retarded child on family integration. *Monographs of the Society for Research in Child Development,* 1959.

Farber, B. Family organization and crisis: Maintenance of integration in families with a severely retarded child. *Monographs of the Society for Research in Child Development,* 1960, *25* (Series no. 75).

Farber, B. *Mental retardation: Its social context and social consequences.* Boston: Houghton Mifflin, 1968.

Farber, B., Jenne, W., & Toigo, R. Family crisis and the decision to institutionalize the retarded child. *CEC Research Monograph,* 1960.

Feldman, M. A., Byalick, R., & Rosedale, M. P. Parent involvement programs—a growing trend in special education. *Exceptional Children,* 1975, *41,* 551–554.

Fotheringham, J. B., Skelton, M., & Hoddinott, B. A. *The retarded child and his family, the effects of home and institutionalization.* Ontario: The Ontario Institute for Studies in Education, 1971.

Fowle, C. M. The effect of the severely mentally retarded child on his family. *American Journal of Mental Deficiency,* 1968, *73,* 468–473.

Fredricks, H. D. B., Baldwin, V. L., McDonnell, J. J., Hofman, R., & Harter, J. Parents educate their trainable children. *Mental Retardation,* 1971, *9,* 24–26.

Gallagher, J. Rejecting parents? In W. Wolfensberger & R. A. Kurtz (Eds.), *Management of the family of the mentally retarded.* Chicago: Follett Educational Corporation, 1969.

Giannini, M. J., & Goodman, L. Counseling families during the crisis reaction to mongolism. *American Journal of Mental Deficiency,* 1963, *67,* 740–747.

Graliker, B. V., Koch, R., & Henderson, R. A. A study of factors influencing placement of retarded children in a state residential institution. *American Journal of Mental Deficiency,* 1965, *69,* 553—559.

Grebler, A. M. Parental attitudes toward mentally retarded children. *American Journal of Mental Deficiency,* 1952, *56,* 475—483.

Grossman, F. K. *Brothers and sisters of retarded children.* Syracuse, New York: Syracuse University Press, 1972.

Holt, K. S. The influence of a retarded child upon family limitations. *Journal of Mental Deficiency Research,* 1958, *2,* 28—34.

Ishtiaq, K. Counseling the parents. *Mental Retardation,* 1972, *10,* 50.

Jolly, D. H. When should the seriously retarded infant be institutionalized? *American Journal of Mental Deficiency,* 1953, *57,* 632—636.

Jordan, T. E. *The mentally retarded* (3rd ed.). Columbus, Oh.: Charles E. Merrill, 1972.

Kanner, L. Parents' feelings about retarded children. *American Journal of Mental Deficiency,* 1953, *57,* 375—383.

Lance, W. D., & Koch, A. C. Parents as teachers: Self-help skills for young handicapped children. *Mental Retardation,* 1973, *11,* 3—4.

Michaels, J., & Schulman, H. Observations on the psychodynamics of parents of retarded children. *American Journal of Mental Deficiency,* 1962, *66,* 568—573.

Patterson, L. L. Some pointers for professionals. *Children,* 1956, *3,* 13—17.

Roos, P. Psychological counseling with parents of retarded children. *Mental Retardation,* 1963, *1,* 345—350.

Ryckman, D. B., & Henderson, R. A. The meaning of a retarded child for his parents: A focus for counselors. *Mental Retardation,* 1965, *3,* 4—7.

Saenger, G. *Factors influencing the institutionalization of mentally retarded individuals in New York City,* Albany, N.Y.: New York State Interdepartmental Health Resources Board, 1960.

Sarason, S. B. *Psychological problems in mental deficiency* (3rd ed). N.Y.: Harper & Row, 1959.

Schonell, F., & Watts, B. A first survey of the effects of a subnormal child on the family unit. *American Journal of Mental Deficiency,* 1956, *61,* 210—219.

Skelton, M. Areas of parental concern about retarded children. *Mental Retardation,* 1972, *10,* 38—41.

Slobody, L., & Scanlon, J. Consequences in early institutionalization. *American Journal of Mental Deficiency,* 1959, *63,* 971—974.

Sternlicht, M., & Sullivan, I. Group counseling with parents of the MR: Leadership selection and functioning. *Mental Retardation,* 1974, *12,* 11—13.

Stewart, J. L. *Counseling parents of exceptional children: Principles, problems and procedures.* New York: MSS Information Corporation, 1974.

Stone, M. M. Parental attitudes to retardation. *American Journal of Mental Deficiency,* 1948, *53,* 363—372.

Stone, N. D. Family factors in willingness to place the mongoloid child. *American Journal of Mental Deficiency,* 1967, *72,* 16−20.

Tizard, J., & Grad, J. C. *The mentally handicapped and their families.* London: Oxford University Press, 1961.

Treatakoff, M. Counseling parents of handicapped children: A review. *Mental Retardation,* 1969, *7,* 31−34.

Wolfensberger, W. Counseling parents of the retarded. In A. A. Baumeister (Ed.), *Mental retardation appraisal education rehabilitation.* Chicago: Aldine, 1967.

Wolfensberger, W., & Kurtz, R. *Management of the family of the mentally retarded.* Chicago: Follett Educational Corporation, 1969.

Wolfensberger, W., & Menolascino, F. J. Framework for management of parents of the mentally retarded. In F. J. Menolascino (Ed.), *Psychiatric approaches to mental retardation.* New York: Basic Books, 1970.

Zudick, L. A conference program with parents of the mentally handicapped. *Exceptional Children,* 1955, *21,* 260−272.

Zuk, G. H. Religious factor and the role of guilt in parental acceptance of the retarded child. *American Journal of Mental Deficiency,* 1959, *64,* 139−147.

Reference Notes

1. Farber, B. Family orientation and marital integration of parents of severely mentally retarded children. Unpublished manuscript presented at the American Sociological Society, Seattle, Washington, 1958.

2. New York Association for Brain-Injured Children. *Parents are partners at Pathfinder.* Unpublished manuscript, the Pathfinder School, Bayside, New York, 1974.

Author Index

Subject Index